Credit Rationing
and the
Commercial Loan Market

"I'm sorry. We don't lend a zillion dollars to anyone."

Drawing by Mulligan;
© 1968 The New Yorker Magazine, Inc.

Credit Rationing and the Commercial Loan Market

AN ECONOMETRIC STUDY

OF THE STRUCTURE OF

THE COMMERCIAL LOAN MARKET

Dwight M. Jaffee

ECONOMICS DEPARTMENT

PRINCETON UNIVERSITY

JOHN WILEY & SONS, INC.

New York • London • Sydney • Toronto

Library of Congress Catalogue Card Number: 72-150611

ISBN 0-471-43705-0

Printed in the United States of America.

10 9 8 7 6 5 4 3 2 1

TO THE MEMORY OF MY BROTHER, *Gilbert B. Jaffee*

Acknowledgments

The research for this study was started as part of my doctoral dissertation at the Massachusetts Institute of Technology. I am indebted to the members of my thesis committee, Professor Franco Modigliani, chairman, and Professors Donald Farrar and Franklin Fisher, for their careful reading of the thesis and for their many helpful suggestions. The original research was also undertaken in conjunction with the Federal Reserve-M.I.T. econometric model project. I thank all participants in this project for help at various times and, particularly, the current directors of the project, Professors Albert Ando and Franco Modigliani, and Dr. Edward Gramlich and Professor Robert Rasche. It is apparent that my debt to Franco Modigliani is double, but this vastly understates the case.

The research was completed and the final manuscript was prepared at Princeton University. I have received many useful comments and suggestions, as well as encouragement, from my colleagues in the Department of Economics, particularly Professors Ray Fair, Stephen Goldfeld, and Burton Malkiel. Paul Haaga and Richard Wolff, Princeton undergraduates, have also served as able research assistants during the preparation of the manuscript.

Some of the preliminary results of the thesis were presented in a paper read at the December 1967 meetings of the Econometric Society. Significant parts of the material in Sections 2.3 to 2.6 and Sections 3.3 and 3.4 have previously appeared in "A Theory and Test of Credit Rationing," *American Economic Review*, December 1969, a paper jointly authored with Franco Modigliani. This material appears here with the permission of the

American Economic Review. The discussion in Section 3.2.2 also includes brief passages from "Methods of Estimation for Markets in Disequilibrium," a paper jointly authored with Ray Fair that is forthcoming in *Econometrica*.

Financial support for the study has been provided at various times by the National Science Foundation, the Social Science Research Council, the Board of Governors of the Federal Reserve System, and the Econometric Research Program and the Financial Research Center at Princeton University. Computations for the study were performed at the computer centers at M.I.T. and Princeton University. The "TSP" computer program for econometric research was used for most of these computations.

Finally, if it were not for the many sacrifices of my wife Annette and my children Jonathan and Elizabeth, this study could not have been completed.

Princeton, 1970   D. M. J.

Contents

Credit Rationing
and the
Commercial Loan Market

CHAPTER 1

Introductory Remarks

1.1 | INTRODUCTION

This study presents an analysis of the structure, functions, and effects of the commercial loan market in the United States economy. The main body of the discussion relates to the formulation and estimation of an aggregate structural model of the demand and supply factors in this market. A special effort is made in developing the model to incorporate the institutional arrangements and constraints that distinguish the commercial loan market from other financial markets, while at the same time maintaining a rigorous theoretical basis for the implied relationships. The emphasis on institutional features leads, in particular, to an extended analysis of the role of credit rationing in the commercial loan market and of the effects of such credit rationing on other financial markets and real investment decisions.

The detailed study at this time of the commercial loan market is motivated by recent developments in the understanding of the monetary and financial structure of the economy, and by recent attempts to incorporate this knowledge in the formulation of large-scale econometric models of the economy. In past discussions of the *modus operandi* of monetary policy, the role of commercial banks and the commercial loan market, as the link between the policy instruments under the control of the monetary authority and the investment and consumption expenditures that were to be controlled, was treated as mechanical and constant. The new view of monetary control, in contrast, stresses the flexibility and variability in this link due to the behavioral relationships underlying bank portfolio

1

management and money supply determination. It then follows as an implication of the new view that the effects of monetary policy can be accurately predicted only to the extent that the structure and parameters of the behavioral relationships are known. It is on this basis that much of the recent effort in monetary economics has been directed at modeling and estimating this structure, and it is as part of this effort that the present study is undertaken.

There are two objectives in this first chapter. The first objective is to develop more fully the considerations already touched upon concerning the role of commercial banks and the commercial loan market in the transmission of monetary policy. These considerations are discussed in the following three sections. The second objective is to provide a summary sketch of the theory and structure of the model of the commercial loan market that is developed in detail in the remainder of the study. This summary is provided in Section 1.5.

1.2 | THE IMPORTANCE OF COMMERCIAL BANKS AND THE COMMERCIAL LOAN MARKET IN THE U.S. MONETARY SYSTEM

Commercial banks have been, and remain, the most important financial intermediaries in the U.S. monetary system. In terms of magnitude, the total assets of commercial banks (over $500 billon at the end of 1969) exceed the sum of the total assets of the next three largest intermediaries, life insurance companies, savings and loan associations, and mutual savings banks. In terms of diversity, the assets of commercial banks include, with the exception of direct corporate securities, the range of assets held by all of the other more specialized intermediaries. Similarly, the liabilities of commercial banks correspond to the range of liabilities of all the other intermediaries with the exception of the life insurance reserves of the life insurance companies.

The importance of the commercial banks in the U.S. monetary system depends, however, not only on the magnitude and diversity of bank assets and liabilities, but also on the essential role of commercial banks in the transmission of Federal Reserve policy. Although it has been debated whether commercial banks *should* be the only financial intermediary directly affected by Federal Reserve policy, there can be little doubt that this *in fact* has been the case. The direct effects of Federal Reserve policy operate on the commercial banks through the well-known instruments of monetary policy: open market operations which affect the total value of bank reserves, the discount rate and the availability of loans from the Federal Reserve, and the setting of reserve requirements. The objectives of monetary policy, as implemented through these instruments, are then achieved by attempting to control the magnitude and composition of the assets held by the commercial banks.

It is in this setting that the importance of commercial loans and the commercial loan market arises. The term *commercial loans* generally refers to credit of short term maturity extended by commercial banks to business firms.[1] The collateral for this credit is typically a short term asset such as inventory stock or accounts receivable. Producers' durable equipment and structures may also serve as collateral for commercial loans, although more typically they are used to back *term loans,* which are commercial loans with a maturity exceeding one year.

It should be stressed that the distinction between commercial loans and term loans on the basis of maturity is less clear, both conceptually and practically, than the definition might indicate. The conceptual difficulty arises from the reluctance of bankers to deny a request from a customer for an extension of a commercial loan beyond the original maturity. To deny such a request from a financially sound firm would jeopardize the bank's "customer relationship" which can be built only over a long period of time.[2] In the case of potential bankruptcy, the large costs of collection also make it expeditious for the bank to extend the loan in hope of obtaining full payment in the future. The consequence of this tendency for "automatic" loan renewal is that both the bank and the borrowing firm view the stated maturity of commercial loans as less than binding.[3] On the practical side, data on the volume of outstanding term loans have been sketchy and there are indications that the available measures of commercial loans include at least some term loans or commercial loans with guaranteed renewal features.[4] The result is that although

---

[1] More technically, the Member Bank Call Report of the Federal Reserve defines commercial and industrial loans as all loans to persons and corporations engaged in manufacturing, mining, oil and gas producing, quarrying, construction, utilities, trade, services, and amusement, and to real estate operators or developers. The loans may be used for financing capital expenditures as well as current operations, and they may be secured or unsecured. We shall refer to commercial and industrial loans as simply commercial loans. See also American Bankers Association [1962], pp. 121–123. (All bibliographical references are provided in the alphabetical list of references at the end of the study. The year of publication is given in the square brackets.)

[2] Hodgman [1963] provides a complete discussion of the implications of "customer relationships" for bank behavior.

[3] This is confirmed by the results of the 1955 Survey of Business Loans at Commercial Banks by the Federal Reserve System. The survey indicated, for the Fourth (Cleveland) Federal Reserve District, that nearly two-thirds of the dollar volume of the commercial loans were outstanding to borrowers who had been continuously in debt to the bank for one year or more, and that half of the amount of the notes represented borrowers in debt for two years or more. See Federal Reserve Bank of Cleveland [1956].

[4] See Budzeika [1964].

the discussion here is concerned primarily with short term commercial loans, the close substitution between commercial loans and the longer maturity term loans must be kept in view.

One measure of the importance of commercial loans for the banking system can be seen in the distribution of commercial bank assets, shown in Table 1.1 for the end of 1969. Among the major categories of assets, loans account for over 50 percent of the total. Within the loan category, commercial and industrial loans represent the largest single class, accounting for over 37 percent of total bank loans. Furthermore, these figures actually understate the true importance of commercial loans in the banks' portfolio. First, the major part of the liquid asset category reflects cash items in the process of collection and required reserves not available for investment. For the category of only earning assets—securities, loans, and other assets—loans constitute about two-thirds of the total. Second, a significant portion of the real estate loans represent mortgages on com-

TABLE 1.1   COMMERCIAL BANK ASSETS (*December 31, 1969*)[a]

	$ Billion	Percentage of Total Assets	Percentage of Subtotal
Cash assets	90.0		90.1
Federal funds sold	9.9		9.9
Total Liquid Assets		99.9	18.8	100.0
U.S. Treasury securities	54.7		43.4
State and local securities	59.2		46.9
Other securities	12.2		9.7
Total Securities		126.1	23.8	100.0
Commercial and industrial loans	108.4		37.8
Agricultural loans	10.3		3.6
Loans for purchasing and carrying securities	9.8		3.4
Loans for financial institutions	17.6		6.1
Real estate loans	70.0		24.4
Other loans to individuals	63.3		22.1
Other	7.4		2.6
Total Loans		286.8	54.0	100.0
Other Assets		17.9	3.4	100.0
Total Assets		530.7	100.0	100.0

[a] Loans and Investments for all commercial banks, *Federal Reserve Bulletin*.

mercial property that substitute for term loans made to the same class of bank customer. Finally, and perhaps most importantly, these figures do not reflect the large magnitude of potential claims on bank funds in the form of outstanding commercial loan lines of credit.

The distinction of commercial loans as the primary asset held by commercial banks and the critical role of the commercial loan market in the transmission of monetary policy have been long recognized. The *real bills doctrine* (or *commercial loan theory of banking*), which first gained prominence in the English banking controversies of the early 19th century, accepted it as axiomatic that the primary function of commercial banks was to supply loans to business firms in order to meet the needs of trade, and that it was the responsibility of the monetary authorities to help the banks serve this function.[5] The same doctrine also later proved an important basis for the institutional change from the National Banking System to the Federal Reserve System in the United States. In terms of the modern theory of central bank policy, the "needs of trade" doctrine has been replaced by more flexible techniques for controlling the cyclical fluctuations in the economy. But in terms of the mechanism and the path of transmission of monetary policy, the commercial loan market still remains key.

1.3 | THE CHANNELS OF MONETARY POLICY

The mechanism by which monetary policy is transmitted through the commercial loan market to the real sectors of the economy can be briefly surveyed by distinguishing two channels of influence: interest rates and credit availability. The interest rate channel is the most orthodox and is in keeping with the neoclassical tradition of perfect markets with well defined demand and supply curves. The operation of the interest rate channel can be illustrated by following through the effects of an open market sale of government securities by the Federal Reserve. The impact effects of the open market sale are an increase in the interest rate on government securities and a decrease in the reserves of the banking system. The increase in the interest rate on government securities is the direct result of the increased supply to this market by the Federal Reserve. A decrease in bank reserves can be avoided only if the Federal Reserve's security sales are paid for solely by the nonbank sector drawing down its cash balances,[6] an unlikely event. Both the increase in the interest rate on government securities and the decrease in bank reserves have the effect of raising the opportunity cost of loanable funds for the bank.

[5] See Burstein [1963], pp. 167–178.
[6] Cash balances refer here to the currency holdings of the nonbank sector, and explicitly exclude the demand deposits of the nonbank sector.

The increase in the interest rate on government securities operates through the substitution in the banks' portfolio between government securities and commercial loans, while the decrease in bank reserves has an effect because it decreases the total amount of funds available for investment. The net effect is then a downward shift in the commercial banks' supply curve in the loan market, and thus an increase in the commercial loan rate. The final effect of the increased commercial loan rate on investment expenditures then follows from the standard neoclassical premise of an interest elastic investment schedule. Since the demand for loans is directly derived from the business firms' demand for investment goods, the quantity of loans outstanding will also be lower in the final equilibrium.

Credit availability, the second channel for the effect of monetary policy through the commercial loan market, is more Keynesian in concept[7] and is based on imperfections in the capital markets, particularly in the commercial loan market itself. More specifically, most arguments for a credit availability channel are based on the existence of special institutional and competitive situations on the supply side of the market. The main tenet of the availability view is that the quantity of loans actually supplied by the commercial banks to the business sector is at least as important as the interest cost of the funds as a determinant of the effectiveness of monetary policy. The use of nonprice means for credit rationing by commercial banks is thus critical to the availability channel. The analyses and arguments that have been used to explain the use of nonprice rationing by commercial banks have been quite varied, and these are discussed more fully in Section 2.2 below. Two points, however, should be stressed in the present context. First, the principal advantage of the existence of availability effects for the efficacy of monetary policy is that, even in the absence of significant interest elasticity in investment demand, control of the quantity of loans supplied by the commercial banks may be sufficient for an effective monetary policy. Second, and an obviously related point, the methods of implementing monetary policy may be quite different depending on whether the main structural link to the real sectors operates through interest rates or the quantity of loans.

1.4 | ECONOMETRIC STUDIES OF FINANCIAL MARKET STRUCTURE

In contrast to the preceding discussion, until quite recently most econometric studies of the monetary mechanism had not given an important place

---

[7] Keynes explicitly introduced the concept of credit rationing in his *Treatise,* Keynes [1930]. In the *General Theory,* Keynes [1936], the emphasis was on disequilibrium in the labor market, and credit rationing was not developed further. Tucker [1970], however, has developed a "Keynesian" macroeconomic model which fully accounts for disequilibrium in all markets.

to the commercial banks and the commercial loan market. The principal role assigned to banks in aggregate economic models was to function as the gearing ratio, transforming an increase in free reserves (supplied by the Federal Reserve) into an increase in the money supply. The commercial bank reserve multiplier was assumed independent of all endogenous economic variables, and thus the Federal Reserve had complete and direct control over the money supply. The result was that although the nature of the influence of the money supply on the real sectors of the economy differed between the Keynesian and Quantity Theory models, in either case the role of the banking system was entirely mechanical.

Recent work by many authors has indicated, however, that the determinants of the money supply are in fact more complex.[8] In particular, the banks' desired level of free reserves depends on Federal Reserve policy parameters and on interest rates, thus making the level of free reserves a function of endogenous variables. It is then but a short step to show that the money supply itself is also an endogenous variable. Stephen Goldfeld [1966] has made even further progress by incorporating the determination of the money supply into a more general theory of bank portfolio choice. His approach emphasizes the banks' demand for each asset in their portfolio, rather than only free reserves. In this way the connection between the commercial loan market and the money supply is made explicit, since commercial loans are among the most important assets held by banks.[9]

Econometric tests of these new theories have been made concurrently with the theoretical advances and have confirmed the value of the new approach. With the exception of Goldfeld's study, however, a commercial loan market has not been included in the available aggregate econometric models. In particular, in the Brookings Model (see de Leeuw [1965]), commercial loans enter only as a residual satisfying a balance sheet constraint, and in the Wharton Model (see Evans and Klein [1968]), the entire commercial bank sector is specified with a single free reserve equation. In addition, even in Goldfeld's work, where attention has been given to the institutional characteristics of the loan market, the possibility of nonprice credit rationing has not been fully incorporated into the estimated model.

In response to this problem, as well as in recognition of the need for a large-scale econometric model incorporating other recent developments in the understanding of the monetary mechanism, work on the

[8] For examples, see Brunner [1961], Brunner and Meltzer [1964], Meigs [1962], Orr and Mellon [1961], and Teigen [1964].

[9] Further research in this area is given in Ando and Goldfeld [1968], and in Modigliani, Rasche, and Cooper [1970].

Federal Reserve-M.I.T.-Penn. (FMP) econometric model project began in early 1966. Reports on the full model will soon be available.[10] The present study was undertaken in conjunction with the FMP project with the goal of providing the necessary model and econometric estimates for the commercial loan sector. Since the commercial loan rate and the volume of commercial loans are important endogenous variables in the FMP model, a complete specification for equations explaining these variables is quite important. In addition, if the FMP model is to portray accurately the structural response of the real sectors to monetary policy, it is critical that the possibility of commercial loan credit rationing be fully tested. Although many of the policy implications of the results of the present study are discussed in general equilibrium framework, it should be noted that a full analysis of the structural multipliers implied by the loan model can be developed only upon completion of the estimation and simulation of the entire FMP model. It is hoped that this analysis will be soon available in the forthcoming reports on the FMP model.

1.5 | THE STRUCTURE OF THE COMMERCIAL LOAN MARKET AND A SUMMARY OF THE MODEL

With this background, we can now turn to a more specific discussion of the structure of the commercial loan market and a summary of the model of the loan market that is developed in the remainder of the study. This discussion also serves as an outline of the material to be presented in the following chapters.

The commercial loan market can be viewed in general terms as the interaction of the supply of commercial loans by banks and the demand for loans by business firms. Were this a "normal" market, the variables to be determined by the supply and the demand would be the quantity of loans outstanding and the price of commercial loans, that is, the commercial loan rate. The existence, or possible existence, of credit rationing, however, rules out this simple interpretation. Credit rationing is said to occur when a bank is unwilling to extend the loan demanded by a customer and supplies only a smaller amount. This can occur in the long run with the commercial loan rate at the level desired by the banks or

[10] The major sponsors of the FMP project, Albert Ando (University of Pennsylvania) and Franco Modigliani (M.I.T.) are currently compiling a volume that discusses and summarizes the model as a whole. The savings deposit, mortgage, and residential construction sectors of the model will also be discussed, in more detail, in Gramlich and Jaffee [1970]. Progress reports on the model are available in de Leeuw and Gramlich [1968], Rasche and Shapiro [1968], de Leeuw and Gramlich [1969], and Ando and Modigliani [1969].

in the short run before the rate has fully adjusted. In technical terms, credit rationing is equivalent to the existence of an excess demand for loans (by at least some customers) at the ruling commercial loan rate. It follows from this definition that even in "equilibrium" one cannot speak of a single quantity of loans, but must distinguish the banks' supply and the firms' demand, the difference being the amount of rationing.

There are thus four endogenous variables to be determined in the commercial loan market: the commercial loan rate, the loan demand, the loan supply, and the amount of credit rationing. Since there is an identity relating three of these variables—credit rationing equals loan demand minus loan supply—only three behavioral equations are necessary to provide a complete system. The formal structure of the loan model developed in this study thus consists of two equations on the supply side, one explaining the amount of credit rationing and one explaining the commercial loan rate, and one equation on the demand side explaining the quantity of loan demand. The quantity of loan supply, the fourth variable in the system, can then be derived by subtracting the amount of rationing from the quantity of loan demand.

In the long run, the model is fully simultaneous. Each of the three endogenous variables depends not only on its own set of exogenous variables,[11] but, in addition, the commercial loan rate depends on the level of loan demand, the level of loan demand depends on the commercial loan rate, and the degree of credit rationing depends on both of these variables. In the short run, however, the model has a recursive property. The commercial loan rate and the degree of credit rationing are set by the banks on the basis of the values of the exogenous variables and the predetermined level of outstanding loans. Loan demand, in turn, is responsive to the commercial loan rate. Finally, the quantity of loans currently received by the firms is a function of the loan demand and the degree of credit rationing.

The recursive feature of the model arises because the banks' decisions on the commercial loan rate and credit rationing are based on the given quantity of loans outstanding. The validity of this assumption rests on two important and related features of the commercial loan market. First, for at least a certain class of prime customers, banks develop and maintain "customer relationships." The value of these relationships for the banks depends in large part on the deposits provided by the customers; the cost is that the banks are under obligation to accommodate loan requests of these customers as they arise. The second feature of the loan market

---

[11] Many of the variables that are included as exogenous for the purpose of this discussion—market interest rates and business expenditures, for example—would of course be endogenous in a complete econometric model.

is the existence of large amounts of lines of credit and other forms of prenegotiated loan contracts. To an important degree lines of credit, together with compensating balance requirements, are a formalization of the customer relationship, and the effect is again that in the short run the banks are obliged to meet the loan requests of these customers.[12]

Although the existence of customer relationships and lines of credit provide the grounds for the assumption that the banks' decisions are based on a given quantity of loans in the short run, there remains an empirical question of the definition of short run and of the time unit used for estimation. The time unit which is actually used in this study, a quarter, appears to be just on the margin: a longer time unit, say a year, would surely contradict the assumption; a shorter time unit, say a month, would almost certainly make the assumption valid. With the technical questions of estimation procedures aside, however, it is helpful from an heuristic standpoint to identify the commercial loan rate and credit rationing with the supply side and the quantity of loans outstanding with the demand side, and we shall continue to discuss the model in this context.

1.5.1 THE SUPPLY OF COMMERCIAL LOANS: CREDIT RATIONING

The possible existence of nonprice credit rationing by the commercial banks has drawn considerable attention since the issue was first raised as part of the Availability Doctrine in the period immediately following World War II. Three basic questions still remain essentially unanswered, however:

1. Is it rational for commercial banks to ration credit by means other than price?
2. Can credit rationing be measured, and, if so, are there significant variations in rationing over time?
3. Is the impact of credit rationing on real expenditure decisions of firms important?

The first of these questions is considered in Chapter 2 which develops a theoretical model of commercial loan supply and credit rationing. The principal criticism of earlier attempts to answer this question is that they focused almost solely on the supply side of the market. Credit rationing, however, can be reasonably defined only as the difference between the quantity of loans demanded and the quantity of loans supplied at the

---

[12] A similar point has been argued at length in Goldfeld [1966], pp. 24–28, and de Leeuw [1965], pp. 45–47. The concept of a customer relationship was first developed by Hodgman [1963]. Shapiro [1964] has been able to implement an econometric model using lines of credit (loan authorizations) as an important variable with Canadian data.

ruling commercial loan rate. The omission of the parameters of loan demand in these earlier studies hence leads to only a partial solution in two senses: first, information on loan supply by itself simply cannot determine the existence of credit rationing; second, the ruling commercial loan rate should be identified in the long run with the banks' desired loan rate, and clearly this is a function of loan demand.

The model of commercial loan supply and credit rationing used in this study assumes that the bank maximizes its expected profits taking into account possible customer default on the loan. The bank's expected income from each loan is formulated as an explicit function of the parameters of the customer's demand function, the probability of default, and the rate of interest charged on the loan. The proof of the rationality of rationing amounts, within this framework, to showing that the bank can increase its expected profits by rationing at least some customers. The discussion in Chapter 2 shows that the institutional characteristics, and particularly the oligopolistic structure, of the commercial banking industry make this result valid.

The empirical problems of verifying the existence of credit rationing, referred to in the second question above, are discussed in Chapter 3. The main problem for previous empirical studies involving credit rationing was a means of measuring the degree of the rationing itself. In fact, a direct measure of credit rationing cannot be obtained, but, fortunately, the theory of credit rationing developed here is suggestive about the nature of an acceptable proxy variable. The empirical tests for the existence of credit rationing are then based on regressions of the credit rationing proxy on variables which the theory suggests should be related to fluctuations in credit rationing. The data for these tests, as well as for the other regression tests discussed below, are based on quarterly observations from the beginning of 1952 to the end of 1969. Taking into account lags in variables, the actual sample used for estimation is generally 1952–3 to 1969–4.[13] This sample has been selected to provide the longest period of observation since the Federal Reserve-Treasury Accord.

Three important conclusions are drawn from the empirical tests of credit rationing. First, the existence of rationing as an empirically important phenomenon is confirmed. Second, the validity of the model of credit rationing that forms the basis of the empirical tests is also supported. Third, the usefulness of the rationing proxy as a measure of the degree of rationing is verified. The credit rationing proxy is used, moreover, in Chapter 6 in the empirical tests of the effects of credit rationing on real expenditure decisions noted in the third question raised above.

[13] The notation 1952–3 is to be read 1952, third quarter. This notation is used throughout the book.

1.5.2 THE SUPPLY OF COMMERCIAL LOANS: THE COMMERCIAL LOAN RATE

The determinants of the desired long run commercial loan rate are developed from a theoretical viewpoint as part of the rationing model (Chapter 2), while the operational counterpart is specified in conjunction with the empirical tests of credit rationing (Chapter 3). In Chapter 4, direct tests of the specification based on a partial adjustment model of the commercial loan rate toward the desired long run level, are provided.

An important part of the formulation of the commercial loan rate equation is the specification of the banking system's desired level for this rate. Two specifications are proposed. First, the desired loan rate can be determined as a function of the opportunity cost of funds for the bank. The bank's equilibrium is then attained when the net yield of all assets in the portfolio are equal, taking into account differences in risk, maturity, and marketability. Alternatively, it is shown in Chapter 4 that the credit rationing proxy variable developed in Chapter 3 can be used directly in the specification of the desired commercial loan rate. The benefit of this alternative specification is that it provides an additional test of the value of the credit rationing proxy.

A second important feature of the formulation is that the parameters of the adjustment process that determine the timing of rate changes are specified as functions of changes in the Federal Reserve discount rate. Changes in the discount rate, in this interpretation, serve as signals for changes in the loan rate that allow communication between the oligopolistic set of banks without direct collusion. The empirical tests confirm the importance of this mechanism and, in fact, changes in the discount rate by themselves explain a substantial percentage of the variance of the changes in the commercial loan rate variable. The existence of the discount rate signal mechanism in the dynamics of rate setting indicates that the commercial loan rate may deviate substantially from the desired level in the short run. This is significant because it confirms the empirical results on the existence of rationing in which short run rationing is based on the spread between the desired loan rate and the quoted rate. Furthermore, with respect to the general model of the loan market, this result is consistent with the proposition that banks act as price setters and in the short run take the level of loan demand as given.

1.5.3 THE DEMAND FOR COMMERCIAL LOANS

The demand for commercial loans is developed in Chapter 5 from a formal model based on the premise that the firm's real expenditure decisions are made prior to the financing decisions except in periods of high and unexpected commercial loan credit rationing.[14] The model emphasizes the firm's choice, in financing its net assets, between commercial loans and long term liabilities (long term debt and equity), together with the balance sheet identity that constrains the total of these two liabilities when all other net assets are taken as given. Furthermore, it is assumed that long-term liabilities adjust only gradually to the desired level, thus creating a buffer function for commercial loans based on the need to fulfill the budget constraint in the short run. In this way the demand for loans is derived as a function of the firm's principal assets—inventory stock, fixed capital stock, and other net liquid assets—as well as a function of the relative cost of commercial loan financing.

This specification is tested for aggregate data, and the results confirm the general structure of the model and indicate a significant substitution between commercial loan and long-term debt financing. Tests of this model are also carried out using data disaggregated by asset size classes from the Federal Trade Commission-Securities and Exchange Commission (FTC-SEC) *Quarterly Financial Report for Manufacturing Corporations*. In general, these results confirm the findings for the aggregate data. One important additional feature of the disaggregated data, however, is that net trade credit between business firms, which essentially cancels out in the aggregate, can be specified separately by asset class. The estimates indicate that net trade credit is a significant element of loan demand for all asset classes and, in fact, it is generally more important than even the inventory stock.

1.5.4 THE EFFECTS OF CREDIT RATIONING ON OTHER MARKETS

In Chapter 6 the effects of credit rationing on sectors of the economy other than the commercial loan market are considered. The most important of these, at least from the standpoint of monetary policy, is the effect of credit rationing on the real investment expenditures of business firms. The effects of credit rationing on other financial markets must also be considered, however, because the effects of credit rationing on investment expenditures will be reduced to the extent that firms rationed in the loan market can still obtain the needed funds from other sources. Among these other sources of funds, trade credit, credit extended by business firms to customers at the time of a sale, appears to be the most important.

Regression equations are estimated in order to evaluate the offsetting effect of trade credit extensions on the impact of credit rationing on investment decisions. In these tests a net trade credit variable is fitted against a distributed lag of the credit rationing proxy variable for each

---

[14] Real expenditures, of course, may still depend on the cost of capital, but it is assumed that the decision to make these expenditures can be taken as given.

of the asset categories in the *FTC-SEC Quarterly Financial Report* data. The results generally confirm the hypothesis in that the credit rationing proxy has a negative effect on the net trade credit issued by the smaller firms and a positive effect on the net trade credit issued by the larger firms. Further confirmation of the redistribution of trade credit in periods of tight money and credit rationing is also developed from surveys of the reactions of business firms to the tight money conditions of 1966.

With this background, the study turns finally to the available empirical evidence for a direct impact of credit rationing on real investment expenditures. Unfortunately, the research studies in this area have been primarily exploratory and the results have been quite mixed. For this reason, it is difficult to make a simple summary evaluation. It does appear, however, that an effect of credit rationing on the investment of small firms is consistent with the evidence, while the case for an effect on the investment of large firms is less clear. Furthermore, because the large firms constitute the major share of the assets and sales of the total economy, this conclusion also implies that the case for an effect of rationing on aggregate investment must remain in doubt. It thus seems that the most important topics for future research in the area of commercial loan credit rationing are empirical studies quantifying the effect of credit rationing on real investment expenditures.

CHAPTER 2

The Theory of Credit Rationing

2.1 | INTRODUCTION

This chapter develops an operational theory of credit rationing consistent with (1) rational behavior by commercial banks, and with (2) the structural and institutional basis of commercial banking in the United States. Credit rationing is defined as the existence of an excess demand for commercial loans at the quoted commercial loan rate.[1] Furthermore, depending on the status of the commercial loan rate, two forms of credit rationing can be distinguished. The term *equilibrium rationing* will be used to refer to credit rationing which occurs when the commercial loan rate is set at the banks' desired long run or equilibrium level. The term *dynamic rationing,* in contrast, wil be used to refer to the transient existence of credit rationing that occurs when the commercial loan rate is set only at the short run desired level.

The theory of credit rationing developed here can be viewed as a logical extension of certain aspects of previous studies in this area. The chapter thus begins with a review of the economic literature relating to the existence of credit rationing. We then proceed to develop a theory of credit rationing. Analytic propositions relating to the existence of credit rationing are first considered under alternative assumptions concerning the institutional basis and the degree of competition in commercial banking. These propositions are then developed, following a discussion of the actual struc-

[1] Throughout this chapter, credit rationing is discussed in the context of commercial banks and commercial loans; this work and the literature of which it is an extension can, however, be interpreted within a broader context.

ture and degree of competition in commercial banking, to provide the complete theory. The chapter concludes with various extensions of the theory.

2.2 | PREVIOUS STUDIES OF THE AVAILABILITY DOCTRINE AND CREDIT RATIONING

The literature on credit rationing includes a large variety of works ranging from empirical attempts to measure the effects of rationing to policy related studies of the implications of the availability doctrine. At this point we are concerned only with the theoretical and institutional studies as they are directed at the questions of the existence and the mechanism of the rationing process. Furthermore, it is important to distinguish at the outset between credit rationing per se and the availability doctrine as a more general theory of commercial loan supply. As John Kareken has pointed out, the failure to make this distinction has led to a substantial confusion on some important points.[2] We will thus first briefly survey the literature on the availability doctrine before turning to a more detailed analysis of the literature on credit rationing and the mechanism of the rationing process, which constitute a main concern of the study.

The two major conclusions to be drawn from this review can be summarized:

1. The availability doctrine has only limited significance independent of a theory of credit rationing. For, in arguing that the banks restrict the availability of credit, the proponents of this doctrine must face the issue why the banks do not simply raise the interest rate they are charging their customers. That is, why not ration by price? This, of course, is precisely the question that a theory of credit rationing must answer.

2. Even those studies with the explicit goal of providing a theoretical justification for credit rationing fail to meet the basic issue, since they consider only the supply side of the market and neglect other very relevant questions. Only when the demand for loans and (hence) the determinants of the commercial loan rate are integrated with the supply can a complete theory be developed.

2.2.1 AVAILABILITY DOCTRINE[3]

The availability doctrine came into prominence at the end of World War II as an alternative to the then accepted theoretical and empirical

---

[2] See Kareken [1957], p. 302, and also Tussing [1961], p. 2.

[3] As noted above, this review of the availability doctrine is brief and highlights only the relevant analytic points. More complete summaries of the availability doctrine are given in Scott [1957b], Lindbeck [1962], and Tussing [1966].

views on the monetary mechanism and the efficacy of monetary policy. The received theory indicated that for monetary policy to be effective, real expenditure decisions should be interest elastic *and* the monetary authority should have the ability to force the necessary fluctuations in the relevant interest rates.[4] The conditions at the end of World War II led to a rather pessimistic evaluation of monetary policy if one accepted this theory. Empirical studies available at the time indicated very little interest elasticity in any important expenditure functions.[5] In addition, severe limitations were placed on the Federal Reserve's ability to influence the level of the interest rate on government debt due to the Treasury's insistence on a low and stable rate to minimize its interest costs and the fear of disrupting the security markets with widely fluctuating rates.

Not surprisingly, the Federal Reserve took an active role in the development of the availability doctrine. The first complete statement of the doctrine, for example, was given by Robert Roosa [1951] at the time he was a vice president of the Federal Reserve Bank of New York. In addition, policy statements by the Board of Governors and the presidents of the various Federal Reserve Banks in 1952 amounted to an official endorsement of the doctrine.[6] On the other hand, as Tussing [1966] has stressed, a rigorous statement (and critique) of the theory of the availability doctrine was developed only later in the professional economic journals.[7]

The principal proposition of the availability doctrine was that small variations in the rate of interest on government securities, achieved through open market operations, would be effective in influencing real expenditures even in the face of relatively interest inelastic expenditure schedules. The mechanism for this effect of monetary policy operated by reducing the availability of funds from the financial intermediaries, rather than through the cost of the funds as in the orthodox theory.

[4] See, for example, papers by Lutz [1945], Ellis [1951], Fforde [1951], and Tobin [1953].

[5] The most important of these empirical studies were the Oxford Surveys of 1938 and 1940; see Henderson [1938], Meade and Andrews [1938], Andrews [1940], and Sayers [1940].

[6] The official Federal Reserve policy statements were originally made in testimony before a joint congressional committee chaired by Wright Patman; U.S. Congress, Joint Committee on the Economic Report [1952a] and [1952b]. These statements were also summarized in the *Federal Reserve Bulletin* of March, 1953, and were reviewed by Tobin [1953].

[7] Tussing cites papers by Tobin [1953], Smith [1956], Kareken [1957], Scott [1957a], Scott [1957b], and Hodgman [1959]. Although Robert Roosa is generally noted as the "founder" of the availability doctrine, Roosa [1951] credits the work of Burgess [1927], Riefler [1930], Williams [1942], and Musgrave [1948] for earlier consideration of similar issues.

It was then assumed, at least implicitly, that this reduction in the availability of credit would reduce real expenditures.[8]

Several lines of argument were used to establish the basic link between variations in government interest rates and the availability of credit to the private sector. The main argument concerned the effects of uncertainty and changing expectations on the supply of commercial loans. Imperfections in the capital markets and the institutional changes brought about by the large amount of newly created Federal debt, however, were also frequently mentioned. Although it is difficult to formalize all of these considerations, Ira Scott [1957a] has developed a relatively simple analytic model of the availability doctrine, and we shall use his model as a framework to discuss the major issues.

Scott considers a financial intermediary, we shall assume a commercial bank, which holds in its portfolio two securities, government bonds and private loans. The bank's expected return and the standard deviation of the return are given by e_g and σ_g and e_p and σ_p for the two securities respectively. Both the expected return and the standard deviation are assumed to be larger for the private loans than for government securities. Two different utility functions are considered. In one case, the bank maximizes its expected return constrained by some maximum level of risk (variance of portfolio). In the second case, following the work of Markowitz, a more general utility function allowing for substitution between risk and return is used.

Scott analyzes how the portfolio composition changes when there is a *ceteris paribus* increase in either the risk or the expected return on the government bonds. The same conclusions are obtained for both of the utility functions, although somewhat restrictive assumptions on the shape of the indifference mapping must be introduced for the more general case.[9] For an increase in the expected return, the standard result is derived: a *ceteris paribus* increase in the yield on government bonds, e_g, leads to an unambiguous increase in the percentage of government bonds held in the portfolio. For an increase in risk, a more surprising result is derived: it is shown that an *increase* in the risk on government bonds will unambiguously *increase* the percentage of government bonds in the portfolio. This is easily seen in the case of the maximum variance utility function. For the initial portfolio composition, the increased risk

---

[8] Modigliani [1963] has shown how the availability doctrine view of monetary policy can be incorporated into a standard macroeconomic model; consideration of this issue was noticeably absent in most earlier discussions of the availability doctrine. The effects of credit rationing, as distinct from the mechanism of the availability doctrine, on the real sectors of the economy are discussed in Chapter 6 below.

[9] Scott *op. cit.*, pp. 46–48.

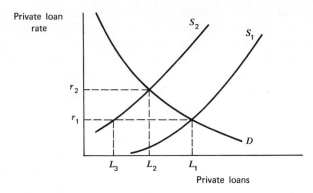

FIGURE 2.1

associated with the government bond portion will increase the risk of the entire portfolio above the acceptable degree. But since the risk on government bonds is assumed, always, to be less than the risk on the private loans, the aggregate risk of the portfolio can be decreased only by transferring funds from the loans to the bonds.

This would appear to confirm the principal proposition of the availability doctrine. Both the increase in yield on government bonds and the resulting increase in uncertainty about their future yield would lead to a decrease in the amount of the portfolio allocated to private loans. But there is a difficulty. The assumption of *ceteris paribus* implies that the commercial loan rate, the rate on private loans, remains fixed when the rate on government bonds changes. Scott, recognizing this point, assumes in a footnote that there is "stickiness in customer loan rates."[10] The implication of this assumption can be easily seen in Figure 2.1.

Figure 2.1 shows the demand and supply schedules for private loans as a function of the private loan rate. The demand curve is drawn under the assumption that there is some elasticity in the demand for private credit, although we shall also consider the case of zero elasticity. The positive slope of the supply curve (S_1) can be derived easily from Scott's results: a *ceteris paribus* increase in the private loan rate causes a redistribution of the bank's portfolio toward private loans. First consider an initial position in which the loan rate (r_1) and loan quantity (L_1) are determined by the intersection of the demand curve and the initial supply curve. Now suppose the Federal Reserve undertakes an open market sale which increases the yield and the risk on government bonds. Both of these changes have the effect of shifting the supply curve leftward, say

[10] Scott *op. cit.*, p. 46.

to S_2. There are then two cases to consider. In the first case, we assume that the loan rate is flexible and adjusts toward the new equilibrium value given by r_2. The amount of credit extended is then reduced to L_2. Under these conditions the availability doctrine differs very little from the earlier theory of the monetary mechanism. An increase in the government bond rate does decrease the amount of credit extended to the private sector, but the amount of reduction depends on the elasticity of the demand curve. In the polar case of a completely inelastic demand for private credit, even after the shift in the supply curve, L_1 credit would still be extended.[11]

Now consider the second case in which the loan rate remains at its initial value of r_1 even after the shift in the supply curve. Under this circumstance the bank would extend loans in the amount of L_3 and there would be an excess demand or credit rationing given by $(L_1 - L_3)$. If this did occur, the availability doctrine would have made a significant contribution, for the amount of credit extended, L_3, would be independent of the shape or slope of the demand curve. But why would the banks leave the rate at r_1? Scott's reliance on "stickiness" in this rate is more a statement of a necessary condition for his conclusion than an explanation.[12] It is precisely this explanation, as well as conclusion, that a theory of credit rationing should attempt to clarify.[13]

In addition to the risk-uncertainty line of argument, Robert Roosa and other early proponents of the availability doctrine stressed portfolio valuation effects on financial intermediary behavior. This aspect of the theory is frequently summarized under the heading of "locked-in" or pinned-in"

[11] The availability doctrine as evaluated here does make one contribution. Given some elasticity in the demand for credit, the reduction in the amount of credit outstanding is achieved with (perhaps) a small change in the level of the government bond rate. The private bond rate would still fluctuate significantly as noted earlier by Kareken [1957], pp. 300–302. This result was no doubt of much greater significance in the milieu of the pre-Accord period in which the availability doctrine first was postulated than it is today. See also Modigliani [1963].

[12] Hodgman [1960] has also noted Scott's reliance on an unexplained stickiness in the commercial loan rate.

[13] Before leaving Scott's model one generalization should be noted. Consider again the basic model with a maximum risk utility function, but with two forms of private loan securities, say P_1 and P_2, where the risk of P_1 exceeds the risk of P_2. Following Scott, assume that the rates on these securities are fixed at some initial values. In this case, should the rate and riskiness of the government bond increase, there would be a substitution away from the most risky security, P_1, as before. Now, however, although we know that the sum of the amount of the portfolio held in security P_2 and in government bonds must increase, the reallocation between these securities depends on the parameter values. In particular, it is conceivable that the amount of the less risky loan, P_2, held by the bank will actually increase.

effects. The situation arises when the Federal Reserve undertakes an open market sale that causes long term bond rates to rise, with the result that capital losses accrue to banks holding these securities. The argument then takes two forms. One variant stresses the reduced liquidity which follows from the capital losses. In analogy with the Scott model, but with liquidity replacing risk, the effect of the reduced liquidity is to cause substitution in the bank's portfolio away from the private securities and to the more liquid government securities. The second variant assumes that banks have regressive expectations with respect to the government bond rate. In this case the banks expect to recoup the capital loss if they continue to hold, or even purchase more, government bonds.[14]

It is thus apparent that with either of these portfolio valuation arguments, there is a tendency for the banks to become locked in to their government bond portfolio. On the other hand, the argument must assume that there is relatively little change in the yield on private loans; if the yield on private loans rises sufficiently in response to the open market purchase, then, of course, private securities may remain attractive even in view of the locked-in effects. Thus there remains an essentially empirical question whether private yields do rise enough to induce banks to extend additional credit to the private sector. Robert Roosa felt they did not; Warren Smith and others felt that they frequently would rise sufficiently.[15] If private yields rise, then the availability doctrine is shorn of much of its impact. If private yields do not rise, we are left with the need to explain why rational profit maximizing banks do not adjust the rates, but instead allow excess demand to develop in the loan market.

Finally, at times the proponents of the availability doctrine appeared to argue that shifts in the demand for credit influenced by the same uncertainty that affected the banks, could be relied on to improve the effectiveness of monetary policy. In terms of our earlier analysis of the Scott paper and Figure 2.1, this would mean that the demand for credit would shift leftward at the same time that the supply curve was shifting. Clearly, the earlier criticism still holds. If the commercial loan rate does adjust, then the availability doctrine differs little from the orthodox theory; and the availability doctrine itself provides little rationale for the loan rate not to adjust.

[14] Another variant of this argument was based on the premise that the banks had a phobia against taking capital losses, perhaps to preserve the appearance of their balance sheets, even though the implied portfolio switch was profitable. The large commercial bank sales of government securities in 1966 would appear, however, to refute this argument once and for all. Also see Smith [1956], pp. 589–598, Lindbeck [1962], pp. 22–25, and Kane and Malkiel [1965], pp. 113–119.

[15] See Roosa [1951], pp. 286–293, and Smith [1956], pp. 589–593.

2.2.2 CREDIT RATIONING

References to credit rationing in England can be traced back as early as the beginning of the 19th century. The issues then centered on the various bullion and currency controversies. Credit rationing became a concern because the usury laws restricted the Bank of England's ability to vary the discount rate, and this resulted in the Bank using a limited loan supply as the instrument of its policy, at least until exemption from some of the provisions of the usury laws was granted in 1833.[16] Later, in his *Treatise on Money,* Keynes [1930] stressed the importance of rationing and the "fringe of unsatisfied borrowers."[17] Unfortunately, the effects of credit rationing were not developed further in the *General Theory* by Keynes [1936]. Ellis [1951] provides one of the earliest links between credit rationing and the availability doctrine. This link was neglected in most statements of the availability doctrine, as stressed in the previous section.

The discussion of credit rationing in the early 1950s was primarily institutional and descriptive in nature, and it centered on the imperfections in the commercial loan market. Essentially three different views on credit rationing can be distinguished during this period:

1. The commercial loan rate adjusts slowly and rationing is important.
2. The commercial loan rate adjusts quickly and rationing is unimportant.
3. The commercial loan rate is sticky in the short run only and hence rationing is primarily a short run phenomenon.

In testimony before the Patman committee in 1952, Paul Samuelson provided a strong statement for the third view, although he also allowed for the existence of credit rationing even in the long run:

". . . It is quite possible therefore that, in the period immediately after open market contractionary operations by the Federal Reserve System or after an increase in legal reserve requirements, the individual bank will react to the credit stringency not by raising his posted interest rates but by rationing out the smaller supply of credit more stringently. Why do I say that after a few months time this rationing aspect will become less important? Do I mean that after a few months time the competitive character of the loan market will change and that the banker will cease to be an administrator of interest rates and a rationer

---

[16] See Viner [1937], pp. 256–257 for a discussion of the arguments used against credit rationing at this time.

[17] Keynes [1930], I, pp. 212–213; II, pp. 364–367.

of credit? No, I definitely do not; rationing and discretionary decisions will always characterize the loan market in the short run and the long run.

What I mean is the following: the extra tightness of rationing that the central banker can induce by his ordinary operations will disappear after a few months and be replaced by a firming of interest charges and a return to normal stringency of rationing."[18]

Samuelson also emphasized the importance of the imperfections in the commercial loan market for the existence of rationing:

"The imperfect competition aspect of banking is absolutely crucial for the recently fashionable doctrine that the central bank gains its leverage not through its effects upon the cost of credit but by its effects upon the availability of credit. I would gladly trade 100 pages of the written and oral testimony before this committee for even a few paragraphs of careful analysis on this point."[19]

Unfortunately, Samuelson's call for a more careful analysis of the market imperfections leading to credit rationing was not immediately met. The speed of adjustment of the commercial loan rate, the element which distinguished the three views, was not discussed within any analytic framework. Acceptance or denial of such phrases as "imperfect markets," "institutional rigidities," and "administered prices" remained the norm. Furthermore, even assuming that these phrases did have some operational meaning, no attempt was made to show that acceptance of "administered prices," for example, would lead to credit rationing as a rational behavior pattern. Steel prices, for example, are generally believed to be administered, but it is doubtful that steel companies ration steel.[20] On the other hand, certainly no attempt was made to give an analytic proof that the lack of administered prices would lead necessarily to the irrationality of credit rationing.

The first significant break from this position can be found in Donald Hodgman's comments on John Kareken's [1957] paper and Kareken's subsequent reply.[21] The important result of this exchange was the realization that, in the absence of price rationing, some other aspect of the

---

[18] Samuelson [1952], p. 695. Samuelson's testimony has sometimes been interpreted as providing an argument against significant credit rationing effects. This quotation clearly contradicts this interpretation.

[19] Samuelson, *ibid.*, p. 694.

[20] In the late 1940s steel was, in fact, rationed; but the issue was then centered on special dynamic circumstances.

[21] Hodgman [1959]; Kareken [1959].

loan or the loan customer would be used by the bank as its rationing criterion. Potential candidates for this function would include:

1. maturity of the loan;
2. collateral required;
3. length and value of the "customer relationship";
4. amount of compensating balance;
5. risk of partial or complete default on the loan.

A theory of credit rationing would then have to face the challenge of showing that rational behavior for banks would lead to their using one of these features of the loan rather than the price of the loan as the rationing device.[22]

Hodgman [*1960*].   In his 1960 article, "Credit Risk and Credit Rationing," Donald Hodgman took up this challenge. His objective was to show that credit rationing was rational even in the absence of the market imperfections assumed in the earlier discussion. His model emphasizes the riskiness of customer loans as the criterion for credit rationing.

He starts his analysis by assuming the existence of a density function, $f[x]$, which gives the bank's estimate of the probability of the firm's end of period value being x.[23] This density function is assumed to be independent of the size of the loan and is bounded in the sense that there exists a finite K such that $f[x] = 0$ for $x \geq K$. The loan contract consists of the principal of the loan L and the interest rate r. It is convenient to define $R = 1 + r$ as the interest rate factor, so that the amount of the contracted repayment is RL. The bank's expected income from the loan can then be written as:

$$(2.1) \quad EY = RL \int_{RL}^{K} f[x]\,dx + \int_{0}^{RL} x f[x]\,dx.$$

The first term in this expression represents the gross receipts of the bank if the outcome x is sufficiently favorable to enable the firm to repay the agreed amount RL in full. The second term denotes the receipts if the outcome for the firm falls short of the contracted amount. In this case, it is assumed the bank receives the entire outcome x, whatever it might be.

As a measure of risk, Hodgman defines EZ as the expected value of

---

[22] Guttentag [1960] appears to miss this point. His theory of credit rationing *assumes* that banks ration credit by altering the maturity of the loan rather than by using the rate. This begs the fundamental question.

[23] We have not directly followed Hodgman's notation at some points in order to retain consistency throughout the discussion.

the loss of principal when the firm fails to earn even the amount L:

(2.2) $EZ = \int_0^L (L - x) f[x]\, dx.$

It is important to note that EZ is independent of the interest rate charged on the loan.

It is assumed that the bank's utility maximization results in its maximizing the ratio EY/EZ.[24] Furthermore, it is assumed that an equilibrium ratio $(EY/EZ)^*$ is determined in a perfectly competitive market. Consequently, for, say, the ith customer to receive a loan of given size, it must be the case that:

(2.3) $\left(\dfrac{EY}{EZ}\right)_i \geq \left(\dfrac{EY}{EZ}\right)^*.$

The customer can bid for the loan by offering an interest rate sufficiently high to satisfy (2.3). This may not be possible, however, since the denominator of the ratio EY/EZ does not depend on the rate of interest, and the numerator, though it does vary with the rate offered, has a finite bound.[25] Thus the case may arise in which the firm cannot offer any rate which will induce the bank to grant a given loan. This is the essence of Hodgman's rationing argument.

The character of this rationing revolves around the riskiness of the firm. To see this, consider two firms similar in all respects except that the expected loss (EZ) of the first firm is higher. Then the less risky firm, with the lower EZ, can be rationed only if the bank is rationing the more risky first customer.

This also points out a very peculiar feature of this sort of rationing. Since customers will receive their demand for some loan size as long as they can promise a sufficiently high EY, it is conceivable that the bank will be making loans to customers even though the firm may be on the brink of bankruptcy in terms of EZ. In this case, the bank will take first lien on all possible returns to the firm, but these returns may barely exceed the principal of the loan. This seems to describe overly risky behavior for bankers typically considered to be conservative investors. Conversely, Hodgman's model also implies that rationing occurs *only* when the loan demanded by the firm is so large that even the promise of the total proceeds from the project cannot induce the bank to grant the loan. Thus we find the firm willing to demand a loan for which

---

[24] Musgrave and Domar [1944] use a similar utility function in analyzing portfolio behavior.

[25] Hodgman bases his argument at this point on the bounds of the density function, though this condition on EY actually holds more generally.

the bank does not think there is any possibility of full repayment. Such an extreme inconsistency in expectations between the bank and the firm would appear grossly unrealistic. The point is that we would never expect firms to demand loans large enough to warrant the type of rationing rationalized in Hodgman's model.[26]

Miller [1962] and Freimer and Gordon [1965]. Hodgman's model did generate a substantial amount of interest in the question of credit rationing, however, and it was the source for the models suggested by Merton Miller, and Marshall Freimer and Myron Gordon. Miller's intent was to construct a model of credit rationing which would avoid the peculiar features of Hodgman's work. Instead of placing a finite bound on the density function, he explicitly acknowledges the additional costs to the bank of collecting the available proceeds in case the firm must partially default. Bankruptcy in this sense is defined whenever the gross recovery x is less than the contracted amount RL. The costs of collection in this case are given as:

$$b_0 + b_1 x, \qquad b_0 > 0, \qquad 0 < b_1 < 1.$$

Within this framework, Miller assumes that the bank maximizes its utility function.[27] Attention is focused on the sign of the term $\dfrac{\partial (EU)}{\partial r}$ where EU is the expected utility from the loan and r is the interest rate charged. If there are no bankruptcy costs then, for Miller's utility function at least, the sign of this partial derivative is positive. When bankruptcy costs are included, however, the expected utility reaches its maximum at a finite interest rate. These two cases are illustrated in Figure 2.2, For the case without bankruptcy costs, the expected utility function rises as the interest rate rises. With bankruptcy costs, the expected utility function reaches a maximum at the rate shown as r^*.

As an alternative to making the loan, it is assumed the bank has the option of investing in a riskless security at an interest rate that implies a specific utility level shown in Figure 2.2 as $\bar{U}$. The firm receives a loan only when it can offer a rate with utility higher than $\bar{U}$. For the case without bankruptcy

---

[26] The preceding argument was stressed very strongly by Sam Chase [1961]. He also pointed out that Hodgman made the strong assumption that the density function, $f[x]$, and the size of the loan were independent. We discuss this aspect of the problem at greater length in Section 2.7.1 below. Ryder [1962] has extended Hodgman's results to the case in which the bank maximizes its long run profits on the premise that a firm once rationed will never return as a customer. See also Hodgman's replies to these comments in Hodgman [1961a] and Hodgman [1962].

[27] Miller actually uses a quadratic utility function. Very similar results can be obtained for a linear (expected value) utility function.

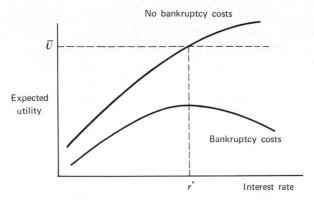

No bankruptcy costs

$\bar{U}$

Expected
utility

Bankruptcy costs

r^* Interest rate

FIGURE 2.2

costs, the utility of the bank rises with the interest rate and thus if the firm
is willing to offer a sufficiently high rate, for example r^* in the figure, it will
receive the loan. This, of course, is the traditional case of price rationing.
In the case with bankruptcy costs, on the other hand, there is a limit to the
utility and if, as illustrated in the figure, the maximum utility for the loan
lies below $\bar{U}$, the customer will not receive the loan regardless of the rate he
offers. Miller calls this phenomenon credit rationing.

One drawback to this approach is the definition of bankruptcy costs.
The bank must incur these costs if the firm cannot repay the contract in full,
and this reduces the bank's expected utility. The likelihood of such bankruptcy in Miller's model is increased if the bank either charges a higher
interest rate or makes a larger principal loan. No attempt is made, however,
to distinguish between failure to repay the principal and failure to repay the
interest on the principal. Once the loan is made, it is true that this distinction
becomes irrelevant, but in trying to explain the bank's *ex ante* behavior it is
of utmost concern. In particular, there should be no *ex ante* cost to the bank
of charging a higher interest rate, since if the firm does in fact default on the
interest payments the bank always has the option of simply ignoring the
default. Thus, although there may be cases in which nothing is gained by
charging a higher interest, the higher interest charge can never lead by itself
to a real reduction in income. As an alternative to Miller's assumption, bankruptcy may be defined only when $x < L$, that is, only when the firm cannot
repay the principal. The costs of collection can still be the same as in Miller's
case. Now, however, the derivative $\dfrac{\partial EU}{\partial r}$ is independent of the bankruptcy
costs, and the marginal utility curve is the same as the case without bank-
ruptcy costs, so that Miller's result no longer holds.

Perhaps an even more interesting point, moreover, is that rationing may occur in Miller's formulation even without bankruptcy costs.[28] The reason is that the utility function has a finite upper bound as long as the expected value of the venture is finite. Under Miller's assumptions it happens that the utility level approaches this bound asymptotically, but the important point is that whenever the utility of the certain asset, $\bar{U}$ exceeds this upper bound on the expected utility of the loan, in Miller's terms the customer is rationed. Consequently, there is really no qualitative difference between the cases with and without bankruptcy costs.[29]

This is not to suggest, on the other hand, that Miller has succeeded in providing a simple general rationale for credit rationing. The problem is that he has not really asked the right question. His analysis concerns a case in which the loan request is an all-or-nothing issue; the bank's only alternative is the risk-free asset. A more realistic situation would allow the bank the alternative of granting a smaller loan to the firm, since in the general case it is certainly true that there is a loan small enough so that its expected utility exceeds $\bar{U}$. This means that the bank generally would supply loans to all customers, but the size of the loans would vary. Whether rationing actually occurs then depends on the interest rate charged by the bank and the shape of the customer's demand curve. The inadequacy of Miller's model is that neither element is integrated with his formulation.

The work of Freimer and Gordon is the most recent model of the Hodgman-Miller form. Whereas Miller determined the optimal interest rate for a given loan size, Freimer and Gordon determine the optimal loan size given the interest rate. The result is a loan offer function that gives the optimal loan size as a function of the interest rate charged on the loan. The distinctive shape of this optimal loan offer function is shown in Figure 2.3 as the curve $\hat{L}_i = \hat{L}_i[R]$.[30] The discussion of "weak credit rationing" by Freimer and Gordon is based on the fact that the size of this optimal loan reaches a finite maximum at some finite interest rate and then declines for higher interest rates.[31] Thus, regardless of the rate the customer offers, he will not receive a loan that exceeds the maximum of the loan offer function.

[28] Of course, bankruptcy costs do affect the "quantitative" character of the solution. This problem is discussed further within our own framework in Section 2.7.3. below.
[29] Freimer and Gordon [1965], p. 403, have raised a similar point, although their argument appears to stress the existence of some finite bound on the density function, an assumption which Miller explicitly disavowed.
[30] The shape of this curve is derived rigorously in Section 2.3.2 below.
[31] Freimer and Gordon actually argue that this is valid only for the case of a "fixed-size" investment project. In Section 2.7.1 below, it is shown that under very reasonable conditions this result can also be derived for the more general case of an "open-end" investment project.

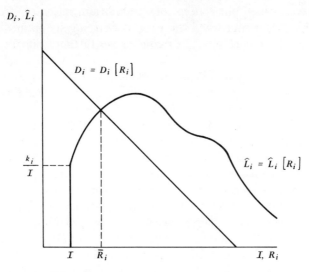

FIGURE 2.3

The analysis presented in this manner differs from Miller's in that the bank does consider offering the firm some smaller alternative loan. But again, the wrong question is posed. To prove that credit rationing will actually occur, it must be shown that the firm's demand exceeds the bank's optimal offer at the rate actually chosen by the bank. Thus, the existence of rationing depends on the rate chosen by the bank and the shape of the demand curve as well as the shape of the optimal loan offer curve. Since the optimal loan offers falls as the loan rate rises for sufficiently high rates, what Freimer and Gordon have shown is the existence of a "backward bending" supply curve in the loan market. This alone is not sufficient to show the existence of rationing.

The Freimer and Gordon case of "strict credit rationing" is a much closer approach to the true problem. This form of rationing occurs when the banker chooses some interest rate and then makes loans at this rate only if the size is less than or equal to the optimal loan. To demonstrate the likely existence of strict credit rationing, they assume that the banks take as given some conventional interest rate—6 percent, in fact—and then show, using numerical examples, that it is unlikely that firms would demand credit at higher rates. Consequently, the bank has no incentive to charge a higher rate. They do not consider, however, whether the bank might do even better by charging a lower rate. In general, this amounts to asking what is the optimal loan rate. It is for this reason that we have defined our concept of "equilibrium rationing" for the case of rationing that occurs when the bank is charging its optimal rate. This is the basic question at stake in trying to verify the rationality of credit rationing.

Hodgman [1961b] and Kane and Malkiel [1965]. The review of the literature concludes with a discussion of papers by Donald Hodgman,[32] and Edward Kane and Burton Malkiel. The common ground for these two papers is that both stress the importance of the "customer relationship" in determining the characteristics of credit rationing. Hodgman's argument is based on the value of the customer's deposit to the bank. With an institutional structure which prohibits interest payment for deposits and which places a floor under the commercial loan rate in the form of the prime rate convention, the bank, Hodgman argues, will compete for the deposits of large corporations by providing other banking services. One of the most important of these services is the provision of bank credit in periods of tight money. Kane and Malkiel take an only slightly different tack. They argue that there is a class of customers for which the denial of a loan request increases the bank's aggregate risk. The fear of the bank is that it will lose these customers and most importantly their deposits for the long run. Thus, both theories indicate that, in periods of tight money, banks will redistribute their loans toward a class of large, stable customers.

Both theories also neglect, however, the very important question of loan rate determination. The crucial problem is why a nonprime customer cannot compete for loans by simply offering a high enough interest rate. Hodgman's argument is that the rate which the nondepositor would have to pay is so high that the firm's demand for loans at this rate is essentially zero. Rather than embarrass the firm with this very high rate, however, the bank goes through the fiction of telling the firm that there is simply no rate high enough to warrant a loan. It should be obvious that this is a classic case of price rationing. The fact that the customer's demand is zero at the equilibrium rate should not cloud the issue, and the fact that the bank saves the customer's face by telling him that he is rationing is clearly irrelevant.

The Kane and Malkiel argument is somewhat different. A good depositor, they argue, is more valuable to his current bank than is his would-be value to some competing bank, since the value of a customer is only developed over time and as a result of a growing confidence in the stability of his deposits. They also note that a bank may be indifferent between a poor depositor of their own bank and a prime customer at some other

[32] See also Hodgman [1963] for a similar discussion.

bank. But the long run profit potential of prime customers in no way implies that a nonprime customer (regardless of whether he is considered prime at some other bank) may not still bid loanable funds away from a bank's prime customers. Indeed, what the Kane and Malkiel study suggests is that the total quantity of loans—to both prime and nonprime customers—may rise in periods of tight money.

Summary. If banks do not use the interest rate as the rationing vehicle, then presumably some other characteristic of the loan contract or loan customer must be used as the criterion. The Hodgman [1960], Miller [1961], Freimer and Gordon [1965] line of argument suggested differential risk characteristics as the criterion. Hodgman [1961b], and Kane and Malkiel [1965], on the other hand, argued that banks give a preference to customers with long run profit potential when it comes to allocating scarce bank funds.

To provide an explanation for credit rationing, a theory must show that at the optimal commercial loan rate it is profitable for the bank to extend a loan smaller than the amount demanded. In fact, this condition holds only if the competitive structure of the industry meets conditions which are developed in the remainder of this chapter. Since the studies reviewed here have generally failed to consider the loan demand and the determinants of the loan rate, it is not surprising that their results are of only limited relevance to the problem.

2.3 | ANALYTIC PROPOSITIONS ON EQUILIBRIUM RATIONING

The remainder of this chapter is concerned with the derivation of a new theory of credit rationing. The present section derives the basic theoretical propositions concerning credit rationing by a rational banker. The following section combines these propositions with the institutional and structural features of the commercial banking industry in order to provide the complete theory. The implications of the model are then derived and a link between the theory and the empirical material of later chapters is provided.

2.3.1 ASSUMPTIONS

The term rational behavior will be used here to mean that the bank maximizes its expected profits. The basic rationale for this assumption is that the bank services a number of customers large enough to allow us to disregard the correlations between the outcomes of sets of loans. Furthermore, since the intent is to show that rationing is a rational policy, it is appropriate to choose a utility function that is not biased toward risk aversion.[33] Finally, the expected profits formulation reduces the number of purely mathematical problems.

We consider a bank faced with n customers. For convenience the demand function of the ith customer is written as:

$$D_i = D_i[R_i], \qquad D_i \geq 0 \qquad \text{for all } R_i,$$

where r_i is the interest rate charged to the ith customer, $R_i = 1 + r_i$ as before, and D_i is continuous and twice differentiable. We assume a downward sloping demand curve, which vanishes for a sufficiently high interest rate factor and is finite even for a zero interest rate (or interest factor equal to unity). That is, there exist R_i^m and D_i^m, each less than infinity, such that:

(2.4) $D_i[R_i] = 0$ for $R_i \geq R_i^m$,

(2.5) $D_i[1] = D_i^m$,

(2.6) $\dfrac{\partial D_i[R_i]}{\partial R_i} = D_i'[R_i] \geq 0$ for $1 < R_i < R_i^m$.

The boundary conditions for the demand curve are based on the characteristics of the underlying investment projects which the firm is financing. It is assumed that each firm has fixed-size investment projects which require D_i^m to finance. Thus even at a zero interest rate, the firm's demand for credit is limited to this amount.[34] At the other extreme, it is assumed that there is a rate sufficiently high to reduce the firm's demand to zero; in this case the projects are financed entirely by nonbank funds. The negative slope of the demand curve is due to the limited access of the firm to alternative means of finance. The implied absence of, or at least limit on, competition between banks for the customer's business is discussed in Secttion 2.4.

The bank's expected profits from granting a loan to the ith customer can be derived following the discussion of Hodgman's [1960] model (Section 2.2.2.). Again x denotes the outcome of the firm's investment projects in terms of its end of period value, and $f_i[x]$ is the bank's subjective evaluation

---

[33] The sufficient conditions for credit rationing developed in this section remain essentially unchanged if a utility function of higher order moments is used, although the amount of credit rationing—if it occurs at all—will be changed. Thus the basic qualitative results hold quite generally.

[34] While this assumption is convenient mathematically, we could in fact allow for what is perhaps a more realistic case of an infinite loan demand at a zero interest rate.

of the probability of different outcomes. It is assumed that the density function is continuous and at least once differentiable, and that there exist k_i and K_i, $0 < k_i < K_i < \infty$, such that:

(2.7) $f_i[x] = 0$ for $x \leq k_i$ or $x \geq K_i$.

If we define $F_i[A] = \int_{k_i}^{A} f_i[x]\, dx$, it then follows that:

(2.8) $F_i[x] = 0$ for $x \leq k_i$,

       $F_i[x] = 1$ for $x \geq K_i$.

We also assume that the end of period outcomes for any two customers of the bank are uncorrelated.

It should also be noted that, in general, the density function $f_i[x]$ will be affected by the size of the customer's investment, which in turn may be expected to depend on the size of the loan granted. For expository convenience, however, our formal analysis will proceed under the restrictive assumption that the size of the projects is fixed and therefore $f_i[x]$ can be taken as independent of the loan size granted. This assumption implies that the firm has alternative means of finance which can be used to complement the bank credit. In Section 2.7.1 below it is shown that the major conclusions reached here can be generalized to the case where the size of the projects is not independent of the loan granted, provided the investment opportunity of the customer is subject to decreasing (expected) returns.

With this basis, we can formulate the bank's expected profits of granting a loan to the ith customer, P_i, as a function of the interest rate factor R_i and the loan size L_i. The expected profits are equal to the difference between the expected repayment on the loan contract (interest plus principal) and the bank's opportunity cost (interest plus principal):

(2.9) $P_i = P[R_i L_i] = R_i L_i \int_{R_i L_i}^{K_i} f_i[x]\, dx + \int_{k_i}^{R_i L_i} x f_i[x]\, dx - I L_i$.

The first two terms in this expression represent the expected repayment and follow directly from equation 2.1 developed for Hodgman's model.[35] The last term represents the bank's opportunity cost, where $I = 1 + j$ and j is the opportunity rate. This rate is for the moment assumed constant on the

---

[35] In cases of partial default on the loan, the bank would incur some collection costs which should be deducted from the outcome x. In Section 2.7.3 below it is shown that the character of the results does not change if this is taken into account. See also discussion in Section 2.2 above.

premise that the bank has unlimited access to a perfect capital market.[36] In Section 2.7.2 below we show that a generalization to the case of an increasing opportunity cost as the loan size increases leaves the basic results unchanged.

The expected profit function (2.9) can be simplified by adding and subtracting $R_i L_i \int_{k_i}^{R_i L_i} f_i[x]\, dx$ and using the fact that $\int_{k_i}^{K_i} f_i[x]\, dx = 1$:

$$(2.10) \qquad P_i = P[R_i L_i] = (R_i - I)L_i + \int_{k_i}^{R_i L_i} x f_i[x]\, dx - R_i L_i \int_{k_i}^{R_i L_i} f_i[x]\, dx.$$

Then, integrating the second term by parts yields:

$$(2.11) \qquad P_i = P[R_i L_i] = (R_i - I)L_i - \int_{k_i}^{R_i L_i} F_i[x]\, dx.$$

The meaning of rational credit rationing can now be formalized. Suppose the bank quotes an optimal interest rate factor R_o. The loan demand is then given by $D_o = D[R_o]$, and the expected profits, $P_o = P[R_o D_o]$, are given by (2.11). Then rationing is rational if, and only if:

$$(2.12) \qquad \frac{\partial P[R_i L_i]}{\partial L_i} < 0 \quad \text{for} \quad L_i = D[R_o] \quad \text{and} \quad R_i = R_o.$$

Thus, rationing is rational if, and only if, expected profits can be increased by decreasing the loan size below the amount that is demanded by the customer at the desired interest factor.

2.3.2. OPTIMAL LOAN OFFER CURVE

Let us now ask the following question: What is the optimal loan size for the bank to grant to a customer, given the interest factor? The locus of these optimal loans as the interest factor varies will be termed the optimal loan offer curve to the firm. It is important to emphasize that the offer curve depends on the firm's ability to repay the loan but not on the firm's demand function. This curve can be determined by using the first order condition for an expected profit maximum, derived by differentiating (2.11):

$$(2.13) \qquad \frac{\partial P[R_i L_i]}{\partial L_i} = R_i(1 - F_i[R_i L_i]) - I = 0.$$

---

[36] The existence of well-developed markets in Federal Funds and certificates of deposits (CDs) make this assumption reasonable in normal periods. If these markets cease to operate in tight money periods, for example when the Regulation Q ceiling hinders the issue of new CDs, then the shadow price of funds would have to replace the market indicator as the opportunity cost. This may lead to dynamic effects, and these are considered below in the discussion of dynamic rationing (Section 2.6) and in the empirical tests.

This condition can be usefully rewritten in the form:

$$(2.14) \qquad F_i[R_iL_i] = 1 - \frac{I}{R_i} = \frac{r_i - j}{1 + r_i}.$$

Since the quantity $F_i[R_iL_i]$ is precisely the probability of default, (2.14) admits the following simple interpretation: the optimal loan is such that the probability of default is equal to the excess of the loan rate over the opportunity cost, normalized by the loan rate factor $R_i = 1 + r_i$.[37]

The offer curve can now be defined as the implicit solution to (2.13) for L_i in terms of R_i subject to the nonnegativity condition $L_i \geq 0$. This solution can be denoted by $\hat{L}_i = \hat{L}_i[R_i]$. From (2.13) several properties of this offer curve can be deduced which will be used in developing the argument.

PROPOSITION I. *The optimal loan offer curve defined by condition (2.13) (and drawn in Figure 2.3) has the following properties:*

(I.1) $\hat{L}_i = 0$ for $R_i \leq I$,

(I.2) $0 \leq \hat{L}_i \leq k_i/I$ for $R_i = I$,

(I.3) $R_i\hat{L}_i \leq K_i$ for all R_i

(I.4) $\lim_{R_i \to \infty} \hat{L}_i = 0$.

Proposition I.1 follows from the nonnegativity condition and condition (2.13). Since the marginal expected profit of an additional loan ($\partial P/\partial L_i$) is negative for all positive loan sizes whenever $R_i < I$, the best the bank can do under this condition is to extend no loan at all. Similarly, when $R_i = I$, condition (2.13) can hold only if $F_i[R_iL_i] = 0$; this implies $R_iL_i = IL_i \leq k_i$ which is equivalent to proposition I.2. This means that the offer curve is a vertical line segment when $R_i = I$. In fact, in the case with no uncertainty in which F_i is identically zero, the offer curve is nothing more than this vertical line.

The logic of Proposition I.3 is that for any given interest rate factor R_i, the bank will not receive additional income from extending loans in amounts that exceed the solution of $R_iL_i = K_i$, because K_i is the maximum amount the firm could conceivably earn. Furthermore, loans cost the bank the opportunity rate I, and hence all solutions must satisfy the condition of Proposition I.3. *Thus the optimal loan is finite no matter*

---

[37] Since the empirically observed spread between the loan rate and the opportunity rate at which banks can secure or invest funds is typically small, this condition implies that banks should tend to assume quite modest default risk. This conclusion seems to be in agreement with bank loss experience on commercial loans.

how high the interest rate offered.[38] Proposition I.4 follows immediately
from Proposition I.3. It implies that as the loan rate grows larger and
larger, the optimal loan does not follow course; to the contrary, at least
after some point, the optimal loan will begin to decline as the rate grows
and will eventually approach zero as the rate grows beyond bounds. The
common sense of this surprising implication can be understood from the
following considerations: (1) by making the size of the contracted repayment R_iL_i sufficiently large, default becomes virtually certain, and
hence the bank can count on becoming the owner of all the net activities
of the firm; (2) as R_i rises, the amount L_i that the bank needs to invest to
achieve this result grows smaller and smaller and approaches zero as R_i
tends to infinity.

Two other properties of the offer curve are also worth developing.

PROPOSITION II. *For a given interest factor R_i, expected profits decrease monotonically as the loan size varies from the optimal size in
either direction.*

The proof follows directly from (2.13), since

(2.15) $$\frac{\partial^2 P[R_iL_i]}{\partial L_i^2} = -R_i^2 f_i[R_iL_i] < 0 \quad \text{for} \quad k_i < R_iL_i < K_i.$$

This also shows that the solution given by (2.13) is, indeed, a global
maximum.

PROPOSITION III. *Expected profits increase along the offer curve for
successively higher interest rate factors.*

To derive this result, first substitute (2.13) into (2.10), which allows
us to write the profit function along the offer curve as:

(2.16) $$P[R_i\hat{L}_i] = \int_{k_i}^{R_i\hat{L}_i} x f_i[x]\, dx,$$

but then,

$$\frac{dP[R_i\hat{L}_i]}{dR_i} = R_i\hat{L}_i f_i[R_i\hat{L}_i]\left(\hat{L}_i + R_i\frac{d\hat{L}_i}{dR_i}\right),$$

and by implicitly differentiating (2.13),

$$\hat{L}_i + R_i\frac{d\hat{L}_i}{dR_i} = \frac{1 - F_i[R_i\hat{L}_i]}{R_i f_i[R_i\hat{L}_i]}$$

[38] Although the maximum is finite, there may be multiple local maxima for the loan
offer curve. In the discussion which follows, we abstract from this complication and
in Section 2.7.4 it is shown that the existence of such local maxima would not affect
our results.

and thus,

$$(2.17) \qquad \frac{dP[R_i\hat{L}_i]}{dR_i} = \hat{L}_i(1 - F_i[R_i\hat{L}_i]) < 0 \qquad \text{for} \qquad k_i < R_i\hat{L}_i < K_i,$$

which proves the proposition. An obvious and reasonable implication of this proposition is that the bank will obtain its maximum potential profits when allowed to charge an infinite interest rate. Of course, this only serves to emphasize that the offer curve is defined independently of the demand for loans, and thus many points on the offer locus may not prove feasible for the lender.

2.3.3 THE BANKER AS A DISCRIMINATING MONOPOLIST

As we have stressed earlier, the existence of credit rationing depends on the loan rate selected by the bank and the shape of the demand function as well as the shape of the bank's offer curve. The interaction of these three elements can be seen clearly in Figure 2.3. The ith firm's demand curve and the bank's offer curve to that customer are assumed to intersect at the interest rate factor $\bar{R}_i$.[39] If the bank chooses to charge an interest factor greater than $\bar{R}_i$, rationing will not occur since the loan demand is less than the loan offer at such an interest factor. In fact, if the firm were willing to accept a larger loan (which it is not by definition of the demand curve), the bank would increase its expected profits by providing such a loan (see Proposition II). On the other hand, if the bank chooses to charge an interest factor less than $\bar{R}_i$, then rationing will occur since in this region the bank's optimal loan offer is less than the amount demanded by the customer. The bank would only reduce its expected profits by increasing the loan offer to meet the demand. Thus the question of the rationality of credit rationing can be reduced to a consideration of the optimal rate factor to be charged by the bank, and its relation to $\bar{R}_i$.

Two critical variables enter into the bank's selection of the loan rate. First there is the question of the time horizon: in the long run, a rational banker would select the rate that maximizes his expected profits; but other constraints may preclude immediate full adjustment in the short run. This leads, of course, to the distinction between the cases of equilibrium rationing and dynamic rationing as already defined. We start by considering only the equilibrium case since it has been the center of the theoretical discussion and because the short run dynamic case is easily derived from the equilibrium case.

The second important variable influencing the bank's choice of rate

---

[39] The existence of at least one point of intersection is assured by the boundary conditions on the demand curve and Proposition I.4. We shall assume that, in fact, only one such point exists. Equivalent results can be obtained for the case of multiple intersections, but only at the cost of more complexity in the analysis. See Section 2.7.4.

is the nature of market competition. Because the degree of competition turns out to be a critical factor in determining the existence of rationing, it is worthwhile considering several different regimes from a purely analytic standpoint.

The first regime considered is the case of a discriminating monopolist. It is assumed that the bank maximizes its expected profits with respect to each customer separately and is free to charge each customer a different interest rate. The determinants of price and quantity for such a monopolist are of course well known in the standard theory of monopoly: the monopolist sets the price at the level at which marginal revenue equals marginal cost, and the quantity is then determined by the customer's demand function.[40] This standard analysis leads to an important problem, however, in considering the possible existence of rationing, because the condition that the demand function determines the quantity simply rules out, by assumption, the possible existence of rationing. Consequently, a more general mode of analysis must be used if the existence of rationing is to be fairly considered. As it turns out, the result of the standard theory is actually correct—a discriminating monopolist will not ration—but to understand the reasons for this result it is worthwhile pursuing the analysis somewhat further.

To allow for the possibility of rationing, a more basic analysis involving the iso-profit curves of the monopolist must be developed. In this case, the iso-profit curves represent the loci of $\{R,L\}$ combinations that provide the bank with constant expected profits. In Figure 2.4 four members of this family of iso-profit curves are shown, in ascending order of expected profits, as the curves p_0, p_1, p_2, and p_3. The optimal loan offer curve $\hat{L}_i$ and the customer demand function D_i are also shown as they were in Figure 2.3. The shape of the iso-profit curves depends on essentially two conditions: (1) expected profits decrease as we move vertically from the optimal loan offer (Proposition II); and (2) expected profits increase as the rate factor increases with a constant loan size until the loan contract equals the maximum possible payment K_i; after that point expected profits remain constant as the rate factor increases further. Condition 1 implies that the iso-profit curves must be vertical as they intersect the offer curve; otherwise a vertical movement, either upward or downward, would result in higher expected profits. Condition 2 implies that the iso-profit curves must be positively sloped where they are above the offer curve and negatively sloped where they are below it. This is true because as the loan size varies from the optimal offer in either direction, the interest rate factor must increase if expected profits are to remain constant. When the loan contract, R_iL_i, reaches the

---

[40] Alternatively, the monopolist can be viewed as a quantity setter, in which case the demand function determines the price.

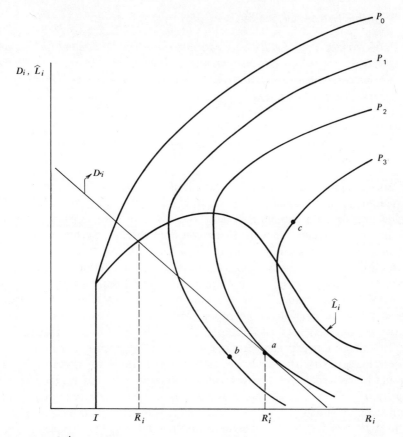

FIGURE 2.4

amount K_i, however, further increases in the interest rate factor do not succeed in increasing the expected profits and thus the iso-profit curves become horizontal at this point. Also, note that the iso-profit curve p_o represents the special case of zero expected profits.[41]

[41] The shape of the iso-profit curves can also be derived algebraically. Setting the expected profit function (2.11) equal to a constant, implicitly differentiating the resulting equation with respect to R_i, and then solving for the slope of the iso-profit curves yields:

$$\frac{dL_i}{dR_i} = \frac{-L_i(1 - F_i)}{R_i(1 - F_i) - I}$$

Noting that the denominator of the fraction is the same as equation 2.13 for the offer curve, and using Proposition II, it is apparent that the iso-profit curves take the form shown in Figure 2.4.

With this framework, we can now prove the following:

PROPOSITION IV.   *Let $\bar{R}_i$ be the rate factor at which the demand function and offer curve for the ith customer intersect, and let R_i^* be the rate factor which maximizes the bank's expected profits when acting as a discriminating monopolist toward the ith customer. Then:*

(IV.1) $R_i^* \geq \bar{R}_i$,
(IV.2)   *Credit rationing is not profitable for a bank acting as a discriminating monopolist.*

With Figure 2.4 before us, the proof is quite straightforward. We can immediately eliminate from consideration all $[R,L]$ points which lie below the demand function, because the shape of the iso-profit mapping insures that such points will always be dominated in terms of expected profits by a point such as a. In other words, starting from a point with rationing, such as b, higher expected profits will be obtained by increasing the interest rate, loan size, or both in a movement toward point a. Proposition IV.2 is thus valid. Next, we can consider points above the demand curve which lie on higher iso-profit curves than a. Point c on iso-profit curve p_3 can serve as an example. Although point c can provide the bank with greater expected profits than a, it will generally not be feasible. The reason is that the bank's customer will be able to increase its own profits by *reducing* the loan toward the amount indicated by the demand function.[42] The bank can thus maintain point c only by a type of negative rationing in which the customer is granted an all or nothing choice of a loan that is larger than he desires at the interest rate associated with c. Although this possibility cannot be ruled out a priori, it is unlikely that banks enjoy this form of extreme monopoly power.[43] Thus, we return to the case of standard monopoly theory in which the bank maximizes its expected profits constrained by the customer's demand function. This maximum will occur at the tangency of the iso-profit map with the demand function as illustrated at point a. It is also apparent that this tangency must occur to the right of the intersection of the demand curve and the offer curve and thus Proposition IV.1 is valid.

Finally, it will be useful to have an algebraic formulation for the optimal

---

[42] By definition, the demand function represents the locus of loan sizes maximizing the firm's profits for given interest rates on the loan.

[43] In the extreme case, a point such as c might imply even negative profits for the bank's customer. In such a case, the point would obviously not be feasible since the customer would prefer to have no loan at all.

interest rate factor R_i^* charged by the discriminating monopolist. This can be derived from the first order condition for the maximum of the expected profits function (2.11) with the constraint of the demand function taken into account. The expected profits function can then be written:

$$(2.18) \qquad P = P[R_iD_i] = (R_i - I)D_i - \int_{k_i}^{R_iD_i} F_i[x]\, dx,$$

where the substitution of D_i for L_i incorporates the constraint. The first order condition is then:

$$(2.19) \qquad \frac{\partial P}{\partial R_i} = D_i'[R_i(1 - F_i) - I] + D_i(1 - F_i) = 0,$$

where

$$F_i = F_i[R_iD_i].$$

Equation 2.19 implicitly defines the optimal rate R_i^* as a function of the opportunity rate factor I and the parameters of the demand function and the density function.

2.3.4 THE BANKER CHARGING ALL CUSTOMERS THE SAME INTEREST RATE

The Case of Two Customers. Now suppose that the banker is constrained to charge all customers the same rate although he can choose that rate freely and can also decide on the size of the loan to be granted each customer. We will show that under these conditions credit rationing may (and very frequently will) be profitable. That is, at the common optimal interest rate, for some customers the most profitable loan for the bank to supply is less than the amount demanded.

To establish this proposition it is convenient to deal first with a subsidiary problem. Suppose that the bank faces only two customers and, for the moment, rule out credit rationing by requiring that the bank *must* satisfy the customers' demand at the chosen common rate.

The bank's expected profits under these conditions can be written, following (2.18), as:

$$(2.20) \qquad P = P_1[RD_1] + P_2[RD_2] = \sum_{i=1}^{2} (R - I)D_i - \int_{k_i}^{RD_i} F_i[x]\, dx,$$

where R is the common rate factor charged both customers and the constraint of satisfying both demand functions is implicit in the notation. By differentiating this profit function with respect to the interest rate factor, the first-order condition for an expected profit maximum is obtained:

$$(2.21) \quad \frac{dP}{dR} = \frac{dP_1[RD_1]}{dR} + \frac{dP_2[RD_2]}{dR}$$

$$= \sum_{i=1}^{2} ((D_i')(R(1 - F_i) - I) + (1 - F_i)D_i) = 0,$$

where

$$F_i = F_i[R_iD_i[R_i]].$$

Equation 2.21 implicitly defines the common optimal rate factor, which is denoted as R^*.

The second-order condition for a maximum is derived by differentiating equation 2.21:

$$(2.22) \quad \frac{d^2P}{dR^2} = \frac{d^2P_1[RD_1]}{dR^2} + \frac{d^2P_2[RD_2]}{dR^2} < 0 \quad \text{at} \quad R = R^*.$$

To simplify the exposition, a stronger assumption must be made:

$$(2.23) \quad \frac{d^2P_i[RD_i]}{dR^2} < 0 \quad \text{for all } R, \quad i = 1, 2.$$

Equation 2.23 clearly implies equation 2.22. In addition, equation 2.23 also implies that the second-order conditions for the problem of the discriminating monopolist will be valid.[44] The second-order conditions for both problems are discussed further in Section 2.7.4 below.

Now let R_1^* and R_2^* be the optimal rate factors the bank would charge customers 1 and 2, respectively, if acting as a discriminating monopolist. Furthermore, assume without loss of generality, that $R_1^* \leq R_2^*$. We can then establish:

PROPOSITION V.   *If R^* is the common rate factor that maximizes the bank's expected profit, we must have:*

$$R_1^* \leq R^* \leq R_2^*.$$

That is, the common optimal rate is bounded by the optimal discriminating monopolist rates for each of the bank's customers. To demonstrate this result, we shall use a proof by contradiction. We assume that either $R^* > R_2^*$ or $R^* < R_1^*$. Then from the definition of R_i^* given in equation 2.19 and

[44] Equation 2.23 insures that the expected profit function of the bank for each of its customers is globally concave for changes in the interest rate factor. The assumption of global concavity is not a necessary condition, however, for Proposition VI to be proven below; the proof can be carried out with weaker assumptions. We shall use the global concavity because it leads, via Proposition V, to a particularly interesting demonstration of Proposition VI.

the second-order condition (2.23), we must have:

$$(2.24) \qquad \frac{\partial P_i[R^*D_1]}{\partial R} + \frac{\partial P_2[R^*D_2]}{\partial R} \gtreqless 0 \quad \text{as} \quad \begin{array}{l} R^* < R_1^* \\ R^* > R_2^* \end{array}$$

Equation 2.24 implies that the bank's expected profits can be increased by raising the rate factor R^* whenever $R^* < R_1^*$ and by lowering the rate factor R^* whenever $R^* > R_2^*$. This clearly contradicts the condition that R^* is the optimal rate (see equation 2.21) and thus Proposition V is valid.

We can now relax the restriction that the bank must satisfy both customers' demand functions and show that, under these conditions, it will never pay to ration customer 1 but it may very well pay to ration customer 2. Specifically, we can establish:

PROPOSITION VI.   *For the common rate regime*

(VI.1) $R^* \geq R_1^* \geq \bar{R}_1$ *implying it is not profitable to ration customer 1.*
(VI.2) $R_2^* \geq R^* \gtreqless \bar{R}_2$, *implying that $R^* < \bar{R}_2$ is possible, in which case, credit rationing is profitable.*

Proposition VI.1 follows directly from Propositions IV and V. Proposition IV implies that a bank customer will not be rationed if the bank is charging this customer an interest rate that equals or exceeds the discriminating monopolist rate R_i^* for this customer. Proposition V insures that the rate being charged customer 1 under the common rate regime, R^*, is in fact greater than the discriminating monopolist rate R_1^*, and thus customer 1 is not rationed. Indeed, as is apparent in Figure 2.4, under these conditions the bank would prefer to extend customer 1 an even larger loan than is made feasible by the customer's demand function.[45]

As for establishing Proposition VI.2, we need only exhibit a concrete example in which the condition holds. That it is, in fact, quite easy to construct such examples can be seen from the following considerations. First, returning to Proposition V and equations 2.19 and 2.21, it is readily apparent that the position of R^* within the range R_1^* to R_2^* depends on the relative size of the two customers (as measured, say, by the size of the loan demanded for any R in the relevant range), on the elasticity of the two demand curves, and on the density functions for the possible outcomes for the two firms. In particular, R^* can be made arbitrarily close to R_1^* by assuming any one or a combination of the following: (1) customer 1 is sufficiently larger than customer 2; (2) the demand curve for customer 1 is sufficiently inelastic in the range of rates above R_1^*; (3) the risk of customer 1 is sufficiently small relative to the risk of customer 2. By the same token, $\bar{R}_2$ can be made arbitrarily close to R_2^* by assuming a sufficiently elastic demand

[45] The role of customer 1 as nonrationed and customer 2 as rationed is of course an arbitrary assignment, depending on our assumption that $R_1^* \leq R_2^*$.

curve for customer 2. Thus by the appropriate choice of these functions, one can readily construct situations where R^* is lower than $\bar{R}_2$. The above construction also provides an interesting interpretation of Proposition VI. The constraint of charging both customers the same rate R^* forces the bank to charge customer 1 a rate which is too high relative to R_1^* and hence, the customer is not rationed. On the other hand, the bank is forced to charge customer 2 a rate which is too low relative to R_2^*. If the rate is sufficiently low relative to $\bar{R}_2$, that is $R^* < \bar{R}_2$, then the second customer will be rationed.

The possibility of credit rationing also adds another dimension to the problem. In the case in which rationing does not occur, R^* is the optimal common rate charged by the bank and the customers receive loans of $D_1[R^*]$ and $D_2[R^*]$, respectively. But when customer 2 can profitably be rationed at R^*, the very existence of rationing changes the conditions of the problem and R^* need no longer be the optimal rate. The bank will now maximize the expected profits function for the two customers under the constraint that only the loan for customer 1 must satisfy the demand function; the loan for customer 2 will be on the bank's optimal loan offer curve for that customer. Thus, instead of (2.20), the banks expected profit function will take the form of:

$$(2.25) \qquad P = P_1[RD_1] + P_2[R\hat{L}_2] = (R - I)D_1 + \int_{k_1}^{RD_1} F_1[x] \, dx$$

$$+ \int_{k_2}^{R\hat{L}_2} f_2[x] \, dx$$

using (2.16) and (2.18). The maximum for (2.25) will be attained at a more general *optimum optimorum* rate, say $\hat{R}$, which allows for the rationing of customer 2. $\hat{R}$ will just equal R^* in cases in which rationing is not profitable, but will generally differ from R^* when rationing is profitable. The fact that $\hat{R}$ may differ from R^* creates some difficulties in deriving the comparative static properties of the model, as will be apparent below. However, it does not affect our basic conclusion; Proposition VI remains valid even if R^* is replaced with the true optimum $\hat{R}$. For, as one can readily verify, $R^* \leq \bar{R}_2$ implies $\hat{R} \leq \bar{R}_2$, and conversely.[46]

Before proceeding to the generalizations of the propositions developed so far, it is worthwhile considering the special case of a risk-free firm, that is a customer for whom the bank's subjective evaluation of default risk is zero.

---

[46] We have previously established that $R^* \geq \bar{R}_2$ implies that R^* is already the optimum optimorum or $R^* = \hat{R}$; hence $R^* \geq \bar{R}_2 \rightarrow \hat{R} \geq \bar{R}_2$. Similarly $\hat{R} \geq \bar{R}_2$ implies that even when rationing is allowed, it is not profitable and therefore $\hat{R}$ must coincide with R^*, the maximum subject to the constraint that rationing is not permissible; that is $\hat{R} \geq \bar{R}_2 \rightarrow \hat{R} = R^*$ and therefore $\hat{R} \geq \bar{R}_2 \rightarrow R^* \geq \bar{R}_2$. But these two propositions together imply $R^* \geq \bar{R}_2 \Leftrightarrow \hat{R} \geq \bar{R}_2$, which in turn implies $R^* \leq \bar{R}_2 \Leftrightarrow \hat{R} \geq \bar{R}_2$.

PROPOSITION VII.   *Neither a banker acting as a discriminating monopolist, nor a banker charging all customers the same rate, will ration a risk-free customer.*

The result of Proposition VII for the case of a discriminating monopolist is simply a special case of Proposition IV and follows directly from that proposition. To prove the proposition for a banker charging a common rate factor, it is important to recall from Proposition I that the bank's offer curve for a risk-free customer is a vertical line at $R = I$. Furthermore, it must be true that R^* (or $\hat{R}$) is greater than I if the bank's expected profits are to be positive. But this implies that $R^* \geq \bar{R}$ for the risk-free customer, which on the basis of Proposition VI rules out the possibility of credit rationing.

Generalization to n Customers.   We can now proceed to generalizations of the propositions developed in this section. First, consider a banker facing n customers and constrained to charge all n customers the same loan rate. Again, let R_i^* ($i = 1, 2, \ldots, n$) denote the rate the bank would charge each customer if acting as a discriminatory monopolist, and let $\hat{R}$ be the common *optimum optimorum* rate the bank charges when allowing credit rationing. Let us number customers in ascending order with respect to the monopolist rate; that is $R_i^* \geq R_{i-1}^*$ for $i = 2, 3, \ldots, n$. Proposition V can then be generalized to:

PROPOSITION V.'   *The optimal common rate $\hat{R}$ charged all customers must lie between the rate charged customer 1 and the rate charged customer n when the bank is acting as a discriminating monopolist. Formally, there exists an integer j, $2 \leq j \leq n$, such that $R_j^* \geq \hat{R} \geq R_{j-1}^*$.*

Similarly, Proposition VI can be generalized to:

PROPOSITION VI.'

    (VI.1')   *For any customers i such that $\hat{R} \geq R_i^*$, we have $\hat{R} \geq \bar{R}_i$ implying that rationing of these customers is not profitable.*

    (VI.2')   *In the case of customers for whom $\hat{R} < R_i^*$, we have $\hat{R} \gtrless \bar{R}_i$, implying that rationing of some of these customers may be profitable.*

The interpretation and proof of these propositions follows directly from the corresponding propositions for the case of two customers, and accordingly are not repeated here.

Generalization to m Customer Classes.   So far we have been restricted in this section to the case in which the banker must charge *all* customers the same rate. Now consider the general case in which the banker sets up a number of customer categories and charges only customers within each category the same rate. With each category is associated an interest factor R_j^{**} ($j = 1, 2, \ldots \ldots m$) and, without loss of generality it can be assumed that $R_j^{**} > R_{j-1}^{**}$ ($j = 2, 3, \ldots m$).

To start, assume that the number of categories and the rate factors associated with each of these categories are beyond the control of the bank and are taken as given. We wish to consider how the bank should classify each of its n customers, given that rationing is not allowed. If it is assumed that the bank's expected profits from each customer are a concave function of the interest factor, then a particularly simple and instructive result is obtained.[47] Under this condition the bank's expected profits from a customer reach their maximum at the monopolist rate for that customer, R_i^*, and decline monotonically as the interest factor deviates from this level in either direction. Consequently, the bank will attempt to charge a customer a rate as close to the monopolist rate for this customer as possible. All the rate categories but the two that bound the monopolist rate for a customer from above and below can then be eliminated from consideration for the classification of that customer. The choice between these two categories depends on the specific shape of the profit function in this interval. If a more general case is allowed, in which the profit function is concave only in the neighborhood of the monopolist rate, the classification of customers becomes more complex, but it is still clear there will always be an optimal category for each customer.

Next, we wish to consider whether there is an optimal set of interest factors, R_j^{**}, for the (still arbitrary) m categories. The answer is obviously, yes. Among all possible sets of classification rates, there must be one set that will maximize the bank's total expected profits. (We rule out the case of ties.) Since this case is linked to the material in the following section, it is worth considering more carefully. Let us assume that the bank has set up its m categories with the corresponding rate factors set to maximize expected profits. Rationing is still not allowed. We know that within each of these classes there must be at least one customer with a monopolist rate lower than the class rate and one customer with a monopolist rate higher than the class rate. If either of these conditions did not hold, then it is clear that the bank could increase its expected profits further by moving the class rate in the direction of the monopolist rates of all customers in the class. But this would contradict the assumption that the class rates were, in fact, the optimal rates.

Now let us ask whether it is profitable to ration any customers under this regime. Fortunately, the necessary results have already been derived. Each of the categories being discussed here can be analyzed in the same manner

---

[47] This assumption is equivalent to requiring that the second order condition, equation 2.23, holds for all values of the interest factor.

as we discussed the single class. In particular, Proposition VI will be valid for each category. Thus it will not be profitable to ration customers whose R_i^* is smaller than its group rate R_j^{**}, but it may pay to ration those for whom R_i^* exceeds R_j^{**}. In particular, rationing will occur whenever a customer's group rate is less than $\bar{R}_i$. Furthermore, the likelihood that it will be profitable to ration at least some customers in a class will be positively related to the heterogeneity of the R_i^* of the customers in that class and hence the likelihood of rationing will be inversely related to the size of m.

Thus, finally, the number of customer categories, m should be allowed as a bank decision variable. The result for this case is clear. The bank's expected profits will be directly and positively related to the size of m since the greater m the greater the power to discriminate between customers. Indeed, in the polar case, the bank would set the number of customer classes m equal to the number of customers n and would be in the position of a discriminating monopolist as already discussed. Thus, without restrictions on the degree of discrimination, credit rationing will not occur.

There remains now to draw the implications of these results by combining the propositions developed so far with a number of considerations arising from the nature of competition in the banking industry.

2.4 | Competition in Commercial Banking

We have just shown that a single bank, free to discriminate between borrowers by charging each customer its monopolist rate R_i^*, would not ration credit. A similar conclusion holds even if there are many banks, as long as they act collusively to maximize joint profits, relying, if necessary, on side payments. If all banks share the identical subjective evaluations of the profitability of borrowers' investment projects, then clearly the optimum rate R_i^* to be charged to the ith customer would be the same no matter which bank served him. Furthermore, even allowing for differences in the subjective evaluation of borrower risk and assuming an arbitrary initial distribution of customers between banks, the device of buying and selling customers would allow each bank and the industry as a whole to maximize profits. In this way a banker's *Pareto optimum* would be reached with each bank charging its customers the monopolist rate, and thus, again, no credit rationing would occur.

In this section we propose to argue that this solution is in fact not feasible, at least in the present American economy. It is suggested, instead, that banks can best exploit their market power, while remaining within the bounds set by prevailing institutions, by classifying customers into a rather small number of classes within each of which a uniform rate is charged, even though the membership of each class will exhibit considerable hetero-geneity in terms of R_i^*.[48]

First, even if there were but a single monopoly bank or a perfectly collusive banking system, the mere existence of usury laws would lead toward the indicated solution.[49] Such laws would prevent the banker from charging any rate R_i^* which is greater than the legal limit. Thus all customers for whom R_i^* is larger than the ceiling would be classified together in the category with the ceiling rate. Since the monopolist rate R_i^* for each customer in this class would equal or exceed the uniform rate set for the class, namely the usury ceiling, it is apparent from the results of the previous section that many, if not all, customers in this class would be profitably rationed.

Even aside from usury ceilings, the pressure of legal restrictions and considerations of good will and social mores would make it inadvisable if not impossible for the monopolist banker to charge widely different rates to different customers. The banker would tend, instead, to limit the spread between the rates and to justify the remaining differentials in terms of a few objective and verifiable criteria such as industry class, asset size, and other standard financial measures. An effort would no doubt be made to choose the criteria for classification so as to minimize the difference between the optimal classification of customers into rate classes and the categories dictated by the objective criteria, but a close approximation might be difficult to achieve.

The inducement to adopt a classification scheme of the type described is likely to be greatly strengthened when we take into account the fact that banks cannot openly collude, although they share a common desire to maintain rates as close as feasible to the collusive optimum. In order to prevent, or at least minimize, competitive underbidding of rates they would need tacit agreement as to the appropriate rate structure for cus-tomers, and thus a classification scheme based on readily verifiable objec-tive criteria would appear as an efficient and effective device. Furthermore, to make the whole arrangement manageable, the number of different rate classes would have to be reasonably small. Finally, one can also readily understand how such tacit agreement on the structure of class rates could be facilitated by tying these rates through fairly rigid differentials to a prime rate set through price leadership.

If we now superimpose the impact of usury ceilings along with the other

---

[48] We do not want to imply that the classification of customers by banks is a novel notion. To the contrary, it appears to be a well-accepted institutional feature of the commercial banking industry. See, for example, Alhadeff [1954], pp. 120–123, and Wojnilower [1962].

[49] The application of usury laws in financial markets has been recently discussed in Blitz and Long [1965] and Goudzwaard [1968].

legal and social constraints, it is clear that the entire structure of rates would tend to be compressed within narrower limits than would otherwise be optimal. This means, in particular, that the rate for each class would tend to the lower limit of the R_i^* spread appropriate for the customers in that class, with the possible exception of the lowest class rate reserved for the riskless or nearly riskless prime customers. The result is that widespread rationing would occur, particularly in the higher rate classes.

Finally, it may be observed that the oligopolistic price setting pattern outlined above is likely to lead to a very sluggish and somewhat jerky adjustment of the entire rate structure as changes in underlying conditions generate changes in the optimal level and structure of rates. The considerations relevant here are well known from the literature on oligopolistic market structure and price leadership. It follows that when conditions are changing rapidly we might expect to find that the entire structure of rates would lag behind, and thus, for a while, would tend to be higher or lower than the optimal structure, depending on the direction of the change. These considerations provide the key to dynamic rationing to be elaborated below.

2.5 | EQUILIBRIUM CREDIT RATIONING

We are now in a position to assemble the propositions of Section 2.3 and the discussion of Section 2.4 into a complete theory of credit rationing. In Section 2.3 it was shown that credit rationing will be profitable even in long run equilibrium, as long as there is uncertainty of loan repayment *and* banks cannot discriminate perfectly between customers. In Section 2.4 both of these conditions were verified as features of the commercial banking industry, and thus we conclude that equilibrium rationing is consistent with rational economic behavior.

2.5.1 COMPARATIVE STATICS OF EQUILIBRIUM RATIONING

It is worthwhile to consider briefly the comparative static properties of the model in order to provide further insight into the structure of equilibrium credit rationing. The amount of equilibrium rationing, E, will be the summation of the difference between loan demand and loan supply for those customers of the bank experiencing credit rationing:

$$(2.26) \qquad E = \sum_{i=1}^{n} \max \, [D_i[\hat{R}_i] - L_i[\hat{R}_i], \, 0].$$

The excess supply of loans to those customers to whom the bank would like to extend additional loans does not, of course, offset the rationing of other customers. The offer curve to a firm depends on the opportunity cost of the bank, I, and the firm's density function of possible outcomes, f_i, and hence E depends on these two factors and the firm's demand function. Consequently, for purposes of comparative static analysis, one may consider the impact of changes in demand, risk, and the opportunity cost on the amount of equilibrium rationing.

Unfortunately, the evaluation of the impact of these changes turns out to be a very difficult process because the rationed or nonrationed status of customers may change following the change in the parameter. In particular, four possibilities must be considered:

1. a rationed customer may continue to be rationed;
2. a rationed customer may cease being rationed;
3. a nonrationed customer may start to be rationed;
4. a nonrationed customer may continue to be nonrationed.

We will consider the case of a change in the opportunity cost in detail to illustrate the possible outcomes. The outcome for changes in the other parameters will then be outlined.

Two important results for the analysis of the comparative static effects of an increase in the opportunity cost are given in the following propositions:

PROPOSITION VIII.   *A ceteris paribus increase in the opportunity cost of the bank causes the optimal loan offer curve to shift downward at every interest rate.*

PROPOSITION IX.   *The common optimal rate factor R^* (applicable if the bank is constrained to satisfy all demand functions) is positively related to the bank's opportunity cost.*

The proof of Proposition VIII follows directly by implicitly differentiating equation 2.13 with respect to I, and then solving:

$$(2.27) \qquad \frac{\partial \hat{L}_i}{\partial I} = \frac{-1}{R^2 f_i[R_i \hat{L}_i]} < 0.$$

Similarly Proposition IX is verified by implicitly differentiating equation 2.21 with respect to I and then solving:

$$(2.28) \qquad \frac{\partial R^*}{\partial I} = \frac{D_1' + D_2'}{\dfrac{\partial^2 P_1}{\partial R^2} + \dfrac{\partial^2 P_2}{\partial R^2}} > 0.$$

This is positive because the slopes of the demand curves insure the numerator is negative and the second order condition (2.23) insures the denominator is negative. It is quite reasonable, of course, that an increase in the opportunity cost should lead to an increase in the optimal rate factor R^*. But it should be noted that this relationship may not be true for the common optimal rate factor allowing for rationing, $\hat{R}$. Because the very act of changing the parameter I may lead to a change in the rationed or nonrationed status of customers, as demonstrated below, special cases may arise in which $\hat{R}$ and I are not positively related, contrary to the relationship between R^* and I. Since such cases are distinctly abnormal,[50] the standard situation being a positive relationship between I and $\hat{R}$, we shall proceed on the premise that Proposition IX is equally applicable to $\hat{R}$.

With the aid of Figure 2.5, we can survey the impact of an increase in the opportunity cost from I_o to I_1. From Proposition VIII, it is known that the offer curve will shift downward from the locus $\hat{L}_o$ to $\hat{L}_1$; and from Proposition IX it is known that the common optimal rate factor will increase, say from $\hat{R}_o$ to $\hat{R}_1$. Thus the net impact of a change in the opportunity cost on the maximum loan offered is the result of a shift in the offer curve and a movement along this curve, and the amount of equilibrium rationing may either rise or fall. These two alternative outcomes are illustrated in Figure 2.5. In the case of the demand curve D_1, the customer would move from a rationed to a nonrationed status, while for the case illustrated by the demand curve D_2, the opposite conclusion holds. Cases in which the rationing status remains unchanged are, of course, equally possible. Thus the effect of an increase in I on the size of rationing must remain uncertain. This result, however, should not be regarded as disturbing. What it implies is that in the long run, *no systematic relationship exists between the extent of equilibrium rationing and the absolute level of interest rates.*

A similar conclusion can be drawn for changes in the parameters of the demand functions and density functions. A change in the density function having the effect of reducing the likelihood of loan repayment will cause a downward shift in the optimal loan offer curve. This shift is similar to the effect of an increase in the opportunity rate except that the vertical portion of the offer curve remains fixed. Thus, the various results illustrated in Figure 2.5 are still possible. Finally, we may assume the bank is displaced

---

[50] This situation may arise because the bank, if it is rationing, finds that it can obtain larger expected profits from the rationed customer by raising the rate, but that it can obtain larger expected profits from the nonrationed customer only by lowering the rate. The first-order condition for the maximization of expected profit function (2.25) thus determines $\hat{R}$ at the point the marginal gains from the two effects are balanced. Now normally an increase in the opportunity rate increases the *marginal* expected profits from both customers and thus the optimal rate will rise. If the rationed customer is operating on the negatively sloped portion of the offer curve, however, the marginal expected profits may fall and this in turn may lead to a lower optimal $\hat{R}$.

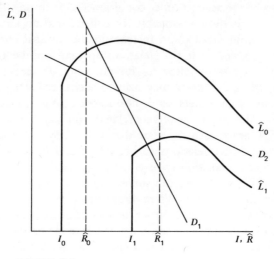

FIGURE 2.5

from the initial equilibrium by an upward shift in the customer's demand function. Since the offer curve is unchanged, the initial effect of the shift in the demand curve would be to cause rationing. In the long run, however, the increase in demand will cause the interest rate $\hat{R}$ to also rise and this movement along the demand curve will tend to offset the initial shift in the function. Thus, again, no systematic relationships exist for the effects of parameter changes on the amount of credit rationing or on even the rationing status of the customer.

2.5.2 SUMMARY OF EQUILIBRIUM RATIONING

It is worthwhile to summarize the results for equilibrium rationing before turning to the discussion of dynamic rationing which follows. The primary objective with respect to equilibrium rationing was to provide a proof of the rationality of this behavior. It was shown that under a regime in which a bank classifies customers into equivalent rate categories, specific parameter values could lead to the profitability of credit rationing. In the two-customer–one-class case, it was demonstrated that one customer would not be rationed while the other customer might be rationed. Similarly, in the n-customer–m-class case, a bank servicing many diverse customers in terms of demand and risk, and forced to classify these customers into a relatively small number of rate categories, would generally find it profitable to ration at least some of these customers.

It is also useful to point out how this theory of equilibrium credit rationing differs from other models of the phenomenon. Two points were stressed in the review of earlier studies of credit rationing. First, it was noted that if bankers do not use the price as the rationing vehicle, then some other characteristics of the customer or loan must be used. Our model stresses the risk characteristics of the customer. Thus in the case of the single class only customers who are risk-free can be ruled out as potential rationing candidates. In the more complex case with several rate categories, a similar result follows. That is, only the class with risk-free customers has no possible rationing. Furthermore, as an empirical approximation, this class of customers might be equated with those customers granted the prime rate. Within each of the other categories some rationing might occur, again depending on the risk characteristics of the customers. Finally, because of usury laws and other social pressures against high interest rates, substantial rationing of high-risk firms is anticipated. In the following chapter on the empirical tests of rationing, the result that the risk-free customers are not rationed is used as an aid in deriving an empirical measure of rationing.

Although our model has stressed these risk characteristics, it would be wrong to interpret this as foreclosing any other rationale for rationing. For example, in Section 2.7.3 it is shown that bankruptcy costs change the quantitative, although not the qualitative, nature of the rationing process. Similarly, the "customer relationship" aspect of the banking industry emphasized by Hodgman, and Kane and Malkiel, is not inconsistent with our model. In an heuristic sense, these characteristics of customers can be thought of as forming part of the bank's evaluation of the customer as characterized by our risk density function. It is not surprising, therefore, that their models lead to the same basic view of the rationing process as our model: that is, a tendency for rationing to result in the reduction of loans to small, risky firms rather than large established corporations. In fact, this interpretation of credit rationing is even found in the early studies by Scott [1957b] and Hodgman [1960].

The second point stressed in the review of the earlier studies was the absence of demand considerations and a theory of the determinants of the optimal commercial loan rate in any of the received theories of rationing. It should be clear that these elements are critical to the rationing process. To propose a theory of credit rationing without this basis is to beg the basic question.

Finally, in terms of the comparative static properties of the model, it was shown that parameter changes that would initially lead to more rationing were offset by the adjustment of the loan rate to its new equilibrium level. Thus in the long run no systematic relationships exist between the amount of rationing and the level of the opportunity rate, or the demand curve, or the risk level of the customer. This has the important implication, which will be used in the empirical tests of credit rationing in Chapter 3, that equilibrium rationing will generally not be the source of cyclical variations in the total amount of observed rationing.

2.6 | DYNAMIC CREDIT RATIONING

Dynamic rationing is defined as the difference between equilibrium rationing and the volume of rationing that arises when the actual rate charged customers, R, differs from the long run equilibrium rate, $\hat{R}$. By this definition, dynamic rationing can be positive or negative, and it will be shown that its magnitude is positively associated with the spread, $\hat{R} - R$. Furthermore, it has already been suggested, in view of the oligopolistic structure of the banking industry, that R is likely to adjust slowly to changes in $\hat{R}$, thus lending credence to the empirical importance of dynamic credit rationing. In fact, in Chapter 4 below, it is indicated how banks tend to rely on some objective signal, such as changes in the Federal Reserve's discount rate, in determining the timing of commercial loan rate changes. In this case dynamic rationing might vary significantly depending upon Federal Reserve policy.

It is helpful to begin by considering a system that starts in long run equilibrium with a rate $\hat{R}_o$ and then receives a shock that changes the equilibrium rate from $\hat{R}_o$ to $\hat{R}_1$ while the quoted rate remains at $\hat{R}_o$. The experiment is thus similar to the comparative static analysis used for the equilibrium rationing except that the quoted commercial loan rate is assumed in the short run not to adjust toward the new equilibrium level. As we have seen, there are three main market forces that can change $\hat{R}$: a change in market interest rates leading to a change in the opportunity cost I; a shift in customer demand schedules; and a change in risk as may be indicated by a shift in $F[x]$. We shall first consider the effects of changing each of these factors, one at a time. Then by combining the results of these *ceteris paribus* experiments, we can examine more realistic situations in which several factors change simultaneously.

1. Consider first a change in market rates of return which, for convenience, may be summarized by some representative rate, r_M; a rise in r_M will directly increase the opportunity rate for funds invested in the loan portfolio. From Propositions VIII and IX, we know that such an increase in I will lower all offer curves and also increase $\hat{R}$. Since the quoted rate remains at $\hat{R}_o$ and all the demand curves are unchanged, *there must be an aggregate increase in rationing*. The model also provides information about the incidence of this increase. At one extreme, the risk-free firms will still not experience any

rationing because the offer curve for them is a vertical line.[51] At the other extreme, firms already rationed in the initial equilibrium will be rationed even more as the offer curve shifts down. Finally, among the risky firms initially not rationed, some will remain unrationed while others will experience new rationing, with the amount depending upon the extent of the shift.

Thus, on the whole, the loan portfolio will shrink and the funds released by rationing will be shifted into other assets whose yield has increased (or be used to repay the now more costly borrowed funds). However, the opportunity cost I is now likely to fall relative to the market rate r_M because loans will be a smaller percentage of the total portfolio. This will tend to moderate, though not eliminate, the initial increase in rationing.

As the loan rate finally adjusts in the long run toward the new equilibrium level the amount of dynamic rationing normally will be monotonically reduced.[52] Thus the amount of rationing is most severe immediately following the initial shock and then gradually returns to the smaller equilibrium rationing level as the loan rate adjusts toward its equilibrium level.

2. Consider next the effect of a downward revision of the anticipated distribution of outcomes; operationally, one may think of the initial distribution $F[x]$ being replaced by a new one $G[x]$ with $G[x] \leq F[x]$. As can be verified from (2.13) and (2.21), such a revision results again in a downward shift in the offer curve, and in an increase in R^* and hence in $\hat{R}$. Since the quoted rate has not changed, the maximum loan offered at that rate must tend to decline. With the demand unchanged, rationing must therefore increase for some of the customers, and the incidence of the increased rationing is entirely analogous to that of case 1. Once more, as loans shift out of the now less remunerative loan portfolio, the opportunity cost I may decline somewhat, mitigating the initial effects.

---

[51] This conclusion would not hold if the shift in I were so large as to exceed $\hat{R}_o$. In this case, the best course of action would be to cut off loans even to the prime firms, and *a fortiori* to all customers. But this case can be disregarded for the banks could be counted upon to respond promptly by raising their quoted rate, that is, $\hat{R}_o$ would not remain unchanged in these circumstances. More generally in the usual theory of monopoly or oligopoly, if the equilibrium price rose because of a shift in either the demand or the cost function, and, for some reason, the market price was prevented from rising, rationing would occur only if the shift were such that the marginal cost would exceed the price. It appears, therefore, that dynamic rationing, just as equilibrium rationing, is intimately related to the uncertainty about the outcome of the loan.

[52] In special cases the adjustment of rationing from the dynamic level to the equilibrium level may not be monotonic. The special cases arise only when the slope of the demand curve exceeds the slope of the offer curve. This can occur over the negatively sloped portion of the offer curve, but since this would generally indicate interest rates and levels of default risk well above the levels bankers would consider acceptable, the case would seem to have little empirical importance.

3. Much the same conclusion can be seen to hold for the case of a shift in all demand schedules, r_M and $F[x]$ constant, except that in this case it is the demand curve which shifts while the offer curve remains unchanged. As long as I remains unchanged the initially rationed customers will experience more rationing because their increased demand is not satisfied at all; the risk-free customers, in contrast, will receive larger loans and remain unrationed; and the initially unrationed risky customers will also obtain larger loans, but possibly not enough to match the increase in their demand. Furthermore, as funds flow into the loan portfolio (because some of the increased demand is satisfied), the opportunity cost of loans will tend to increase giving rise to additional rationing of the type under case 1.

Normally, an increase in loan demand will tend to occur in periods of buoyant economic activity and hence will be associated with a rise in r_M (partly reflecting the higher demand in all markets and partly causing, in turn, a higher demand for bank funds), and also with an increase in the anticipated profitability of the investment projects, the latter producing a decrease in risk as measured by $F[x]$. The outcome is then a combination of the *ceteris paribus* results under cases 1, 2, and 3. The shift in $F[x]$ tends to raise the loan offered at the unchanged rate, $\hat{R}_o$; at the same time, the quantity demanded at the rate rises, and if I were unchanged, the effect on $\hat{R}$, as well as on rationing, would depend on the relative amount of the two shifts. Even on this basis, one would anticipate an increase in rationing because the demand curve is likely to shift further than the offer curve, reflecting an increase in the optimism of firms relative to that of the banks. But more fundamentally, I must rise, both because with I constant, more funds would flow into the loan portfolio causing I to rise relative to r_M, and because r_M itself will be rising. Hence the final outcome will tend to be the same as in the previous three cases. The extent of increased rationing will depend on the relative shift in $F[x]$, in the quantity demanded at the unchanged rate, and in r_M, and on whether, on balance, these shifts will cause funds to flow in or out of the loan portfolio. It is apparent, however, that the rise in I and in rationing will tend to be greater the smaller the elasticity of supply of funds to the banking system. The effect might be particularly severe if the ability of banks to attract funds were actually reduced, as happened in some recent episodes in which the certificates of deposit rates in secondary markets exceeded the Regulation Q ceiling.

We may thus conclude quite generally that as $\hat{R}$ rises relative to $\hat{R}_o$, rationing will tend to increase; and the incidence of the increased rationing will tend to fall most heavily on customers who would be rationed in equilibrium, and will tend to affect the least, if at all, the riskless, or nearly riskless, prime customers. One implication of this result is worth stressing since it provides the key to the operational measurement of credit rationing set forth in the next section. Suppose that we were to classify all customers into two broad classes, the prime customers and all others. We should then expect that as the gap between $\hat{R}$ and $\hat{R}_o$ widens and dynamic rationing becomes more severe, loans to the riskless customers will tend to represent a growing share of the total loan portfolio.

This result can be given the following useful interpretation, which also serves to bring to light the common nature of equilibrium and dynamic rationing. In the presence of risk as to the outcome of the loan, reducing the size of the loan will increase the expected rate of return by reducing the expected loss from insolvency of the firm. It is therefore quite understandable that a bank, faced with a higher opportunity cost (whether from a rise in the market rate or in lending opportunities) and unable to raise the return by raising rates, will find it profitable to raise its return at least by upgrading the quality of its portfolio through a reduction in risk; the upgrading may take the form of shifting funds toward less risky customers, and/or of reducing loans made to risky customers, depending on the nature of the shift in underlying conditions.

2.7 | EXTENSIONS OF THE MODEL

The analysis in this chapter has been based so far on three simplifying assumptions: (1) a fixed-size investment project; (2) a constant opportunity cost to the bank for loanable funds; and (3) no costs attendant with collecting the available proceeds in case of the firm's bankruptcy. In this section we derive results showing that the conclusions of the basic model are not altered when each of these assumptions is removed individually. For each case we will show that the properties of the offer curve corresponding to Propositions I, II, and III remain unchanged in their essential characteristics. Propositions IV to VII in the text then follow immediately because the assumptions that are changed here have no effect on the demand curve or on any other features of the problem beside the offer curve. The chapter concludes with a brief discussion of the implications of the second-order conditions used in the analysis and a summary of the results of this section.

2.7.1 OPEN-END INVESTMENT OPPORTUNITY

The assumption of a fixed-size investment opportunity for the firm has been used to insure that the potential end of period value of the firm is independent of the size of the loan contract. It has been suggested that a more realistic assumption would make the potential outcome a function of the size of the loan.[53] Freimer and Gordon[54] have also considered this problem for the special case of a rectangular density function. The analysis provided here is of substantially greater generality, since the density function is not restricted. Furthermore, the emphasis of the Freimer and Gordon work appears to have been misplaced, since they conclude that the likely result is for there to be infinite optimal loan sizes for this problem. It will be shown here that, on the contrary, under reasonable assumptions the loan size will always be finite.

We consider a firm with a fixed equity base, H, and a loan supplied by the bank, L, such that the firm's total assets are:

$$(2.29) \quad A = H + L \quad H, L \geq 0.$$

The end of the period value of the firm is given, as before, by a random variable x. Now, however, it is assumed that the end of period value depends on the firm's total assets and can be expressed as:

$$(2.30) \quad x = (\rho[A]y)A,$$

where y is the random rate of return with a probability distribution independent of the scale of the project, and $\rho[A]$ is a nonrandom function of total assets which adjusts the rate of return y for the scale of total assets. Thus, for $\rho[A] \equiv 1$ we would have a constant expected rate of return to scale, while $\rho'[A] < 0$ would imply a decreasing expected rate of return to scale.

The properties of $\rho[A]$ assumed here are, formally:

$$(2.31a) \quad \rho[H] = 1,$$

$$(2.31b) \quad \rho'[A] \leq 0,$$

$$(2.31c) \quad \gamma = \gamma[A] = \frac{d(A\rho[A])}{dA} = \rho[A] + A\rho'[A] \geq 0,$$

$$(2.31d) \quad \delta = \delta[A] = \frac{d\gamma[A]}{dA} = 2\rho'[A] + A\rho''[A] \leq 0.$$

Condition (2.31a) provides a convenient scaling for $\rho[A]$ in that it implies that $y = x[H]/H$. Condition (2.31b) rules out cases of increasing returns to scale. Condition (2.31c) is equivalent to requiring $dx[A]/dA \geq 0$; that is, the random total return is a strictly nondecreasing function of the size of the investment. Condition (2.31d) requires that the marginal return be a nonincreasing function of A.

---

[53] See Chase [1961], pp. 322–325; and Hodgman [1961a], pp. 327–328.

[54] Freimer and Gordon [1965], pp. 405–408.

The density function for the random rate of return y is given by $g[y]$. We assume there exist v and V, $0 \leq v < V < \infty$, such that:

(2.32) $\quad g[y] = 0 \quad$ for $\quad y \leq v \quad$ or $\quad y \geq V$.

Letting $G[W] = \int_v^w g[y]\, dy$, we also have:

(2.33) $\quad \begin{aligned} G[y] &= 0 \quad \text{for} \quad y \leq v, \\ G[y] &= 1 \quad \text{for} \quad y \geq V. \end{aligned}$

Following the analysis of Section 2.3.2, we start by considering the bank's expected profits from a customer as a function of the interest factor R and the loan size L, independent of demand:

(2.34) $\quad P = P[RL] = A\rho \int_v^\beta yg[y]\, dy + LR \int_\beta^V g[y]\, dy - IL,$

where $R = 1 + r$, $I = 1 + j$, and $\beta = RL/A\rho$. For notational convenience the i subscript for the ith customer and the functional dependence of ρ on A have been omitted. β is, of course, the necessary value for y if the loan plus interest is to be fully repaid. The similarity of the structure of equation 2.34 with that of equation 2.9 should be apparent. Thus it is clear that (2.34) can be rewritten as:

(2.35) $\quad \begin{aligned} P = P[RL] &= L(R - I) - RLG[\beta] + A\rho \int_v^\beta yg[y]\, dy \\ &= L(R - I) - A\rho \int_v^\beta G[y]\, dy, \end{aligned}$

in analogy with (2.10) and (2.11).

The optimal loan size offer curve is then given by the condition:

(2.36) $\quad \begin{aligned} \frac{\partial P[RL]}{\partial L} &= R(1 - G[\beta]) + \gamma \int_v^\beta yg[y]\, dy - I \\ &= R(1 - G[\beta]) + \gamma \left(\beta G[\beta] - \int_v^\beta G[y]\, dy \right) - I = 0. \end{aligned}$

The optimal loan $\hat{L}$ is the implicit solution of (2.36).

The second-order condition for a maximum is given by:

(2.37) $\quad \frac{\partial^2 P[RL]}{\partial L^2} = \frac{\partial \beta}{\partial L} g[\beta](\gamma\beta - R) + \delta \int_v^\beta yg[y]\, dy < 0.$

This will be valid for all L and all finite R since the last term is clearly negative and:

(2.38) $\quad \beta = \frac{RL}{A\rho} \leq \frac{R}{\rho} \leq \frac{R}{\gamma} \quad$ for all L and all finite R,

and

(2.39) $\quad \frac{\partial \beta}{\partial L} = \frac{R(A\rho - L\gamma)}{(A\rho)^2} > 0 \quad$ for all R and L.

The case for an infinite R is discussed below. It should also be clear that (2.37) also insures that as we move further from the offer curve in either direction the bank's expected profits will be decreasing monotonically (Proposition II).

We now can describe the shape of the offer curve. For the case $R < I$ we must have the corner solution of a zero loan, since $\dfrac{\partial P[RL]}{\partial L}$ (from equation 2.36) is negative even at this point. Second, we must have:

$$(2.40) \qquad \hat{L} \le \frac{vA\rho}{R} \qquad \text{for} \qquad R = I,$$

since condition (2.36) can be met for this case only if $\beta \le v$. Moreover, this implies that:

$$(2.41) \qquad \hat{L} < \frac{vH\rho[A]}{I - v\rho[A]} \qquad \text{when} \qquad R = I \qquad \text{and} \qquad I - v\rho[A] > 0$$

Since $\rho[A]$ is a decreasing function of A, the maximum loan size when $R = I$ will be finite as long as there exists some finite loan size, M say, such that $I > v\rho[M + E]$. This means that the bank's opportunity cost must exceed the certain rate of return from the firm's project (as adjusted by the scale factor) at some finite scale of investment. Conversely, if this condition did not hold, then the bank could realize a certain return greater than its opportunity cost, regardless of the size of its investment in this asset. Since this would imply that a certain return v should be, in fact, the bank's proper opportunity cost in evaluating the return on other bank assets, there would be an obvious contradiction of the definition of I.

For $I < R < \infty$ we must rule out the possibility that at some rate factor in this range the optimal loan may be infinite. To insure that an infinite loan will not be optimal, the marginal profits, evaluated at $L = \infty$, must be negative, that is:

$$(2.42) \qquad \frac{\partial P[RL]}{\partial L}\bigg|_{L=\infty} = R\left(1 - G\left[\frac{R}{\rho[\infty]}\right]\right) + \gamma \int_v^{\frac{R}{\rho[\infty]}} yg[y]\,dy - I < 0.$$

To understand the meaning of this condition, it is helpful to consider, for the moment, the constant return to scale case in which $\rho = \gamma = 1$. In general, by differentiating (2.36) with respect to R, we obtain:

$$(2.43) \qquad \frac{\partial^2 P[RL]}{\partial L \partial R} = (1 - G[\beta]) + \frac{\partial \beta}{\partial R} g[\beta](\gamma\beta - R) \qquad \text{for all } R \text{ and } L.$$

For the constant return case, this reduces to:

$$(2.44) \qquad \frac{\partial^2 P[RL]}{\partial R \partial L} = (1 - G[R]) \geq 0 \qquad \text{as} \qquad R \leq V \qquad \text{and} \qquad L = \infty.$$

Therefore the marginal profit is increasing as R increases up to the point $R = V$, evaluated along the locus $L = \infty$.[55] Consequently, in this case a sufficient condition ruling out infinite optimal loans for $I < R < \infty$ is the condition ruling out an infinite optimal loan at $R = V$. This condition is easily derived from (2.42) to be:

$$(2.45) \qquad I > \int_v^V yg(y)\, dy.$$

Thus, for this special case, as long as the opportunity cost is greater than the expected value of the rate of return on the venture, only finite optimal loans can occur. This condition is also very reasonable. Since the bank is an expected profit maximizer, it is assumed indifferent to risk. Thus, if there were a project with an expected return greater than the opportunity cost, it is clear that this project's rate of return would be, in fact, the relevant opportunity cost. Other assets would be evaluated using this project's rate of return as the standard.[56]

In the general case under study here, an even weaker condition, already given as (2.42), will be sufficient to rule out the possibility of infinite optimal loans. That is, instead of the strict condition given by (2.45), we need only require that the adjustment factor for the rate of return, ρ, decline sufficiently fast so as to insure that (2.42) does hold.

With infinite optimal loans now ruled out, we can proceed with the analyses of the shape of the offer curve when $R \to \infty$. Because of the bound on the potential rate of return, we must have

$$(2.46) \qquad \lim_{R \to \infty} R(1 - G[\beta]) = 0.$$

Therefore, at $R = \infty$, the first-order condition (2.36) is:

$$(2.47) \qquad \frac{\partial P[RL]}{\partial L}\bigg|_{R=\infty} = \gamma[A] \int_v^V yg[y]\, dy - I = 0.$$

---

[55] The reason for choosing this special case is that this statement is not valid for the general case under consideration. That is, in the general case, expected profits may rise and fall as R rises, the loan size given.

[56] Freimer and Gordon, *op. cit.*, pp. 406–407, implicitly argue that just the opposite is true. Their conclusion is valid only if condition (2.45) does not hold. That is, only if the expected rate of return exceeds the opportunity cost. Only then does the open-end investment case lead to infinite optimal loans.

This means that $\lim_{R \to \infty} \hat{L} = N$, where N is defined by:

$$(2.48) \quad \gamma[N + E] \int_v^V yg[y]\, dy \leq I.$$

An interesting interpretation of this condition comes from the fact that at an infinite interest rate the banker is, in essence, taking over the firm. Thus, he will invest capital (N, that is) in this project up to the point at which the marginal expected return just equals the opportunity cost. The inequality arises only because of the nonnegativity assumption requiring that $\hat{L} \geq 0$. Furthermore, in general, the optimal loan reaches its maximum at some interest rate in the closed interval $(V\gamma[N + E], \infty)$. From this it should be clear that the offer curve just described is equivalent to the curve for the fixed-investment case in its essential characteristics.[57]

The only property of the offer curve that remains to be verified is that $\partial P[RL]/\partial R > 0$ when evaluated along the offer curve. This result can be obtained easily by substituting (2.36) into (2.35) and then taking the derivative with respect to R.

In summary, the purpose of this section has been to show that the properties of the loan offer curve remain unchanged even when the size of the loan granted by the bank is allowed to influence the profitability of the firm's investment projects. The only restrictive assumption introduced in the discussion was the condition ruling out an increasing rate of return to scale for the firm's investment projects. The intuitive basis for this assumption is clear, since if the condition did not hold then the bank might obtain progressively greater expected profits as the size of the loan offer increases, and thus infinite loan offers could not be ruled out. We can thus conclude that although the existence of open-end investment opportunities for the firm may result in larger loans being offered by the bank, the conditions for the existence of credit rationing remain qualitatively unchanged from the analysis already presented.

2.7.2 INCREASING OPPORTUNITY COSTS

It has been assumed that the bank could invest and borrow at a fixed and exogenously determined opportunity rate factor I. This is reasonable since the bank has the options of lending or borrowing in the Federal Fund's market, issuing certificates of deposit, buying or selling government securities, and finally, borrowing from the Federal Reserve. To a first approximation the yields on these alternative securities are equal when adjusted for risk and maturity. Furthermore, under moderate mone-

---

[57] The results stated in this paragraph are equally true for the simple case $\rho = \gamma = 1$ given that condition (2.45) holds.

tary conditions, a bank would have access to these markets at the given market price. Under more extreme conditions, however, a bank may find the relevant opportunity cost rising as its demand for credit increases. That is, the Federal Reserve becomes reluctant to discount, the certificate of deposit rate reaches its ceiling, and so on.

The goal here is to show that even under these latter conditions the basic formulation remains valid. We shall characterize these conditions by the assumption that $I = I[L]$ where L is the total loans outstanding for the bank. The properties of this function are:

(2.49a) $I[0] = I_o,$

(2.49b) $\dfrac{\partial I[L]}{\partial L} = I'[L] \geq 0,$

(2.49c) $\dfrac{\partial^2 LI[L]}{\partial L^2} = 2I'[L] + LI''[L] \geq 0.$

Condition (2.49b) implies that the bank's costs, $(LI[L])$, are increasing as the loans increase and condition (2.49c) means that the rate of increase is also rising.

We want to consider the properties of the bank's optimal offer curve for the ith customer and thus assume that the loans to all customers but the ith are fixed at some given value. The general formulation for the bank's expected profits from the ith customer follows directly from equation 2.11 with the exception that the opportunity cost is now a function of the total loans granted:

(2.50) $P[R_iL_i] = (R_i - I[L])L_i - \displaystyle\int_{k_i}^{R_iL_i} F_i[x]\, dx.$

Similarly, the loan offer curve is derived by differentiating (2.50) with respect to L_i and setting the result equal to zero:

(2.51) $\dfrac{\partial P[R_iL_i]}{\partial L_i} = R_i(1 - F_i[R_iL_i]) - I[L] - L_iI'[L] = 0.$

Equation 2.51 implicitly defines the optimal loan offer $\hat{L}_i$ as a function of the rate factor and opportunity cost.

The second-order condition for a maximum is derived by differentiating (2.51) with respect to L_i:

(2.52) $\dfrac{\partial^2(P[R_iL_i])}{\partial L_i^2} = -R_i^2 f_i[R_iL_i] - \dfrac{\partial^2 I[L]L_i}{\partial L_i^2} < 0.$

This holds by virtue of assumption (2.49c).

The properties of the offer curve now follow directly from (2.51). Since $I'[L] \geq 0$, it is clear that $\hat{L}_i = 0$ for $R < I_o$. In fact, even with $R = I_o$, we have $\hat{L}_i = 0$. This differs from the constant cost case, but does not require any modifications in the basic model except as noted below. For $I_o < R \leq \infty$, the shape of the offer curve is also very similar to the basic case. The slope of the offer curve in this range can be determined by implicitly differentiating equation 2.51 with respect to R_i:

$$(2.53) \quad \frac{\partial L_i}{\partial R_i} = \frac{(1 - F_i) - R_i f_i \hat{L}_i}{R_i^2 f_i + 2I'[L] + \hat{L}_i I''[\hat{L}_i]},$$

with f_i and F_i evaluated at $R_i \hat{L}_i$.

In the case with constant opportunity costs the last two terms in the denominator are zero whereas in the current case their sum is positive. The effect of introducing the rising opportunity cost is thus to reduce the slope of the offer curve at every rate factor. That is, if the constant opportunity cost of the basic case equals the initial opportunity cost here, I_o, then the optimal offer curve for rising costs will lie below the optimal offer curve for constant costs. It is equally clear that $\lim_{R \to \infty} \hat{L}_i = 0$ is true for both cases.

Thus, the shape of the offer curve is in its essential aspects unchanged when we introduce rising opportunity costs.

Finally, to show that profits increase along the offer curve, we differentiate (2.50) with respect to R_i, while constraining $L_i = \hat{L}_i[R]$. If we then use (2.51), the result simplifies to:

$$(2.54) \quad \frac{\partial P[R_i \hat{L}_i]}{\partial R_i} = (1 - F_i)\hat{L}_i \geq 0,$$

with F_i evaluated at $R_i \hat{L}_i$, which is the same result obtained for the basic model.

Although the similarity in the structure of the problem for the constant and increasing cost cases is clear, it should be pointed out that rising opportunity costs do necessitate one caveat with respect to the dynamic rationing of riskless customers. It was argued above that dynamic rationing of riskless customers could be ruled out, for practical purposes, since it was unlikely that the commercial loan rate would ever fall below the bank's opportunity cost. When we allow for rising opportunity costs, however, the case becomes less certain. The point to be stressed, however, is that if we do find that the riskless customers are rationed, then we can be sure that the risky customers are being rationed all the more. Thus, even under these conditions, rationing takes the form of a redistribution of loans toward the less risky customers.

2.7.3 COSTS ATTENDANT WITH BANKRUPTCY OF THE FIRM

The possibility of the bank incurring special costs when collecting the loan proceeds from a bankrupt firm has already been touched on in the discussion of Merton Miller's [1962] model in Section 2.2. For Miller, bankruptcy occurs when the firm cannot fully repay the loan contract, that is, when the available proceeds x are less than the contracted amount RL. For this case Miller assumes the bank's costs of collecting the available proceeds are given by $b_o + b_1 x$. In our earlier discussion, it was suggested, however, that bankruptcy might be more reasonably defined as the case when the available proceeds x are less than the amount of the loan principal L.[58] The collection costs may remain as assumed by Miller.

In this section it will be shown that including these bankruptcy costs in the problem does not affect the qualitative nature of the rationing solution. When bankruptcy costs are taken into account, the bank's expected profit function becomes:

$$(2.55) \quad P[RL] = \int_k^{RL} x f[x]\, dx + RL \int_{RL}^{K} f[x]\, dx - IL$$
$$- \int_k^{L} (b_o + b_1 x) f[x]\, dx,$$

where we have omitted the i subscript for the ith firm. Following the previous analysis, we next differentiate (2.55) with respect to L to obtain the optimal offer curve:

$$(2.56) \quad \frac{\partial P[RL]}{\partial L} = R(1 - F[RL]) - I - (b_o + b_1 L) f[L] = 0.$$

For $R < I$ the optimal loan is zero and for $R = I$ the optimal loan is defined by $\hat{L} \leq k/I$, just as without bankruptcy costs. In general, for $I < R < \infty$, the effect of the existence of the bankruptcy costs is to lower the offer curve below the level for no bankruptcy costs. The $\lim_{R \to \infty} \hat{L} = 0$, however, just as it does without bankruptcy costs. Thus the shape of the offer is essentially unchanged when bankruptcy costs are added. To insure the conditions for a maximum, note that:

$$(2.57) \quad \frac{\partial^2 P[RL]}{\partial L^2} = -R^2 f[RL] - (b_o + b_1 L) f'[L] - b_1 f[L].$$

In general, the sign of this derivative may be either negative or positive. It will be positive if $f'[L]$ is sufficiently negative so that the expected value of the bankruptcy costs, $(b_o + b_1 L) f[L]$, declines sufficiently fast when the loan size is being increased. The issue is not of any important consequence, however, and to simplify matters one could assume that (2.57) is, in fact, negative for all values of R and L. Finally, note that if we differentiate (2.55) with respect to R, evaluate the result at $L = \hat{L}[R]$, and then substitute (2.56)

---

[58] Although this definition of bankruptcy is used in the analysis, similar results would be obtained using Miller's definition.

into the result, we obtain

(2.58) $$\frac{\partial P[R\hat{L}]}{\partial R} = (1 - F)\hat{L} \geq 0,$$

with F evaluated at $R\hat{L}$.

2.7.4 SECOND-ORDER CONDITIONS

A significant portion of this chapter has been concerned with the solution of maximization problems and the derivation of the properties of the first-order conditions. The second-order conditions, however, were generally simply assumed to be valid. The primary purpose of this section is to provide some insight into the implications of these assumptions for the underlying density functions and demand functions.

Multiple (Local) Maxima for the Optimal Loan Offer Curve. The discussion in Section 2.2 proved that there was a finite maximum to the optimal loan offer curve $\hat{L}_i = \hat{L}_i[R_i]$. The purpose of this part is to show (1) that multiple local maxima can occur, and (2) that the existence of local maxima does not change the essential conclusions of the basic analysis.

Implicitly differentiating equation 2.13 with respect to the interest rate factor, we obtain the slope of the offer curve:

(2.59) $$\frac{\partial \hat{L}}{\partial R} = \frac{1 - F - R\hat{L}f}{R^2 f},$$

where the i subscript for the customer has been omitted, and f and F are to be evaluated at $R\hat{L}$. Equation 2.59 can be rewritten:

(2.60) $$R\frac{\partial \hat{L}}{\partial R} + \hat{L} = \frac{(1 - F)}{Rf}.$$

Differentiating (2.60) with respect to R and substituting (2.59) then yields:

(2.61) $$R\frac{\partial^2 \hat{L}}{\partial R^2} + 2\frac{\partial \hat{L}}{\partial R} = \frac{-(1 - F)(2f + (1 - F)f')}{R^2 f^3}.$$

To prove the existance of multiple maxima, we must show that $\dfrac{\partial^2 \hat{L}}{\partial R^2} > 0$ can occur when $\dfrac{\partial \hat{L}}{\partial R} = 0$. From (2.60) and (2.61) we obtain:

(2.62) $$\frac{\partial^2 L}{\partial R^2} = \frac{-2\hat{L}}{R^2 f} - \frac{\hat{L}^2 f'}{Rf} \qquad \text{when} \qquad \frac{\partial L}{\partial R} = 0,$$

and hence,

(2.63) $$\frac{\partial^2 L}{\partial R^2} > 0 \qquad \text{if} \qquad f' < \frac{-2}{R\hat{L}},$$

There appears to be no economic rationale for restricting f' in this manner; thus multiple local maxima can occur.

The effect of the existence of local maxima on the basic analysis of the problem is quite minor. For example, consider the case of the discriminating monopolist. The existence of local maxima implies the possibility of multiple intersections of the offer curve and the demand curve; thus the rate factor defined above as $\bar{R}$ need not be unique. Only the largest of these rates, however, is relevant for the monopolist because profits increase as we move along the offer curve (Proposition III) and the largest of the rates is feasible by definition. Thus Proposition IV remains valid with the exception that $\bar{R}$ must be redefined as the largest rate factor at which the offer curve and demand curve intersect. In a similar fashion the analysis of a banker charging all customers the same rate factor can be amended.[59]

The Discriminating Monopolist. The second-order condition for the maximation of expected profits for the discriminating monopolist, is derived by differentiating equation 2.19 with respect to R_i:

$$(2.64) \quad \frac{\partial^2 P}{\partial R_i{}^2} = D_i''(R_i(1 - F_i) - I) + 2(1 - F_i)D_i'$$

$$- (R_i D_i' + D_i)^2 f_i < 0.$$

This can be rewritten as:

$$(2.65) \quad D_i'' < \frac{2(1 - F_i)D_i}{(R_i(1 - F_i) - I)^2} + \frac{(D_i')^2 I^2 f_i}{(R_i(1 - F_i) - I)^3} > 0.$$

The second-order condition thus amounts to an upper bound on the second derivative of the demand function. The bound, in turn, depends on the parameters of both the demand and density functions. It is interesting to note that in the case of certainty, condition (2.65) reduces to:

$$(2.66) \quad D_i'' < \frac{2D_i}{(R_i - I)^2}.$$

Since the demand curve is below the offer curve at the equilibrium rate, it follows that $R_i(1 - F_i) - I$ must be positive (see equations 2.13 and 2.19) and thus condition (2.66) does in fact imply condition (2.65). Thus our solution will be a maximum as long as the corresponding solution for the case without uncertainty is a maximum.

---

[59] The possibility of local maxima does make the concept of "weak credit rationing" of Freimer and Gordon [1965] (see Section 2.2) ambiguous, however, since credit rationing will then occur only in specific intervals. This possibility is not mentioned by Freimer and Gordon, possibly because they work with a rectangular density function with the property that $f' = 0$ in the relevant range.

The Bank Charges All Customers the Same Rate. The second-order condition for this case is derived by differentiating equation 2.21 with respect to the interest rate factor R. This can be written as:

$$(2.67) \qquad \frac{\partial^2 P}{\partial R^2} = \sum_{i=1}^{n} \frac{\partial^2 P_i}{\partial R^2} < 0,$$

where $\dfrac{\partial^2 P_i}{\partial R^2}$ has already been defined in equation 2.64. Thus the second-order condition for the bank charging all customers the same rate has essentially the same interpretation as the condition for the discriminating monopolist. In particular the relationship between the second-order conditions for the cases with and without uncertainty is the same as just discussed for the discriminating monopolist.

2.7.5 SUMMARY

The discussion in this section has shown that the basic model can be easily extended to incorporate more general assumptions than those used in the main body of the analysis. The primary effect of allowing for open-end investment projects, increasing opportunity costs, and bankruptcy costs was that the specific shape of the loan offer curve might be changed. In all cases, however, the basic qualitative features of the loan offer curve, in particular the conditions derived in Propositions I, II, and III, remain valid. The discussion of the second-order conditions and multiple solutions indicated that the assumptions necessary for the solution to be a maximum were no more severe, and might even be more easily met, than those generally encountered in similar economic problems. The primary conclusions of this section are thus that the conditions developed in the basic model for the existence of credit rationing remain generally valid and that the conclusions concerning the mechanism and form of credit rationing will continue to hold.

CHAPTER 3

Measures and Tests of Credit Rationing

3.1 | INTRODUCTION

In this chapter the empirical evidence for the existence of credit rationing by commercial banks is examined and evaluated. The major difficulty in establishing the empirical existence of credit rationing is with problems of measurement. In Section 3.2, the problems of measuring the amount of credit rationing are considered. As examples of various possible solutions to the problems of measurement, earlier studies by G. L. Bach and C. J. Huizenga [1961(a)], D. Hester [1962], J. Hand [1968], W. L. Silber and M. E. Polakoff [1970], R. Fair and D. Jaffee [1970], and the Federal Reserve System are summarized and discussed. In Section 3.3 a new proxy for the degree of credit rationing is developed. This proxy measure is based on the theoretical framework already developed in Chapter 2. In Section 3.4 the proxy variable is used in time series regression tests for the existence of credit rationing. The chapter concludes with an Appendix which contains data for the proxy variable and other unpublished series used in the chapter.

It should be stressed that the material developed here relates solely to the existence of credit rationing as a phenomenon of commercial bank loan supply. A second question, which concerns the effects of credit rationing on the expenditures of business firms and household units, is considered in Chapter 6.

3.2 | THE MEASUREMENT OF CREDIT RATIONING AND A REVIEW OF PREVIOUS STUDIES

Credit rationing has been defined as the existence of an excess demand for commercial loans at the quoted interest rate. Excess demand is defined as the difference between the customer's demand and the bank's offer for those firms being rationed. Consequently, the direct measurement of credit rationing requires *ex ante* observations for both the demand and offer functions of each customer of the bank or, alternatively, direct observations for bank acceptances and rejections of loan requests. Although in principle these types of data are obtainable, in practice it is clear that they are not available now, nor are they likely to be available in the near future.

A discussion of the measurement and existence of credit rationing thus requires recourse to indirect techniques and methods of analysis. That is, measures of credit rationing must be inferred from direct observations on variables known or theorized to be closely associated or related to the actual rationing. This leaves considerable latitude in the construction of measures of credit rationing and in the form of tests for the existence of rationing. Essentially four indirect techniques have been used for the measurement of credit rationing:

1. *Cross-Section Analysis.* Bank loan supply functions are analyzed with cross-section data over periods of differing monetary tightness for evidence of differential bank behavior (credit rationing) in the tight money periods.

2. *Time Series Analysis.* Demand and supply functions for loans are estimated over time with explicit allowance for the existence of credit rationing. The significance of "rationing variables" is then used as the test for the existence of rationing.

3. *Survey Techniques.* Commercial banks or business firms are questioned by survey concerning the existence and amount of credit rationing.

4. *Proxy Measures.* Variables expected to be highly correlated with credit rationing are used as proxy measures of the actual phenomenon.

In the following discussion, earlier studies that have used these techniques are summarized and evaluated.

3.2.1 CROSS-SECTION ANALYSIS

The principal source of cross-section data is the Federal Reserve's sample surveys of commercial and industrial loans made by member banks.

The Federal Reserve surveys were conducted in October 1955 and October 1957 and were based on a stratified probability sample of about 2000 banks which included all banks with deposits over $50 million and declining proportions of smaller banks. The data provide extensive information on the terms of loan contracts, such as the size of the loan, the interest rate, and the maturity, for loans granted or approved in the month preceding the survey.[1] Complete call report data is also available for each bank in the survey. The timing of the surveys is particularly useful for studying the effects of tight money on loan supply since in October 1955 the economy was beginning its recovery from the 1953–1954 recession and interest rates were relatively low, while in October 1957 the economic expansion was reaching its cyclical peak and interest rates were relatively high. The Federal Reserve data were used extensively in the cross-section studies of Bach and Huizenga, Hester, and Silber and Polakoff.

Bach and Huizenga [*1961a*]. Bach and Huizenga used the Federal Reserve data to classify banks, for the period October 1955 to October 1957, into three groups: loose, medium, and tight. A necessary condition for a bank to be classified as tight was that it have a relatively low ratio of free reserves and government bills and certificates to total deposits in October 1955. In addition, the bank's growth in deposits over the period had to be low relative to other banks'. It was further assumed that the relative demand for loans of small and large firms was independent of the classification of the bank and that there was relatively little shifting of customers from tight banks to loose banks over the period.

The data were used to test the hypothesis that tight money leads to discrimination against small firms in the availability of loan funds. Discrimination can be interpreted here in the sense of credit rationing of small firms. The test was based on the notion that if discrimination against small firms occurs in periods of tight money, then the discrimination should be observable in terms of relatively greater discrimination against small firms at the tight banks compared to the medium and loose banks. That is, assuming the demand for loans remains constant across banks, the discrimination or rationing of small firms should show up as a relatively slow growth in loans granted to small firms at tight banks.

The results of the Bach and Huizenga analysis indicated that loans to large firms increased more rapidly than loans to small firms for all categories of banks. The relative growth rate of loans to small firms

---

[1] Detailed discussions of the data are available in the *Federal Reserve Bulletin* issues of April, 1956, pp. 327–340, and April, 1958, pp. 393–408. Analysis of the data by the Federal Reserve System is available in *Financing Small Business,* U.S. Congress, Committee on Banking and Currency [1958].

was greatest, however, at the tight banks. Consequently, Bach and Huizenga were lead to reject the hypothesis of discrimination against small firms.

The Bach and Huizenga study has been strongly criticized for its assumptions concerning the relative growth of the loan demand of large and small firms and the arbitrary definitions of bank tightness.[2] It is clear for example that if discrimination by tight banks against small firms leads the small firms to request and in some cases to obtain loans at loose banks, then discrimination could occur although the Bach and Huizenga measure would indicate otherwise. Similarly, the data do indicate that the loans of large firms grew faster than the loans of small firms. Thus, if the demand of the two classes of customers remained constant in relative terms, then the faster growth of loans to large customers would indicate overall discrimination against small firms regardless of the distribution of loans between loose and tight banks. Deane Carson [1961] has also suggested that the Bach and Huizenga results may be quite sensitive to the definitions used in the classification of banks; unfortunately, the data were not tabulated for other possible definitions.

The theory of credit rationing developed in Chapter 2 provides additional grounds for evaluating the Bach and Huizenga test. In terms of the earlier analysis, the various degrees of bank tightness measured by Bach and Huizenga can be interpreted as variations in the opportunity cost of funds to banks over the cross section. This raises a basic question concerning the source of this variation. In equilibrium one important source of such variation is the tendency for banks to specialize and service only one or a few classes of customers. This implies that the relevant optimal or long run equilibrium interest rate on loans would differ between banks in the same manner that the optimal rate differs between various classes of customers. In the polar case, in which each bank services only one class of customers, only banks which service the same class would have equal equilibrium loan rates. Moreover, in Chapter 2 it was shown that there is no systematic relationship between the amount of equilibrium rationing and the level of the opportunity cost. This means, in terms of the Bach and Huizenga study, that differential "equilibrium" tightness need not imply differential equilibrium rationing, and thus the Bach and Huizenga results are not necessarily inconsistent with the existence of such discrimination.

This suggests that differential tightness, as defined by Bach and Hui-

---

[2] The Bach and Huizenga study has been criticized in comments by Carson [1961] and Tussing [1963] and by Silber and Polakoff [1970]. See also the replies by Bach and Huizenga [1961b] and [1963].

zenga, may have implications for rationing only in essentially dynamic situations. Problems of interpretation still arise in this case however. Dynamic rationing has been shown to depend on the spread between the equilibrium loan rate and the rate actually quoted. Now, in general, there is no reason why the speed of adjustment of the loan rate toward its equilibrium level should be equal for all loan classes, particularly if banks do tend to specialize in servicing specific classes of customers. Consequently, if the tighter banks were able to adjust the quoted rate more quickly, then we would not expect to find a strong relationship between tightness per se and dynamic rationing. In fact, Bach and Huizenga themselves provide very clear evidence supporting the contention that the tight banks adjusted (raised) their rates faster than the loose banks. Thus, to the extent that the classification of banks by tightness is correlated with the type of customers serviced by the banks, one would not expect the Bach and Huizenga experiment to provide strong evidence of credit rationing.

Hester [1962]. In his study of commercial bank loan offer functions, Donald Hester has also used the Federal Reserve survey data to examine the effects of tightening monetary conditions between 1955 and 1957 on credit rationing. Specifically, he considers two sets of hypotheses:

"5.   *Ceteris paribus,* when rates of interest on competing assets are higher, borrowers of any particular size:
   (a)   pay a higher rate of interest on their loans.
   (b)   receive loans with shorter maturities.
   (c)   receive smaller loans.
   (d)   are more frequently required to provide security.
 6.   *Ceteris paribus,* when rates of interest on competing assets are higher the deposit coefficient (elasticity) of:
   (a)   the loan rate of interest is more positive.
   (b)   the maturity of the loan is more negative.
   (c)   the amount of the loan is more negative.
   (d)   the likelihood of security is more positive."[3]

Hypothesis 5(a) reflects the standard market response of the loan rate to an increasing opportunity cost of bank funds. The remaining hypotheses all indicate bank reliance on nonprice factors and/or credit rationing as interest rates attain higher levels.

Hester tests these hypotheses by fitting regressions for each of the contract terms appearing in the hypotheses, the loan rate, the maturity, the

---

[3] Hester [1962], pp. 156–157.

size of the loan, and the use of security for the loan. The data sample includes pooled observations from the 1955 and 1957 Federal Reserve surveys for banks in the Cleveland Federal Reserve district using individual loans as the unit of observation. As an example, his results for the loan size variable A were:

$$(3.1) \quad \log A = -.243 + .222C_{57} + .075 \log D_{55} + .071 \log D_{57}$$
$$(.034) \quad (.013) \qquad (.015)$$
$$+ .638 \log H_{55} + .690 \log H_{57},$$
$$(.012) \qquad (.011)$$

$R^2 = .591$; standard errors in parentheses.

The independent variables are a dummy shift variable taking the value 1 for 1957 observations (C_{57}), deposits of the bank (D) and the total assets of the borrower (H). The subscripts for D and H indicate the data correspond to the year shown; for example for loans made in 1955, D_{55} and H_{55} take the values for D and H in that year and D_{57} and H_{57} are unity. Regressions with the same independent variables were also fitted for the three other contract term variables.

On the basis of these results Hester accepts hypothesis 5(a) for the interest rate effect, but rejects the hypotheses concerning the existence of credit rationing. Hypothesis 5(a) is accepted because the shift parameter is significant and positive in the loan rate equation. The remaining hypotheses were rejected because the coefficients did not take on the appropriate values. In particular, hypotheses 6 were rejected because the deposit variables did not change significantly between 1955 and 1957; this is very clear in the example of the loan size equation shown in (3.1).

Before evaluating these results, it is worthwhile to first consider the closely related tests performed by Silber and Polakoff.

Silber and Polakoff [1970]. In the most recent study using the Federal Reserve Survey data, Silber and Polakoff have attempted to improve upon the tests of Bach and Huizenga, and Hester. The model used by Silber and Polakoff is based on Hester's specification of the commercial bank loan offer function. The individual bank is used as the unit of observation and regressions are fitted for the supply of loans disaggregated into five asset size classes for the years 1955 and 1957. Thus ten regressions are fitted in all. The independent variables in these regressions are the deposits of the bank, the own rate and other rate, the own maturity and other maturity, and the own security requirement and the other security requirement. The "other" variables are represented by weighted averages of the relevant variables for the other asset size classes at the bank. As an example, the equation fitted by Silber and Polakoff for the smallest customer class 1 in 1955 was:

$$(3.2) \quad L_1{}^{55} = 564.3 + 1.78\,D + 132.9\,i_1 - 234.2\,i_o - 114.4\,M_1$$
$$\phantom{(3.2) \quad L_1{}^{55} = 564.3 +} (.15) \qquad (175.5) \quad (117.6) \quad (53.8)$$
$$\phantom{(3.2) \quad L_1{}^{55} = 56} + 52.1\,M_o + 1037.1\,S_1,$$
$$\phantom{(3.2) \quad L_1{}^{55} = 564.} (52.1) \qquad (521.8)$$

$$R^2 = .44, \qquad \text{standard errors in parentheses.}$$

The subscript 1 indicates an own-class 1 variable and the subscript o represents an "other" variable. The independent variables are deposits (D), interest rates (i), maturity (M), and security (S). It should be noted that in the nine other equations only the deposit variable invariably received the correct sign, and in some equations it is the only variable with the correct sign.

The Silber and Polakoff test for discrimination is based on the ratio of the deposit variable coefficients between 1955 and 1957 for each of the asset size categories. If discrimination against small firms occurred between 1955 and 1957, then they postulate that the ratio of the 1955 to the 1957 deposit variable coefficient should decline for larger asset size classes. The results for this test are shown in Table 3.1. It is apparent from Table 3.1 that, except for the smallest asset class 1, the ratio of deposit coefficients does decline for larger classes. Furthermore, there is a fairly distinct break at the class 3 level. Consequently, Silber and Polakoff conclude that discrimination against small firms does occur, and that in particular the discrimination is most severe against firms with assets of $5 million or less.

Perhaps the most striking feature of the results of Silber and Polakoff is that although their basic theoretical model follows directly from the work of Hester, their conclusions are essentially just the opposite from the conclusions drawn by Hester on the basis of his own estimates. Several

TABLE 3.1

		Silber and Polakoff Deposit Coefficients		
	Asset Class	1955	1957	Ratio
1	Less than $\tfrac{1}{4}$ million	1.78	1.43	1.30
2	$\tfrac{1}{4}$ to $1 million	3.89	2.22	1.80
3	$1 to $5 million	16.88	14.02	1.20
4	$5 to $25 million	50.79	64.97	.78
5	Over $25 million	137.05	221.40	.61

plausible explanations for this are available. First, the Silber and Polakoff study uses data from the New York City Federal Reserve District whereas Hester's study, as already noted, uses data from the Cleveland Federal Reserve District. It is quite possible that the New York City banks, consisting in part of major money market banks, will be more sensitive to tight money conditions, and thus may ration, while the Cleveland banks do not.[4] Second, the basic unit of observation for the two studies differs; Silber and Polakoff use individual banks, while Hester uses individual loans. In particular, the dependent variable in the regressions of Silber and Polakoff is the total amount of loans made to firms of a given size, whereas the dependent variables in Hester's equations are the terms of individual loan contracts, for example, the size of individual loans. It is, of course, possible that the total amount of loans and the size of individual loans could move in opposite directions over a time interval if the number of customers within a size class is also changing. Third, Silber and Polakoff separate their sample by asset size and use the relative movements in the deposit variable coefficient in deriving their conclusion, while Hester uses only aggregate equations.

It is to be stressed that these points should not be taken as negative criticism of either of the two studies. Rather, the points indicate that the two studies are addressing different questions. Silber and Polakoff are concerned with the differential effects of discrimination in terms of the total amount of loans granted to small firms in the New York City Federal Reserve District, whereas Hester is concerned with the reductions in loan size for firms of all asset sizes in the Cleveland District. With this interpretation the two sets of results are not necessarily inconsistent.

More generally and more critically, however, there are two important problems that relate to cross-section studies and that are particularly disturbing in a credit rationing context. The basic Hester loan supply formulation assumes both equilibrium and perfect competition in the loan market. The assumption of equilibrium can be avoided only by explicitly introducing dynamic market adjustment mechanisms into the study. Such a task would appear very difficult for a cross-section study given the limited amount of data that are available. The assumption of perfect competition is equally difficult to avoid since in its absence the supply of loans is determined jointly with the parameters of the demand schedules, and data for the latter are not available from the Federal Reserve surveys. While both of these problems are, of course, common to all cross-section studies, and thus one might be sympathetic to the plight, the force of

---

[4] This suggests that a study of a third Federal Reserve District such as Chicago might be helpful if it provides results intermediate to those for New York City and Cleveland.

much of the argument of Chapter 2 was that credit rationing is a phenomenon that arises most clearly in the dynamic adjustment of an imperfect market. Furthermore, as noted above, similar problems also arise with the cross-section study of Bach and Huizenga. Thus, as ingenious as the three studies summarized here are, one is lead to conclude that cross-section analysis has not provided conclusive evidence on the existence of credit rationing.

3.2.2 TIME SERIES ANALYSIS

Although time series analysis is more amenable than cross-section analysis to the explicit specification of dynamic and disequilibrium structures for market behavior, time series techniques have rarely been used for this purpose. The primary exceptions to this rule appear in studies of the mortgage and housing markets, but even then the availability of funds is typically specified as a determinant of demand or supply rather than as a characteristic of the basic structure of the market.[5] This neglect appears to be due to the practical problems of implementing econometric techniques that can explicitly incorporate disequilibrium markets. A recent study by Fair and Jaffee [1970], however, describes various econometric techniques for estimating aggregate demand and supply schedules and the extent of rationing in disequilibrium markets. In this section the theoretical framework for these techniques is summarized.

The general model consists of an aggregate demand and an aggregate supply function:

$$(3.3) \qquad D_t = \alpha_0 X_t^D + \alpha_1 P_t + \mu_t^D, \qquad t = 1, 2, \ldots, T,$$

$$(3.4) \qquad S_t = \beta_0 X_t^S + \beta_1 P_t + \mu_t^S, \qquad t = 1, 2, \ldots, T.$$

D_t denotes the quantity demanded during period t, S_t the quantity supplied during period t, and P_t the price of the good during period t. X_t^D and X_t^S denote the variables, aside from P_t and the error terms μ_t^D and μ_t^S, which influence D_t and S_t respectively. Equations 3.3 and 3.4 are standard demand and supply equations: price is assumed to have a negative effect on demand ($\alpha_1 < 0$) and a positive effect on supply ($\beta_1 > 0$). In the context of the commercial loan market, the quantity of course refers to the quantity of loans and the price refers to the interest rate on the loans.

The distinguishing feature of the model is that P_t is *not* assumed to adjust each period so as to equate D_t and S_t. The market, in other words, is

---

[5] This is the approach used in studies by Maisel [1965], Sparks [1967], Smith [1969], and de Leeuw and Gramlich [1969]. Other studies by Huang [1966], Sparks [1968], and Jaffee [1970] assume that the quantity of mortgages is determined by supply factors, while the mortgage interest rate adjusts as a function of excess demand.

not assumed to be always in equilibrium. Consequently, some assumption has to be made about how the actual quantity is determined. Let Q_t denote the actual quantity observed during period t. Then Q_t is asumed to be:

(3.5) $Q_t = \min \{D_t, S_t\}$, $t = 1, 2, \ldots, T$.

Equation 3.5 replaces the general equilibrium condition that D_t equals S_t for all t and states that the actual quantity observed is equal to the minimum of the quantity demanded and the quantity supplied: thus generally some demanders or some suppliers will go unsatisfied during any one period.

The primary econometric problem in estimating the system of equations 3.3 to 3.5 is that the observed data on quantity will represent either the demand function or the supply function (from equation 3.5), but not both, for any given observation. Consequently, standard techniques that estimate both schedules over the entire sample cannot be used in this case. Instead, two alternative approaches to the estimation problem are considered. One approach is to separate the sample of observations into demand and supply period regimes depending on the minimum of the demand and supply functions. Each schedule may then be fitted against the observed quantity for those sample points falling within its regime. A second approach is to adjust the observed quantity for the effects of rationing and then fit both schedules over the entire sample period using the adjusted quantity.

Three techniques for implementing the first approach are suggested. One technique is to use a maximum likelihood criterion for the determination of the demand and supply regimes. This technique may be difficult computationally, however, so a second possibility is also suggested. The second technique assumes that the price in the market changes as a function of excess demand:

(3.6) $\Delta P_t \gtreqless 0$ as $D_t - S_t \gtreqless 0$.

Consequently, the change in price may serve as an indicator of the excess demand status of the market, and it may be used in the selection of the demand and supply regimes. The third technique for implementing the first approach uses the information of equation 3.6 to reduce the number of doubtful demand and supply regime sample points to a manageable number, and then the maximum likelihood criterion is used to choose among these remaining points.

The technique for implementing the second basic approach to the estimation problem relies on a more specific assumption concerning the adjustment of price:

(3.7) $\Delta P_t = \gamma(D_t - S_t)$, $0 \leq \gamma \leq \infty$.

Equation 3.7 implies that the *amount* of excess demand is strictly proportional to the change in price. Consequently the change in price may be used as a *quantitative* surrogate for excess demand, and this allows both the demand and supply schedules to be estimated over the entire sample, as shown in Fair and Jaffee.

3.2.3 SURVEY TECHNIQUES

Questionnaire surveys of commercial banks and their loan customers provide a third potential source of information for the measurement of credit rationing. Such surveys have in the past been generally concerned with determining the effectiveness of monetary policy in influencing investment and other expenditure decisions. The effectiveness of monetary policy in the 1966 money crunch, for example, was surveyed in studies by the OBE-SEC and Donaldson, Lufkin & Jenrette, Inc.[6] Since these studies are concerned primarily with the effects of credit rationing, rather than with its actual existence, they are discussed in Chapter 6 below.

More recently, the Federal Reserve System has started a *Quarterly Survey of Changes in Bank Lending Practices* which attempts to directly ascertain changes in nonprice lending policies of commercial banks. The survey is taken quarterly during the first two weeks of the second month of each quarter and data are available starting with the February 1967 survey. The sample includes approximately 125 commercial banks and duplicates the panel used for the *Quarterly Survey of Interest Rates on Business Loans* (see Section 3.3). The questions cover four principal types of loan supply: commercial and industrial loans, loans to nonfinancial business firms, loans to independent finance companies, and bank willingness to make other types of loans. In all, 23 questions are asked. A senior loan officer at each respondent bank is asked to judge whether changes in the bank's lending policies for each of these loan categories would be considered "essentially unchanged" or "moderately" or "much" firmer or easier.

The questions in the category of loans to nonfinancial business firms are of primary interest for the credit rationing of commercial loan customers. These questions, together with the responses for the February 1967 survey, are shown in Table 3.2. It can be seen that the questions cover a wide range of topics relevant to the level and variability of loan contract terms and availability policies. The February 1967 survey indicates, for example, that the policy on loans to nonfinancial business firms, tended to be either "essentially unchanged" or "moderately easier" when

---

[6] See Crockett, Friend, and Shavell [1967] and Donaldson, Lufkin & Jenrette, Inc. [1967].

TABLE 3.2 CHANGES IN BANK LENDING PRACTICES AT SELECTED LARGE BANKS: POLICY ON FEBRUARY 15, 1967, COMPARED WITH POLICY 3 MONTHS EARLIER (*Number of Banks; Figures in Parentheses Indicate Percentage Distribution of Total Banks Reporting*)

	Total	Much Firmer Policy	Moderately Firmer Policy	Essentially Unchanged	Moderately Easier Policy	Much Easier Policy
Loans to nonfinancial businesses:						
Terms and conditions:						
Interest rates charged	133 (100.0)		6 (4.5)	33 (24.8)	100 (75.2)	
Compensating or supporting balances	132 (100.0)	1 (0.8)	13 (9.8)	121 (91.7)	4 (3.0)	
Standards of credit worthiness	132 (100.0)		4 (3.0)	118 (89.4)	1 (0.8)	
Maturity of term loans	132 (100.0)	1 (0.8)	4 (3.0)	118 (89.4)	8 (6.0)	1 (0.8)
Practice concerning review of credit lines or loan applications:						
Established customers	133 (100.0)		4 (3.0)	106 (79.7)	22 (16.5)	1 (0.8)
New customers	133 (100.0)	3 (2.3)	8 (6.0)	60 (45.1)	58 (43.6)	4 (3.0)
Local service area customers	131 (100.0)		2 (1.5)	104 (79.4)	23 (17.6)	2 (1.5)
Nonlocal service area customers	130 (100.0)	3 (2.3)	8 (6.2)	94 (72.3)	25 (19.2)	
Factors relating to applicant:*						
Value as depositor or source of collateral business	132 (100.0)	4 (3.0)	7 (5.3)	117 (88.6)	3 (2.3)	1 (0.8)
Intended use of the loan	132 (100.0)	3 (2.3)	7 (5.3)	95 (72.0)	25 (18.9)	2 (1.5)
Loans to independent finance companies:						
Terms and conditions:*						
Interest rate charged	133 (100.0)		4 (3.0)	59 (44.4)	70 (52.6)	
Compensating or supporting balances	133 (100.0)	2 (1.5)	5 (3.7)	125 (94.0)	1 (0.8)	
Enforcement of balance requirements	133 (100.0)	3 (2.3)	10 (7.5)	120 (90.2)		
Establishing new or larger credit lines	133 (100.0)	6 (4.5)	14 (10.5)	92 (69.2)	20 (15.0)	1 (0.8)

Source: Quarterly Survey of Changes in Bank Lending Practices, questions on loans to nonfinancial businesses, *Federal Reserve Bulletin*, April, 1968.

* For these factors, firmer means the factors were considered to be more important in making decisions for approving credit requests, and easier means they were considered to be less important.

compared with the policy three months earlier, although in three categories—compensating balances, standards of credit worthiness, and value of depositor—policy became moderately firmer.

As the basis for a comparison with the credit rationing proxy variable to be developed in Section 3.3, the results for the twelve surveys taken during the period 1967 to 1969 are summarized in Table 3.3. For each question, the numbers tabulated in the table indicate the net percentage of respondents pursuing a firmer or easier policy relative to policy three months earlier. The net percentage was calculated by subtracting the percentage of respondents indicating an easier policy from the percentage of respondents indicating a firmer policy; thus positive numbers indicate a net firmer policy and negative numbers indicate a net easier policy. The answers of "much" firmer (or easier) have not been distinguished from answers of "moderately" firmer (or easier) because no adequate basis could be found for weighting the "much" category, although the cases in which over 15 percent of the respondents indicated a "much" firmer policy are noted with an asterisk in the table (there were no cases in which over 15 percent of the respondents indicated a "much" easier policy).

As tabulated in Table 3.3, the results of the survey indicate signifiant variations in the nonprice terms of business loan contracts. On a general level, the pattern of firming and easing on these contract terms is consistent with more qualitative interpretations of the changing stance of monetary policy during this period. Following the credit crunch of 1966, the contract terms were generally easier during the first two quarters of 1967, and then gradually tightened between 1967–3 and 1968–1. During 1968–2 monetary policy was significantly tighter, and this is reflected in firmer policies on nonprice terms and the interest rate charged on business loans. Following the enactment by Congress of the tax surcharge, there is an indication of some easing by the banks during 1968–3, although in some categories further tightening is still indicated. Finally, starting in 1968–4 and continuing through the last survey in 1969–4, there is a continuous and significant firming in all nonprice contract terms.

As will be apparent below, the general pattern indicated by these surveys is broadly consistent with the new proxy variable to be developed in Section 3.3. There are two problems, however, that make the quantitative use of the survey data difficult. First, there may be a bias toward a response of firmer policy in some of the reporting. This is particularly clear for the categories of compensating balances, standards of credit worthiness, and the value of a depositor, all of which show continuous firming over the three year period. Second, the responses to the question on the interest rate charged are not always consistent with the observed

TABLE 3.3 SUMMARY OF QUARTERLY SURVEY OF BANK LENDING PRACTICES (*Percentage of Respondents Reporting Net Firmer Policy*)

	1967				1968				1969			
	Feb.	May	Aug.	Nov.	Feb.	May	Aug.	Nov.	Feb.	May	Aug.	Nov.
Terms and conditions												
Interest rate charged	−75.2	−69.8	21.6	30.4	34.4	*93.6	0.8	−27.2	*86.2	*91.1	*78.3	49.6
Compensating or supporting balance	2.3	2.3	20.8	25.0	16.1	*56.8	4.8	10.4	*64.3	*75.8	*68.3	*57.6
Standards of credit worthiness	9.0	9.5	12.0	8.8	7.3	32.8	4.8	4.8	32.8	42.7	*40.6	36.0
Maturity of term loans	−3.0	−3.1	5.7	12.1	1.6	32.8	1.6	1.6	30.3	*42.7	*42.2	35.2
Practice concerning review of credit lines or loan applications												
Established customers	−14.3	−14.2	1.6	6.4	−0.8	30.0	−5.6	−1.6	32.5	47.5	*51.6	36.8
New customers	−38.3	−23.1	16.8	21.6	10.4	*64.8	−5.6	6.4	*61.7	*80.3	*81.4	*60.8
Local service area customers	−17.6	−12.1	0.8	6.5	−2.5	30.1	−5.6	−4.1	30.9	47.2	48.8	32.0
Nonlocal service area customers	−10.7	−4.0	16.2	18.8	11.7	*56.9	10.6	15.4	*49.5	*70.8	*68.8	*56.5
Factors relating to applicant												
Value as depositor or source of collateral business	5.2	6.3	25.6	20.0	19.2	*54.4	12.8	16.0	*58.6	*67.5	65.0	*46.0
Intended use of loan	−12.8	−13.4	10.4	14.4	12.0	*44.3	8.1	6.4	*54.5	*72.6	*68.5	*39.2

* More than 15% of respondents indicated "much" firmer policy.

changes in the commercial loan rate. The most obvious cases occur in 1967–3, 1967–4, and 1969–4: in these quarters the commercial loan rate changed by small amounts, —1, 3, and 1 basis points respectively (see Appendix), while the survey responses indicated that 21.6, 30.4, and 49.6 percent of the banks were pursuing moderately firmer policies during these quarters. In contrast, in 1968–1 when 34.4 percent of the banks reported moderately firmer policies, the commercial loan rate actually rose about 40 basis points.

3.2.4 PROXY MEASURES

The fourth technique available for the measurement of credit rationing is the use of proxy measures. This approach has been considered most carefully in work by John Hand [1968]. Hand developed a list of 24 variables, shown in Table 3.4, which in principle might be highly correlated with credit rationing. The variables include measures of the level and spreads of various interest rates, measures of commercial bank tightness, and characteristics of loans granted and of the loan customers. From these variables he attempted to extract a summary index measure that could stand proxy for the actual amount of credit rationing.

More specifically, his statistical technique was to use the methods of principal components and factor analysis to find sets of these variables that might be taken as indicators of credit rationing. The success of such tests relies importantly on the ability to identify the resulting "factors" in terms of the more intuitive concepts that they are intended to measure. In general, Hand was not able to achieve this identification. That is, the factors and components that resulted from his analysis could be interpreted in terms such as general credit tightness and general economic activity, but none of the factors were clearly representing purely credit rationing phenomena.

Hand's results thus suggest that the number of potential variables for use in any proxy must be limited to those that can be directly interpreted in terms of established theory. In the following section the theory of credit rationing developed in Chapter 2 is used in this way in order to derive a new proxy variable for credit rationing.

3.3 | A NEW PROXY VARIABLE FOR CREDIT RATIONING

It has been already noted that in principle the volume of credit rationing should be measured as the difference between the loan demand and bank supply of rationed customers as defined by E in equation 2.26. The degree or relative incidence of credit rationing could then be measured by the

TABLE 3.4   VARIABLES USED IN FACTOR ANALYSIS: JOHN HAND [1968]

1. Percent of commercial loan extensions that were over $10,000 in size
2. Percent of commercial loan extensions that were over $200,000 in size
3. Percent of commercial loan extensions over $200,000 granted at the prime rate
4. Percent of commercial loan extensions that were granted at the prime rate
5. Commercial paper rate minus prime loan rate
6. Treasury bill rate minus prime loan rate
7. Prime loan rate minus average rate on nonprime loans
8. Rate on loans over $200,000 in size minus rate on loans under $10,000 in size
9. Moody's AAA rate
10. Deviation of Treasury bill rate from trend
11. Federal Funds rate minus Federal Reserve discount rate
12. Treasury bill rate minus Federal Reserve discount rate
13. Treasury bill rate minus average rate on commercial loans
14. Treasury bill rate minus Moody's industrials rate
15. Deviation of noncorporate trade credit liabilities from trend (flow of funds data)
16. Accounts payable of firms with assets under $10 million divided by sales
17. Borrowings from the Federal Reserve by noncountry banks
18. Net borrowed reserves of noncountry banks
19. Loan to deposit ratio of weekly reporting banks
20. Average rate on commercial loans
21. GNP, not seasonally adjusted, current dollars—deviation from trend
22. Treasury bill rate
23. Change in the commercial loan rate
24. Change in the Treasury bill rate

ratio of the volume of rationing to the potential demand of rationed customers, or:

$$(3.8) \qquad \hat{H} = \frac{E}{E + L_2} = \frac{D_2 - L_2}{D_2},$$

where D_2 denotes the demand of rationed customers and L_2 the volume of loans actually granted to them. Unfortunately, as the discussion in Section 3.2 indicated, the direct measurement of E and L_2, the components of $\hat{H}$, requires information that is not available on the *ex ante* customer demand and bank supply functions.

The analysis of Chapter 2, however, points to a possible operational proxy measure for the actual degree of credit rationing indicated by $\hat{H}$ in (3.8). As developed in Chapter 2, the credit rationing model suggests that there should be a positive association between variations in dynamic credit rationing and variations in the proportion of the total loan portfolio accounted for by loans to risk-free prime customers. To be complete, the distribution of credit rationing over all risk (or interest rate) classes should be considered, but in deference to the practical problems of implementation, only risky and risk-free firms are distinguished. Let L_1 ($= D_1$) denote the volume of loans granted (and demanded) to risk-free firms and L_2 and D_2 denote the loans granted and loans demanded respectively by risky firms. The proposed operational proxy for the nonobservable $\hat{H}$ is either of the following two:

$$(3.9a) \qquad H_1 = \frac{L_1}{L_1 + L_2}$$

or

$$(3.9b) \qquad H_2 = \frac{1}{H_1} = \frac{L_1 + L_2}{L_1}.$$

The first measure, H_1, is simply the percentage of total loans that are granted to risk-free customers; hence it is positively related to the degree of rationing. The alternative proxy is its reciprocal and hence is negatively related to the degree of rationing.

To see the relation between either proxy and the ideal measure $\hat{H}$, let $B_2 = D_2/D_1$. Then from (3.9) we obtain:

$$(3.10a) \qquad H_1 = \frac{1}{[1 + B(1 - \hat{H})]}$$

and

$$(3.10b) \qquad H_2 = 1 + B(1 - \hat{H}),$$

since $L_1 = D_1$. Differentiating (3.10) with respect to $\hat{H}$, yields:

$$(3.11a) \qquad \frac{\partial H_1}{\partial \hat{H}} = \frac{B}{[1 + B(1 - \hat{H})]^2} > 0$$

and

$$(3.11b) \qquad \frac{\partial H_2}{\partial \hat{H}} = -B < 0.$$

Equation 3.10 shows that for a given value of B, the proxies are monotonic functions of the ideal measure H, and equation 3.11 confirms that the relation is in the desired direction.[7]

---

[7] Expression 3.11 can be also written in elasticity form as:

$$\frac{\partial H_1}{\partial \hat{H}} \frac{\hat{H}}{H_1} = \frac{B\hat{H}}{1 + B(1 - \hat{H})} \qquad \text{and} \qquad \frac{\partial H_2}{\partial \hat{H}} \frac{\hat{H}}{H_2} = \frac{-B\hat{H}}{1 + B(1 - \hat{H})}.$$

Equation 3.10, which relates the proxies H_1 and H_2 to $\hat{H}$, involves the relative demand factor B as a parameter essentially because the nonobservable D_2 was replaced with the observable D_1. This of course implies that any changes in B will give rise to variations in H_1 or H_2 that do not correspond to variations in $\hat{H}$. In particular, if there were sizable variations in B over time, the proxy measures of $\hat{H}$ could be subject to appreciable errors in measurement. The implications of this possible error can be seen most clearly, using H_2 as an example, by rewriting (3.10b):

$$(3.12) \qquad H_2 = 1 + \bar{B}(1 - \hat{H}) + \epsilon(1 - \hat{H}),$$

where $\bar{B}$ is the mean of B and ϵ is the deviation from this mean. If $\hat{H}$ and ϵ are uncorrelated, then the expected value of the second term in (3.12) will be zero. In this case, the error of measurement will not tend to generate bias in estimated regression coefficients when the proxy measure is used as the dependent variable as will be done in Section 3.4.[8] Fortunately, the conclusions of Chapter 2 concerning the comparative static properties of the model and the classification of customers suggest that, at least in principle, these variables will not be correlated. Further empirical verification of this point is also provided in the discussion of the demand for commercial loans in Chapter 5.

In attempting to implement the credit rationing proxies given in equation 3.9, further problems of data availability must be considered. Both proxies require data on the percentage of loans granted to risk-free firms. Data of total loans are, of course, readily available. To obtain data on loans to risk-free firms it is necessary to identify risk-free firms with those firms that obtain commercial loans at the prime rate. This correspondence of low risk and the lowest rate class is easily verified as both an institutional fact and as an important feature of the theoretical model of Chapter 2.

The source of data for total commercial loans granted and for loans granted at the prime rate is the Federal Reserve System's *Quarterly Survey of Interest Rates on Business Loans*. Until December 1966 the survey was taken during the first two weeks of the last month of each quarter; starting in February 1967 the timing of the survey was changed to the first two weeks of the second month of the quarter.[9] The survey records the volume of new loans granted, with disaggregation by loan sizes and interest rate classes, during the period of the survey for a sample that

---

[8] Because (3.10a) is nonlinear in $\hat{H}$, this statement will be true only for a linear approximation of H_1. If either proxy were being used as an independent variable, the problem of bias would be more serious. See, for example, Malinvaud [1966], Chapter 10.

[9] The survey was changed at this point to allow for changes in coverage and timing as described in detail in the May 1967 *Federal Reserve Bulletin*. This change necessitates splicing of the data if they are to be used on a time series basis and these splices are described in the Appendix.

now numbers approximately 125 banks. With this data the proxy H_1 can be measured as the percentage of loans granted at or below the prime rate and the proxy H_2 can be measured as the inverse of H_1.[10] Unfortunately, in several instances the prime rate changed during the period of the survey with the effect that loans made at the new prime rate cannot be distinguished from loans made at this same rate level while the old prime rate was in effect. To circumvent this problem and secure a more reliable measure these quarters were smoothed as well as possible (see Appendix). In addition, in order to provide easy comparability with other measures of credit rationing, the two proxy series were seasonally adjusted and normalized to have a mean of zero and a standard deviation of unity.

As an alternative, and possibly more complete measure for the credit rationing proxy, an attempt was also made to incorporate the data on the percentage of loans granted at the prime rate with the data available from the survey on the size classes of granted loans. In particular, it was postulated that large loans might generally also represent loans to risk-free firms. In order to merge the prime rate and loan size data into a single measure of credit rationing, the first principal component of the following four series was computed:

1.   The proportion of total loans granted at the prime rate.
2.   The proportion of total loans over $200,000 in size.
3.   The proportion of loans over $200,000 in size granted at the prime rate.
4.   The proportion of total loans $1,000 to $10,000 in size.[11]

The first three variables should enter the principal component positively and the fourth series, representing the percentage of small loans, should enter negatively. The computed factor loadings of the four series for the principal component were, respectively:[12]

1.   .980
2.   .969
3.   .921
4.   −.959

---

[10] The possibility of loans being granted below the prime rate arises primarily in cases where the loan was contracted in an earlier period with a lower prime rate. By necessity these loans are treated as prime rate loans.

[11] These are the same as the first four series listed in Table 3.4 that were used by John Hand in his earlier work on credit rationing. We are grateful to Hand for making his data available.

[12] The time series for the principal component is calculated by summing the four series weighted by the factor loadings and then dividing the entire time series by the sum of the squared factor loadings. The factor loadings shown here are slightly different from those shown earlier in Jaffee and Modigliani [1969] because the data sample now extends through 1969.

These results indicate the four series enter the principal component with the expected sign and that they are about equally weighted. The principal component has, by construction, a mean of zero and a standard deviation of unity. The final series was also seasonally adjusted. This measure, of course, corresponds to the H_1 proxy since series 1 is analogous to the basic series used for the H_1 measure. A principal component proxy in the form H_2 was also derived using the inverse of the four series and the factor loadings were similar to the ones listed above.

To summarize, four possible proxy measures for credit rationing have been developed. The two measures for the H_1 form of the proxy are based on the percentage of loans granted at the prime rate and the principal component of four series respectively, the latter series including information on the size of the loans. The two measures for the H_2 form of the proxy are based simply on the inverse of the data used for the H_1 proxies. All four series have a mean of zero and a standard deviation of unity and are seasonally adjusted. The data for the four series over the period 1952–1 to 1969–4 are shown in the Appendix.

On the basis of tests to be discussed in the following section the proxy in the form of the H_1 principal component was selected as the best measure of credit rationing, and it will be used in describing the qualitative characteristics of the proxy. It is apparent from Table 3.7, however, that the four proxy series are very similar (except for sign) and that essentially the same conclusions are valid for the other three forms of the proxy. Figure 3.1 shows a plot of the principal component proxy H_1 from 1952–1 to 1969–4. The pattern of rationing indicated by the proxy seems quite credible throughout the sample period. The tight money periods of 1957, 1966, and 1969, for example, all stand out as cyclical peaks for the degree of credit rationing. In addition the pattern of credit rationing indicated for the period 1967 to 1969 is very similar to the pattern indicated by the earlier analysis of the Federal Reserve survey of nonprice terms on loan contracts: following the 1966 credit crunch, the proxy falls during 1967–1 and 1967–2, is essentially flat through 1968–1, rises in 1968–2, falls again in 1968–3, and then rises through to the end of the sample, reaching a level in 1969–4 that is slightly higher than the previous peak in 1966–3.

3.4 | A Test of Credit Rationing

3.4.1 SPECIFICATION OF THE TESTS

In this section, the credit rationing proxy variable is used to test the implications of the model developed in Chapter 2 as to the forces controlling variations over time in the extent of credit rationing. The test,

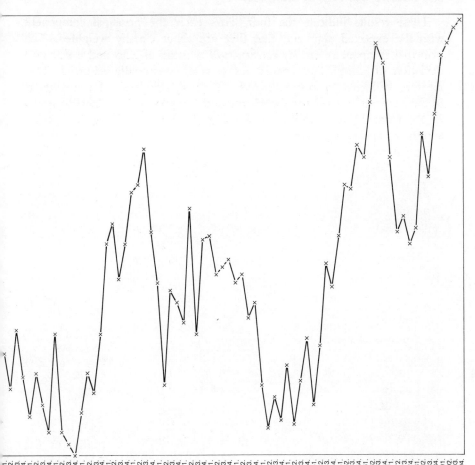

FIGURE 3.1   *Credit rationing proxy: 1952–1 to 1969–4 (principal component proxy H_1).*

relying on quarterly time series data for the years 1952 to 1969, will serve to shed light on three main problems discussed in this chapter: (1) the value of the credit rationing proxy variable; (2) the validity of the theory of credit rationing developed in Chapter 2; and (3) the existence of credit rationing as an empirically significant phenomenon.[13]

---

[13] It is important to note that success in this test will confirm the value of the proxy as a variable to be used in testing for the impact of credit rationing on the real sectors of the economy.

The principal implication of the theoretical model is that the main source of systematic variations in credit rationing is to be found in changes in dynamic rationing; and that these changes in turn are positively associated with the spread between the long run optimal or equilibrium loan rate, denoted hereafter by r_L^*, and the rate actually prevailing, r_L.[14] If it is further assumed that, to a first approximation, this association can be formulated as a linear relationship within the empirically relevant range, then:

$$(3.13) \qquad H = a_0 + a_1(r_L^* - r_L) + \epsilon.$$

The specification of equation 3.13 accounts for both equilibrium and dynamic rationing. When the commercial loan rate is set at its long run optimal level, then only equilibrium rationing is observed. On the micro-economic level, equilibrium rationing depends on the specific parameter values for the demand functions, density functions, and opportunity cost. The investigation in Chapter 2 indicated, however, that no systematic relationship existed between the degree of rationing and changes in these parameters. Accordingly, in equation 3.13 the constant term a_0 is interpreted as a measure of equilibrium rationing up to a stochastic error term which is included in the overall error term ϵ. It should also be recalled at this point that the proxy measures of credit rationing to be used as the dependent variables in (3.13) have been scaled to have a mean of zero over the sample period. This arbitrary choice of origin will of course be reflected in the constant a_0, and consequently it will not be possible to distinguish the level of equilibrium rationing from the scaling effect embodied in the constant.

Dynamic rationing enters the specification of equation 3.13 as the interest rate spread between the optimal rate r_L^* and the quoted rate r_L. When the quoted rate is below the optimal rate level, the amount of dynamic rationing will be positive in the sense that the amount of credit rationing will exceed the equilibrium level. When the quoted rate is above the equilibrium level, dynamic rationing will, in the same sense, be negative. The total amount of rationing cannot be less than zero by definition, however, and the difference in scaling between the total amount of rationing and the proxy variables (which will take on negative values) is included in the constant term as already mentioned.

To complete the specification of equation 3.13, the determinants of the optimal rate r_L^* must now be discussed. The theory of Chapter 2 indicated

---

[14] r_L^* denotes an empirical approximation to the theoretical construct $\hat{R}$ developed in Chapter 2. In particular, r_L^* must stand proxy for the spectrum of optimal rates corresponding to the respective risk classes. Similarly, r_L stands for the spectrum of actual rates and is measured as the average rate on commercial loans compiled from the *Quarterly Interest Rate Survey*.

that the optimal commercial loan rate would be set at that level at which the marginal proceeds from a commercial loan, after adjustment for risk, would just equal the opportunity cost. It is also known that this relationship will be valid for all other assets in the bank's portfolio. This means that the optimal commercial loan rate will tend to equal the market yield on any other asset held in the bank's portfolio after adjustment for risk, maturity, liquidity, and, possibly, any expectations concerning future levels of that rate. We are free, then, to choose as the standard of comparison any security that is widely held by banks; the obvious criterion being practical expedience. The choice, on this basis, is the bank's holdings of Treasury bills.

On the basis of these considerations, the desired commercial loan rate is specified:

$$(3.14) \qquad r_L^* = c_0 + c_1[r_T + b_1((DEP/TB) - 1) - b_2D + b_3L'/(A - L') \\ + b_4\Delta(L'/(A - L'))],$$

where the notation will be defined as we proceed.

Consider first the bank's return on Treasury bills. It may be regarded as consisting of essentially two components. The first component, the market yield on Treasury bills, r_T, is straightforward. The second component, the liquidity value of Treasury bills, is more involved and accounts for the next two terms inside the brackets in equation 3.14. The basic premise is that the liquidity yield of Treasury bills should decrease as the bank's holdings of these bills (TB) rises relative to its deposit (demand and time) liabilities (DEP). The specification for this first part of the liquidity yield takes the form $b_1((DEP/TB) - 1)$ where $b_1(>0)$ is an estimated parameter.[15] The specification thus implies that the liquidity yield of Treasury bills becomes zero when deposits are invested only in bills and the liquidity yield becomes infinite as bill holdings approach zero. Preliminary tests indicated that this specification is slightly better than a linear form such as $b_1(1 - (TB/DEP))$.

A second consideration relating to the liquidity yield of Treasury bills is the development of a broad and active market in certificates of deposit (CDs) starting about 1962. The previous analysis has taken the level of the bank's deposits as given in the short run since the bank has little

[15] The legal requirement that banks must maintain government securities in their portfolio as collateral for government deposits raises one conceptual problem. To the extent that this requirement necessitates holding Treasury bills of some required amount, the correct variable for our analysis would be the free bills; that is, the bills held above the required amount. It has been suggested that, at least in 1966, such a restriction was a restraining influence on bill holdings. Legally, however, a wide variety of Federal and Local Government securities are acceptable as collateral and it is unlikely that more than a few banks, probably centered in New York City, held Treasury bills only to satisfy collateral requirements, even in 1966.

immediate control over them. CDs on the other hand can be purchased and sold in an active market, and thus afford the banks an important means for changing their total assets at short notice. For this reason the existence of CDs can be interpreted as causing a reduction in the liquidity value accruing to a bank from holding a given amount of Treasury bills. It is to be stressed that it is the potential of using CDs, that is the existence of the CD market, rather than the extent to which CDs are actually used, that affects the liquidity yield of Treasury bills. Consequently, the negative effect of the CD market on the liquidity yield is included in the specification of equation 3.14 by a dummy variable, D, which takes on the value 1 for the period of an effective CD market.[16] For present purposes, the CD market is assumed to arise as an important force affecting the supply of commercial loans beginning in the first quarter of 1962.

The value of the CD market in providing banks liquidity is, of course, severely limited in those periods in which the Regulation Q ceiling on CD interest rates inhibits the issue of new CDs. The effect of a binding Regulation Q ceiling can be taken into account in equation 3.14 by including an additional dummy or dummies which counteract the effect of the CD dummy D. Unfortunately, it is difficult to specify accurately the periods with a binding CD ceiling, and thus regressions testing equation 3.13 using data for the period starting in 1965-4, the first quarter in which the ceiling was likely to be binding,[17] may reflect as much on the specification of the dummies as they do on credit rationing. For this reason, in the results presented below, the regressions of equation 3.13 are first fitted over the period 1952-3 to 1965-3 in order to test directly the hypotheses concerning credit rationing. The sample is then expanded to include the period 1965-4 to 1969-4 and the effect of the Regulation Q ceiling on credit rationing is considered.

Continuing with the specification of the determinants of r_L^* in equation 3.14, the next to last term in that equation measures the share of the loan

---

[16] Specifications in which the CD dummy D was multiplicatively interacted with the Treasury bill rate and liquidity yield terms were also tested, but the simple linear form proved preferable.

[17] During the period from the inauguration of the CD market in 1962 through 1965-3 the Regulation Q ceiling does not appear to have significantly restricted the issue of new CDs. There were short periods during which the secondary market rate on particular maturities of CDs exceeded the ceiling (in 1963-3 and 1964-4 for example), but the Federal Reserve moved to promptly raise the ceiling in these cases. In addition, during these periods the commercial banks were still able to issue CDs in the maturity ranges in which the Regulation Q ceiling was not binding. In 1965-4, however, the secondary market rate rose unequivocally above the ceiling for all maturities of CDs. Also see Willis [1968].

portfolio in total assets. This variable is included because the opportunity cost of funds used for loans is likely to rise relative to market interest rates when the share of the bank's assets allocated to loans increases. In addition, this variable may be considered as an adjustment of the required rate on loans for the relative illiquidity of loans due to the absence of a secondary market. It is anticipated that this illiquidity should increase at an increasing rate as the ratio of loans to assets (or liabilities) grows and thus we measure this effect as $b_3(L'/(A - L'))$ where $b_3(> 0)$ is an estimated coefficient, A is total loans and investments, and L' is the commercial loan portfolio of the banks. The specification implies that the illiquidity cost of loans approaches zero as the loan portfolio approaches zero and approaches infinity as loans approach total assets. Finally, changes in the liquidity ratio should also be considered, since a dynamic short run increase in loans that is beyond the control of the bank would have additional (although only transitional) liquidity costs, and this effect is accounted for by the last term in (3.14).[18]

The task of specifying the optimal commercial loan rate in equation 3.14 is now essentially completed. As the last step, the rate r_L^* is specified as a linear function of the terms in the square brackets which have just been discussed. The need for the linear function arises because differences in risk and maturity between commercial loans and Treasury bills have not been formally taken into account.

The basic equation to be estimated can now be derived by substituting equation 3.14 into 3.13, which yields:

$$(3.15) \quad H = (a_o + a_1 c_0 - d_1 b_1) - a_1(r_L) + d_1(r_T) + d_1 b_1(DEP/TB) \\ - d_1 b_2(D) + d_1 b_3[L'/(A - L')] + d_1 b_4 \Delta[L'/(A - L')],$$

where $d_1 = a_1 c_1$. To summarize, the degree of credit rationing has been specified as a linear function of the spread between the desired commercial loan rate and the quoted loan rate. The quoted loan rate r_L thus enters the equation with a negative sign, while the remaining variables, determining the desired rate, enter with a positive sign except for the CD dummy D. We now turn to regression tests based on this formulation.

3.4.2 RESULTS OF THE TESTS

The results of testing the specification contained in equation 3.15 are shown in Table 3.5. The equations have been estimated with two-stage

[18] The loan variable used in the regression test is the sum of industrial and commercial loans and nonresidential mortgage loans of all commercial banks (see Appendix). The mortgage loans are included since they are made to the same customers as the shorter maturity commercial loans.

TABLE 3.5 ESTIMATED COEFFICIENTS FOR CREDIT RATIONING EQUATION

Dependent Variable:	Con-stant	r_L	r_T	(DEP/TB)	$L'/(A-L')$	$\Delta[L'/(A-L')]$	D	G_1	G_2	R^2	S_e	D.W.
Sample 1952–3 to 1965–3												
(a) Principal component H_1	-2.96	-1.15	.32	.006	23.50	2.63	-1.17			.820	.319	2.08
	(6.1)	(5.4)	(2.5)	(1.2)	(7.8)	(.27)	(7.7)					
(b) Principal component H_2	2.96	1.14	-.30	-.006	-23.49	-5.17	1.19			.814	.326	2.14
	(6.0)	(5.2)	(2.3)	(1.1)	(7.7)	(.53)	(7.6)					
(c) Percentage of prime rate loans H_1	-2.40	-1.01	.36	.003	19.42	5.21	-1.14			.770	.334	2.04
	(4.8)	(4.5)	(2.7)	(.60)	(6.2)	(.51)	(7.1)					
(d) Percentage of prime rate loans H_2	2.83	1.09	-.36	-.003	-22.32	-9.77	1.32			.781	.372	2.23
	(5.0)	(4.4)	(2.4)	(.48)	(6.4)	(.87)	(7.4)					
Sample 1952–3 to 1969–4												
(e) Principal component H_1	-3.04	-.97	.38	.007	20.48	1.05	-1.13	.87	.46	.913	.315	2.03
	(7.3)	(5.6)	(3.6)	(1.7)	(9.0)	(.16)	(8.1)	(5.1)	(2.7)			

Notes: R^2 is not corrected for degrees of freedom; S_e is the standard error of estimate corrected for degrees of freedom; D.W. is the Durbin-Watson statistic; and absolute values of T-statistics are shown in parentheses.

least squares.[19] The interest rate variables are not seasonally adjusted and are measured in percentage points. All other variables are seasonally adjusted and all dollar magnitudes are in billions of dollars. A complete set of variable definitions is provided in the Appendix.

The first four equations in Table 3.5 have been estimated over the sample period 1952–3 to 1965–3 using the complete specification of equation 3.15, but with different versions of the credit rationing proxy variable used for the dependent variable. Equations (a) and (b) in the table use the principal component version of the H_1 and H_2 proxies respectively, and equations (c) and (d) use the percentage of prime rate loans version of the H_1 and H_2 proxies respectively. It is apparent from these results that the variations in the magnitude and statistical significance of the coefficients are small for the different proxy measures, although the signs of the coefficients of course change for the H_1 and H_2 measures. Because of these striking similarities, the choice of the best measure becomes much less important. On the basis of the slightly better fit, however, the proxy measure H_1 using the principal component basis (equation (a)) will be used in analyzing the results and extending the estimates through the end of 1969.

The coefficient estimates shown in equation (a) in the table confirm the implications of the model in that all coefficients have the correct sign and the goodness of fit is respectable taking into account the noise in the dependent variable discussed above.[20] The very significant negative coefficient of the commercial loan rate r_L deserves specific note since it supports one of the most distinctive implications of the model, namely that a rise in the commercial loan rate, given the optimal level of this rate as measured by the remaining variables in the equation, tends to reduce rationing as it reduces the demand and increases the supply of loans. Similarly, the opportunity cost as measured by the Treasury bill rate r_T and the loan illiquidity variable (the share of loans in the bank's portfolio) appear as the most significant factors tending to increase rationing given the commercial loan rate. Although the Treasury bill liquidity term and the change in the commercial loan illiquidity term are not statistically significant, this may be due to multicollinearity since in the short run, with the level of total assets essentially fixed, banks may have to

[19] Only variables of *first causal order* (see Fisher [1965], pp. 625–628) for the commercial loan model have been treated as endogenous. In the present instance these variables are the commercial loan rate r_L and the quantity of loans L. The instruments include all the exogenous and predetermined variables appearing in the final specification for the estimated equations for credit rationing, the commercial loan rate (Chapter 4) and commercial loan demand (Chapter 5).

[20] These results differ slightly from the estimates shown earlier in Jaffee and Modgliani [1969] because of minor data revisions and sample changes.

sell Treasury bills to meet unexpected loan demands. This constraint would be valid only in the short run, however, which explains why the level of the bank illiquidity terms remains significant. The remaining variable in the equation is the dummy D intended to measure the effect of the existence of the CD market beginning in 1962. The coefficient of the dummy is both very significant and large (since the dependent variable has approximately unit variance). This suggests that the newly acquired ability of banks to attract and shed funds through CDs contributed appreciably to a reduction in the degree of credit rationing.

It was indicated above that the sample period for estimation could be extended through the end of 1969, the last period of available data, only if the effect of a binding Regulation Q ceiling is added to the specification. The periods of a binding Regulation Q ceiling can, in principle, be determined by comparing the secondary market rate on CDs with the Regulation Q ceiling since if the secondary market rate exceeds the ceiling, then this should preclude the issue of new CDs.[21] In Table 3.6 the secondary market rates on three months CDs and the corresponding Regulation Q ceilings for the period 1965–4 to 1969–4 are shown. Both the ask-bid range and the mean rate for the secondary market CDs are averaged over the two week period of the Federal Reserve interest rate survey; that is, for 1965 and 1966, the first two weeks of the last month of the quarter, and for 1967 to 1969, the first two weeks of the second month of the quarter. This raises a special problem for the 1965–4 observation since the Regulation Q ceiling was raised on December 6, 1965, essentially in the middle of the survey period for that quarter, with the effect that the ceiling was binding during the first week of the survey, but it was not binding during the second week after the ceiling was raised. It is difficult to measure the relative effects during these two weeks and thus in the last column of the table, which shows the spread between the average secondary market rate and the Regulation Q ceiling, the spread for 1965–4 is set at zero.

On the basis of the rate spreads between the secondary market yield and the Regulation Q ceiling, it is apparent that six quarters—1966–3 to 1966–4 and 1969–1 to 1969–4—definitely had binding ceilings. In addition, 1965–4 should be counted as half a period with a binding ceiling.

---

[21] It has been observed that even in periods of a clearly binding Regulation Q ceiling, new CDs continue to be issued in small amounts. This is due to either a very inelastic demand on the part of some CD purchasers or, perhaps more likely, to the use of CDs as an alternative to compensating balance requirements normally met by demand deposits. This suggests that even a fully binding Regulation Q ceiling might not completely offset the advantages to the banks of the CD maket.

TABLE 3.6 SECONDARY MARKET AND CEILING RATES ON THREE MONTH
CDs: 1965-4 TO 1969-4

| | CD Yields[a] | | Regulation Q | Average Rate |
Quarter	Ask-Bid Range	Average	Ceiling	Minus Ceiling
1965-4	4.54–4.59	4.57	4.00 to 5.50	0.00[b]
1966-1	5.03–5.16	5.10	5.50	−.40
1966-2	5.40–5.54	5.47	5.50	−.03
1966-3	5.78–5.98	5.88	5.50	.33
1966-4	5.60–5.80	5.70	5.50	.20
1967-1	5.11–5.23	5.17	5.50	−.33
1967-2	4.35–4.60	4.48	5.50	−1.02
1967-3	4.79–5.20	5.00	5.50	−.50
1967-4	5.25–5.36	5.31	5.50	−.19
1968-1	5.30–5.43	5.37	5.50	−.13
1968-2	5.93–6.05	5.99	6.00	−.01
1968-3	5.80–5.95	5.87	6.00	−.13
1968-4	6.00–6.10	6.05	6.00	.05
1969-1	6.40–6.63	6.52	6.00	.52
1969-2	7.00–7.34	7.17	6.00	1.17
1969-3	8.30–8.63	8.47	6.00	2.47
1969-4	8.23–8.50	8.37	6.00	2.37

[a] *Source:* Federal Reserve Bank of New York.
[b] See discussion in text.

Decisions on binding ceilings for some of the other quarters raise more
difficult questions. The quarters 1966–2, 1968–2, and 1968–4, for example,
would appear likely candidates since the average rate just about equals
the ceiling and part of the ask-bid range is actually above the ceiling
for these periods. On the other hand, quarters such as 1968–1 and 1968–3
would not appear that different in terms of the spread between the CD
rate and the ceiling. Part of the difficulty here, of course, is that the
secondary market for CDs becomes thin after the supply runs out in
periods in which the Regulation Q ceiling is effective; thus the market
quotations may not be indicative of the true status of the market. Consequently, additional information in terms of new offering rates, secondary
market rates on other maturities of CDs, and changes in the outstanding
stock of CDs was also considered, with the result that only the quarters
1966–2, 1968–2, and 1968–4 were added to the list of quarters with bind-

ing ceiling rates.[22] The qualitative nature of this decision makes it important, however, to distinguish these periods from those periods in which the ceiling was unequivocably binding. In order to do this, two additional dummy variables accounting for the Regulation Q ceiling have been added to the specification of equation 3.15 for the estimation over the sample 1952–1 to 1969–4. The first dummy, C_1, takes the value 1 in periods of a binding ceiling—that is, 1965–4, 1966–2 to 1966–4, 1968–2, and 1968–4 to 1969–4—except that 1965–4 is counted as half a period and is entered in the dummy with the value $\frac{1}{2}$. The second dummy, C_2, takes on the value of the spread between the three month CD secondary market yield and the corresponding Regulation Q ceiling, as shown in the last column of Table 3.6, for these same quarters. The second dummy is included in the equation in order to distinguish, albeit imperfectly, between the different degrees of binding ceilings.

The results of estimating this specification are shown in equation (e) of Table 3.5. It can be seen that both dummies obtained the expected positive coefficient and that the coefficients are statistically significant. In addition, the coefficient estimate for the C_1 dummy (.87) is somewhat less in magnitude than the estimate for the basic CD dummy D (−1.13), suggesting that a binding Regulation Q ceiling tends to counteract, but not completely negate, the effect of the existence of the CD market in reducing the degree of credit rationing. Taking into account the spread effect as incorporated in the C_2 dummy as well, however, it can be calculated that the secondary market rate must exceed the ceiling by about 55 basis points before the sum of the C_1 and C_2 dummies eliminates the effect of the basic CD dummy. Presumably, at this point all the advantages of a developed CD market, in terms of reduced rationing, are lost.[23] It can thus be concluded that variations in the level of the Regulation Q ceiling provide the Federal Reserve with very potent control over the degree of credit rationing.

Finally, it should be noted that only the coefficient estimates for the

---

[22] The estimated regression reported below was also tested with the quarters 1968–1 and 1968–3 treated as binding ceiling quarters. The residuals indicated that this treatment of 1968–3 improved the fit while 1968–1 reduced the fit. In all cases, however, the coefficient estimates for the variables in the equation changed very little.

[23] Indeed, Table 3.6 shows that the spread between the secondary market rate and the ceiling rate actually exceeded the critical level of 55 basis points during the last three quarters of 1969. This overkill in terms of the countervailing effect of a binding Regulation Q ceiling on the functioning of the CD market can be interpreted if the development of the CD market has lead to other institutional changes which become irreversible over time. One example with possible relevance for the 1969 experience is the increased interest rate sensitivity of even passbook savings account holders brought about by the well publicized disintermediation by holders of larger accounts.

commerical loan rate and the loan illiquidity variable show any significant change when compared to the estimates of equation (a) for the shorter sample period ending in 1965–3. Even this variation is not disturbing, however, since by extending the sample period through 1969–4, we have introduced observations on the level of the commercial loan rate and loan asset ratio that exceed by a large margin any contained in the shorter sample. Indeed, the coefficient estimates for these two variables are actually more significant in the longer sample as one would expect.

3.4.3 SUMMARY

The principal goal for this chapter was to provide evidence verifying the existence of credit rationing. The model suggested that credit rationing would be positively related to the spread between the desired commercial loan rate and the loan rate actually being quoted. The empirical results confirmed the existence of credit rationing in that the signs of coefficients were correct and they were generally statistically significant; the goodness of fit also seemed very reasonable in view of the known noise in the dependent variable. This same evidence also substantiates, of course, the underlying theory of credit rationing and the proxy measure which was derived from it. In the following Chapters 4 and 5 the proxy measure is used in obtaining structural estimates of the demand and supply for commercial loans. Then in Chapter 6, again with the aid of the proxy measure, the impact of credit rationing on the expenditures of business firms and households is considered.

APPENDIX ON DATA SOURCES

All dollar magnitudes are measured in billions of current dollars and are seasonally adjusted. Interest rates are measured in percentage points and are not seasonally adjusted. Unless otherwise noted, data are available in the *Federal Reserve Bulletin*. The actual data for selected series are shown in Table 3.7.

A Total loans and investments for all commercial banks; two month average centered on end of quarter.

C_1 Dummy variable taking the value 1 in 1966–2 to 1966–4, 1968–2, and 1968–4 to 1969–4, the value $\frac{1}{2}$ in 1965–4, and zero elsewhere.

C_2 Dummy variable taking the value of the spread between the secondary market rate on three month CDs and the Regulation Q ceiling (see Table 3.6 for data) for the 10 quarters listed for C_1, and zero elsewhere.

D Dummy variable taking the value 1 from 1962–1 through 1969–4, and zero elsewhere.

DEP   The sum of demand deposits and time deposits at all commercial banks; two month average centered on end of quarter.

H   The credit rationing proxy variable was developed in four different forms, which can be noted as (a), (b), (c), and (d) corresponding to their use in the equations shown in Table 3.5:

H_a: principal component of four series;
H_b: principal component of inverse of four series;
H_c: proportion of total loans granted at the prime rate;
H_d: inverse of proportion of total loans granted at the prime rate.

The four series used in the principal component were:

1.   proportion of total loans granted at the prime rate;
2.   proportion of total loans over $200,000 in size;
3.   proportion of loans over $200,000 in size granted at the prime rate;
4.   proportion of total loans $1,000 to $10,000 in size.

The data for the four proxy variables for the period 1952–1 to 1969–4 are shown in Table 3.7. A description of the construction of these variables follows.

The data for the four series used in the principal component were obtained from the Federal Reserve *Survey of Interest Rates on Business Loans.* The data from these surveys were available in the Federal Reserve's statistical release E.2 for the period 1952–1 to 1966–4 and in the *Federal Reserve Bulletin* since 1967–1. Because of changes in the timing and coverage of the survey (see *Federal Reserve Bulletin,* May, 1967) two splices in these series are necessary between 1966–4 and 1967–1. First, starting in 1967–1 the category of loans over $200,000 in size was replaced by loans over $500,000 in size because the former was no longer available. Overlapping data at the point of the change, made available by the Federal Reserve, allowed a smooth splicing of the two series. Second, because of the change in coverage, there was an abrupt change in all four series between 1966–4 and 1967–1. The overlapping data suggested, however, that the levels of the four old series in 1967–1 were about the same as the levels in 1966–1; thus the new series starting in 1967–1 were set equal to the 1966–1 value for the old series.

A second set of adjustments were necessary in series 1 and 3 because the prime rate changed several times during the period of the survey. For these periods it is not possible to distinguish loans made at the new prime rate and loans made at this same rate while the old prime rate was in effect. The value of series 1 and 3 for these quarters was determined by using series 2 as the standard for an interpolation. The average value of the series interpolated from the previous quarter forward and the next quarter backward was used.

The four series were then seasonally adjusted. Proxy measure H_c is identical to series 1 in its spliced and seasonally adjusted form and proxy measure H_d is the inverse of series 1. Proxy measure H_a was obtained by determining the first principal component of the four series 1 to 4 and proxy measure H_b was obtained by determining the first principal component of the inverse of the four series.

L' $= L + M.$

L Commercial and industrial loans at all commercial banks; last month of quarter; unpublished Federal Reserve System series; data are shown in Table 3.7.

M Nonfarm, nonresidential, commercial bank mortgage loans; seasonally adjusted by ratio to moving average.

r_L Average rate on commercial loans from the Federal Reserve *Survey of Interest Rates on Business Loans*. Because of changes in coverage, 5 basis points are subtracted from the published series since 1967–1 (see *Federal Reserve Bulletin*, May, 1967). Data are shown in Table 3.7.

r_T Rate on three month Treasury bills, average of monthly data.

TB Treasury bills held by commercial banks included in the Treasury Survey of Ownership as published in the *Federal Reserve Bulletin*; seasonally adjusted by ratio to moving average. The principal drawback of this series is that it comes from only a partial sample of all commercial banks. In Loans and Investment by Class of Bank, *Federal Reserve Bulletin*, data on the universe of commerce banks are available, but only on a semiannual basis. Since the totals for the smaller Treasury Survey do not appear to have drifted relative to the total for all commercial banks, the former quarterly series was used.

TABLE 3.7   SELECTED DATA SERIES: 1952–1 TO 1969–4

		H_a	H_b	H_c	H_d	L	r_L
1952	1	−0.69	0.64	−0.47	0.41	23.10	3.45
1952	2	−1.00	0.92	−0.69	0.68	22.90	3.51
1952	3	−0.49	0.46	−0.40	0.33	23.40	3.49
1952	4	−0.88	0.95	−0.96	1.02	24.40	3.51
1953	1	−1.25	1.30	−1.18	1.32	24.50	3.54
1953	2	−0.86	0.83	−0.68	0.66	24.50	3.73
1953	3	−1.14	1.09	−0.92	0.97	24.70	3.74

TABLE 3.7   (*Continued*)

		H_a	H_b	H_c	H_d	L	r_L
1953	4	−1.39	1.50	−1.44	1.70	23.90	3.76
1954	1	−0.51	0.47	−0.43	0.36	23.70	3.72
1954	2	−1.39	1.48	−1.46	1.75	23.30	3.60
1954	3	−1.48	1.43	−1.22	1.39	23.20	3.56
1954	4	−1.58	1.56	−1.33	1.55	23.50	3.55
1955	1	−1.20	1.11	−0.92	0.97	24.10	3.54
1955	2	−0.87	0.81	−0.67	0.65	25.00	3.56
1955	3	−1.04	1.00	−0.95	1.01	26.30	3.77
1955	4	−0.53	0.50	−0.36	0.29	27.90	3.93
1956	1	0.27	−0.27	0.05	−0.16	29.90	3.93
1956	2	0.44	−0.43	0.41	−0.52	31.30	4.14
1956	3	−0.03	0.02	0.03	−0.13	32.50	4.35
1956	4	0.27	−0.27	0.14	−0.25	33.70	4.38
1957	1	0.72	−0.71	0.54	−0.63	34.30	4.38
1957	2	0.80	−0.77	0.77	−0.84	35.30	4.40
1957	3	1.09	−1.01	1.24	−1.23	35.50	4.83
1957	4	0.37	−0.37	0.45	−0.55	35.20	4.85
1958	1	−0.06	0.06	−0.24	0.15	34.90	4.49
1958	2	−0.96	1.01	−1.11	1.23	34.50	4.17
1958	3	−0.13	0.15	−0.31	0.23	34.80	4.21
1958	4	−0.25	0.26	−0.39	0.32	35.40	4.50
1959	1	−0.41	0.43	−0.59	0.55	35.70	4.51
1959	2	0.57	−0.56	0.47	−0.57	37.40	4.87
1959	3	−0.53	0.54	−0.54	0.49	38.50	5.27
1959	4	0.31	−0.31	0.33	−0.44	39.40	5.36
1960	1	0.33	−0.33	0.28	−0.39	40.70	5.34
1960	2	−0.01	0.01	−0.01	−0.09	41.40	5.35
1960	3	0.06	−0.06	−0.10	−0.01	41.80	4.97
1960	4	0.14	−0.15	0.11	−0.22	42.10	4.99
1961	1	−0.07	0.06	−0.18	0.09	42.50	4.97
1961	2	−0.01	−0.01	0.00	−0.11	42.40	4.97
1961	3	−0.39	0.38	−0.42	0.35	43.00	4.99
1961	4	−0.24	0.18	−0.04	−0.07	43.90	4.96
1962	1	−0.98	0.96	−0.96	1.03	44.60	4.98
1962	2	−1.33	1.38	−1.29	1.48	45.50	5.01
1962	3	−1.08	1.12	−1.08	1.19	46.70	4.99
1962	4	−1.26	1.27	−1.20	1.35	47.60	5.02
1963	1	−0.79	0.84	−0.92	0.97	48.50	5.00
1963	2	−1.30	1.32	−1.12	1.25	49.40	5.01
1963	3	−0.92	0.97	−1.01	1.09	50.10	5.01
1963	4	−0.56	0.54	−0.51	0.46	52.00	5.00

TABLE 3.7   (*Continued*)

		H_a	H_b	H_e	H_d	L	r_L
1964	1	−1.12	1.12	−1.06	1.16	53.00	4.99
1964	2	−0.61	0.63	−0.69	0.68	54.50	4.99
1964	3	0.12	−0.13	0.09	−0.20	56.10	4.98
1964	4	−0.10	0.08	−0.10	−0.01	58.40	5.00
1965	1	0.36	−0.35	0.25	−0.36	61.80	4.97
1965	2	0.80	−0.80	0.64	−0.72	64.40	4.99
1965	3	0.75	−0.75	0.44	−0.54	66.90	5.00
1965	4	1.12	−1.11	0.89	−0.94	69.40	5.27
1966	1	1.03	−1.06	0.83	−0.89	72.20	5.55
1966	2	1.53	−1.53	1.39	−1.34	75.70	5.82
1966	3	2.03	−2.09	1.87	−1.69	78.10	6.30
1966	4	1.87	−1.92	1.75	−1.61	78.60	6.31
1967	1	1.03	−1.06	0.83	−0.89	80.80	6.08
1967	2	0.39	−0.41	−0.05	−0.05	82.90	5.90
1967	3	0.53	−0.56	0.26	−0.37	84.20	5.89
1967	4	0.27	−0.27	−0.19	0.10	86.30	5.91
1968	1	0.42	−0.43	0.59	−0.68	87.80	6.31
1968	2	1.23	−1.20	1.77	−1.62	89.60	6.79
1968	3	0.84	−0.89	0.88	−0.93	92.40	6.84
1968	4	1.39	−1.44	1.45	−1.39	94.70	6.56
1969	1	1.92	−1.83	2.35	−2.01	99.60	7.27
1969	2	2.01	−1.98	1.74	−1.60	102.30	7.81
1969	3	2.16	−2.10	2.65	−2.19	103.60	8.77
1969	4	2.23	−2.18	2.72	−2.24	104.90	8.78

CHAPTER 4

The Determinants of the Commercial Loan Rate

4.1 | INTRODUCTION

The commercial loan rate is important in this study both as a link in the overall model of the commercial loan market and as a structural determinant of the degree of credit rationing. Within the full loan market model, it may be recalled from Chapter 1, the commercial loan rate and the degree of credit rationing are the banks' supply side decision variables. The specification of the commercial loan rate equation must thus include the variables that account for the variations in the interest cost of the credit made available to the banks' commercial customers. With respect to the structural determinants of credit rationing, the discussion in the two previous chapters has shown, both theoretically and empirically, that the spread between the banks' desired level for the commercial loan rate and the level actually quoted for this rate is the principal determinant of the degree of credit rationing. In particular, variations in credit rationing are primarily a function of the speed with which banks adjust the commercial loan rate. It is thus important that the commercial loan rate equation accurately depict the dynamics of this short run adjustment process. The purpose of this chapter is to specify and estimate these determinants of the commercial loan rate, thereby completing the structural description of the supply side of the loan market.

4.2 | REVIEW OF THE THEORY OF THE COMMERCIAL LOAN RATE

The principal theoretical considerations for the formulation of a commercial loan rate equation have already been developed in the two previous

104

chapters on the degree of credit rationing, and the discussion here is mainly a review and summary of these considerations. In terms of the long run equilibrium properties of loan supply, the determinants of the loan rate can be derived as a corollary of standard portfolio theory. The bank's expected return on commercial loans must equal, after adjustment for varying risk, liquidity, and maturity, the return on other assets or liabilities held in the bank's portfolio. In the formulation of the desired commercial loan rate for the credit rationing equation in Chapter 3, this specification centered on the yield on Treasury bills. More generally, however, the yield on commercial loans can be compared to the yield on other assets such as long term government or corporate bonds, or to the cost of funds for liabilities such as certificates of deposit or Eurodollars. In each case, however, the differences in risk, liquidity, and maturity must be taken into account. The assets or liabilities actually used in formulating the commercial loan rate equation will thus depend largely on the accuracy with which the variables determining the variations in these characteristics of the securities can be specified.

A second important consideration in the formulation of the determinants of the commercial loan rate is the imperfect competitive character of the industry. In the polar case of a single discriminating monopolist bank, the rate charged on each loan would be such that the expected *marginal* income from the loan would equal the bank's *marginal* opportunity cost. The bank would thus charge each customer a different rate depending on the risk of the customer and on the elasticity of the customer's demand function. In this case, as in the standard theory of monopoly, it is not possible to define a supply function independent of the parameters of the risk and demand functions.

Fortunately, in a more realistic setting, the banks should be viewed as an oligopolistic cartel in terms of the determinants of the commercial loan rate. In this case the determinants of the loan rate can be handled more directly, although the relationship may still be complex. If open collusion and side payments between banks in the cartel are allowed, then, of course, the monopolistic solution still pertains, although the distribution of customers among the banks will depend on initial conditions. It is clear, however, that the degree of explicit collusion necessary for such a system to operate would not be tolerable, either socially or legally. On the other hand, it is well agreed that banks do have sufficient market power to avoid a perfectly competitive solution. It could thus be expected that the banks would find a practical method for enforcing at least some of their market power, while remaining within the social or legal constraints. The solution to this problem, as discussed in Chapter 2, lies in the ability of the banks to distinguish between loan customers on the basis of the objective characteristics of the firm's financial condition and industry group. These objective criteria provide the banks a means of discriminating between customers that is not available in industries selling a homogenous product to essentially homogenous customers.

In practice, the ability to discriminate between customers leads to a solution in which banks classify customers into categories such that, within each class, all customers are charged the same commercial loan rate. In Chapter 2, the formal properties of such a system of classification were developed. In brief, the optimal classification of firms would be determined by the elasticity of demand and the bank's subjective evaluation of the risk, as under a monopoly or perfectly colluding oligopoly. In practice, however, the number of customer categories must be relatively small, and the categories that are determined must be rationalized in terms of the objective criteria already mentioned. Furthermore, it will be difficult to change a firm's category, once it is set, unless there are changes in the objective criteria. Consequently, the actual pattern of classification and discrimination will only approximate the ideal, and changes in the classification will be less frequent than under an unconstrained profit maximizing system.

In addition to determining the desired long run level for the commercial loan rate, the oligopolistic cartel must also decide when to change the rate in the short run. It is well known that the commercial loan rate tends to lag behind other important market rates in adjusting to new conditions, and the reasons are clear. Imperfect forecasting, inadequate information, and similar factors all argue for at least a gradual adjustment in the rate. Perhaps even more important is the fact that it will generally take a significant amount of time before even the principal commercial banks will be able to agree that a change in the rate is warranted. The absence of a single price leader indicates, moreover, that some form of indirect communication between banks would be very important in determining the level and the timing of changes in the loan rate.

These considerations suggest the hypothesis that the banks rely on an objective signal in determining the timing and the amount of rate changes. That is, in periods in which the signal indicates the need to change the loan rate, the rate adjusts very quickly; at other times the speed of adjustment is very slow and the prime rate might not change at all. A graph of the changes in the actual commercial loan rate for the period 1952–2 to 1969–4, shown in Figure 4.1 as the solid line, lends additional support to this view. The changes in the loan rate cannot only be very large, but, more importantly, they tend to be sporadic. This is consistent with a pattern of rate determination dependent on an outside signal. If the underlying adjustment process occurred at a constant or continuous rate, in contrast, one would expect a much smoother cyclical pattern to the rate changes.

The pattern of changes in the commercial loan rate also suggests the nature of the signal. In Figure 4.1, changes in the Federal Reserve discount rate over the period 1952–2 to 1969–4 have been graphed with the symbol "*", along with the changes in the commercial loan rate as already described.[1] The correspondence of periods in which the commercial loan rate had a significant change, and of periods in which the discount rate changed, is apparent from the figure. In particular, the commercial loan rate changed by more than 10 basis points in 25 of the quarters from 1952–2 to 1969–4, and for all but two of these quarters the discount rate changed in the same or in the preceding quarter. The two exceptions are 1966–3, when the loan rate rose by 48 basis points, and 1967–1, when the loan rate fell by 23 basis points. Furthermore, the simple correlation between changes in the commercial loan rate and changes in the discount rate is .62 over this period.

In addition to the correlation between changes in the Federal Reserve discount rate and the commercial loan rate, the discount rate would appear to fit the banks' need for a signal very well on a number of grounds. First, as a policy instrument of the Federal Reserve, changes in the discount rate are evident to all banks, are unambiguous in direction, and are relatively infrequent. This means there will be no misunderstanding among the banks that a signal has occurred. Second, the use of the discount rate as the signal has the advantage that the Federal Reserve, or other government agencies, can scarcely criticize changes. Third, and perhaps most importantly, in an environment in which banks value customer relationships, timing loan rate changes to coincide with discount rate changes allows the banks to shift the onus of the rate change onto the Federal Reserve policy and the resulting market conditions.

Two further points with respect to the use of the discount rate as a signal should be noted however. First, the above argument does not require that the discount rate be the sole signal for rate changes. It is clear that the loan rate may tend to change even in the absence of a discount rate change or other signal. Also, the loan rate may respond to other signals as well. Both of these possibilities are considered in the empirical tests below. The hypothesis remains, however, that changes in the discount rate are the most frequent signal for changes in the loan rate. Second, it should be emphasized that the underlying logic of this formulation assumes that the Federal Reserve does continue to change the discount rate in a manner that allows the commercial banks to use

---

[1] A description and listing of the data for these variables is presented in the Appendix.

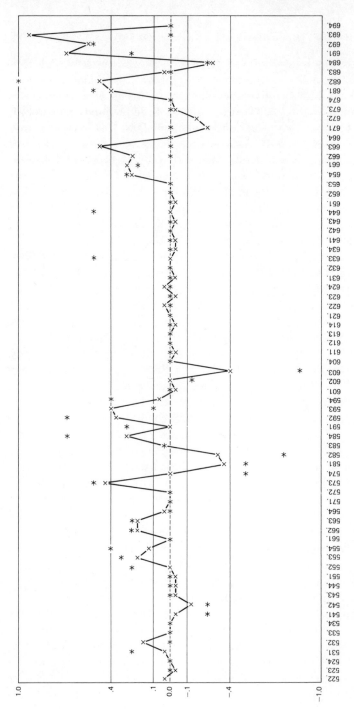

FIGURE 4.1   *Changes in commercial loan rate* (———) *and discount rate* (*): *1952–2 to 1969–4 (percentage points).*

it as an indicator. Clearly the Federal Reserve could easily thwart this use of one of its policy instruments by stubbornly refusing to change the discount rate. More realistically, the establishment of a mechanism tying the discount rate to the Treasury bill or Federal Funds rate would eliminate the discount rate as an acceptable signal. In this sense, the hypothesis should be interpreted as an explanation of past commercial bank and Federal Reserve behavior, rather than as a true prediction of behavior in the future.

4.3 | SPECIFICATION OF THE STRUCTURAL EQUATION

The preceding theoretical considerations and hypotheses can be formally incorporated into an equation explaining the changes in the commercial loan rate:

$$(4.1) \quad \Delta r_L = g + h[r_L^* - (r_L)_{-1}],$$

where r_L^* is the long run desired level for the commercial loan rate and r_L is the rate actually quoted in the short run. The desired rate can be considered, as already noted, to be an approximation to the optimal set of rates corresponding to the various rate classes. The amount of the actual change in the rate is then determined by the spread between the desired loan rate and the rate actually quoted at the end of the preceding period. The timing of the adjustment process depends on the signal used for determining the agreement of the banks to the need for a change. Consequently, the coefficients of the adjustment process, g and h, cannot be specified as constants, but must instead be formulated as functions of the signal variable, that is as functions of changes in the discount rate. In order to make the equation testable, both of these elements, the determinants of the desired rate and the determinants of the short run adjustment, must be explicitly specified, and it is to this specification that we now turn.

4.3.1 THE ADJUSTMENT PROCESS

The functional dependence of the parameters of the adjustment process in equation 4.1, g and h, on changes in the discount rate can be most simply postulated as linear relationships:

$$(4.2) \quad h = h_o + h_1 |\Delta r_D| + \text{lagged terms in } |\Delta r_D|,$$

$$(4.3) \quad g = g_o + g_1 \Delta r_D + \text{lagged terms in } \Delta r_D,$$

where r_D is the Federal Reserve discount rate. Substituting equations 4.2 and 4.3 into equation 4.1 then yields:

$$(4.4) \quad \Delta r_L = g_o + g_1 \Delta r_D + h_o[r_L^* - (r_L)_{-1}] + h_1[r_L^* - (r_L)_{-1}] |\Delta r_D|$$
$$+ \text{lagged terms in } \Delta r_D \text{ and } |\Delta r_D|[r_L^* - (r_L)_{-1}].$$

Equation 4.2 implies that the speed at which the banks adjust the commercial loan rate toward its desired level increases when the discount rate changes. The absolute value of the discount rate is used in order to allow this effect to work for both increases and decreases in the discount rate; that is, the speed of adjustment will increase whichever direction the discount rate changes. One difficulty with this formulation arises if the change in the discount rate and the spread between the desired and actual rate are of opposite sign. In this case the direction indicated by the signal opposes the basic movement of the adjustment process. Such behavior by the Federal Reserve, however, would be contrary to the basic premise of the model that the discount rate can be used as a signal. As a practical matter, moreover, it seems clear that the discount rate would not be changed in one direction when the banks desire a change in the opposite direction. The rationale for the lagged terms in equation 4.2 is given below.

Equation 4.3 indicates that a change in the discount rate has an effect on the commercial loan rate independent of the basic adjustment process. The relevance of such an effect arises from the following reasoning: when the Federal Reserve raises the discount rate, it is likely that the spread between the desired rate and the rate actually being charged will vary among banks, and some banks may, in fact, be satisfied with their current rate. If the signal mechanism is to function effectively, however, it is important that even those banks with a small spread raise their rates. Indeed, it is the essence of the model that, in the absence of collusion, banks will rely at least in part on an exogenous signal for the timing of rate increases. This can lead, in the polar case, to a situation in which all banks are in equilibrium ($r_L^* = r_L$), while the Federal Reserve still persists in changing the discount rate. In this case each individual bank, due to its ignorance of the status of other banks, would voluntarily move away from the equilibrium. In the long run, equilibrium would be regained, of course, because of the continuing effect of the term $h_0[r_L^* - (r_L)_{-1}]$.

The lagged terms in equations 4.2 and 4.3 indicate that the effect of a discount rate change on the commercial loan rate may be distributed over time. One would, of course, expect the predominant effect, say the *impact effect*, of the discount rate change on the loan rate to occur almost immediately if the signal mechanism is operating correctly. But there may also be *secondary effects*, which take as long as a quarter to work out. The secondary effects may arise because nonmajor banks respond more slowly to the signal, and, further, because some loans may have been previously negotiated. In this context it should also be noted that the commercial loan rate is being measured as the average rate on commercial loans, rather than by the prime rate. The main reason for specifying the lagged terms, however, is due to data restrictions, and, particularly, the timing of data observations. The details of the problems of timing and data restrictions are given in the Appendix, Section A.1, but the main point can be illustrated directly. Assume the commercial loan rate is observed only once during the quarter, and for simplicity assume this observation is on the last day of the quarter. Now, if the discount rate change occurs on the first day of the quarter, for example, then one can reasonably assume that all the effects of the discount rate change will be fully developed by the end of the quarter when the change in the commercial loan rate is observed. Alternatively, however, the discount rate change could occur on the next to last day of the quarter; in this case it is clear that the main effects of the discount rate change may not be included in the commercial loan rate observation of the following day. This suggests that the total effect of a change in the discount rate can only be adequately measured by using at least two variables. For the impact effect that occurs in the current quarter, the current change in the discount rate, Δr_D, is used as specified in equation 4.4. For the secondary effects that occur in the following quarter, the change in the discount rate is distributed over two quarters by taking the first difference of the average discount rate during the quarter, the average discount rate being determined by the numbers of days the rate is in effect during the quarter. This latter variable will be denoted as $\Delta \overline{r_D}$.[2]

Two further aspects of the specification of the discount rate as a signal for loan rate changes should be mentioned. First, it is possible that the discount rate changes may only be standing proxy for general changes in the level of interest rates, rather than serving the role of the signal. If this is true then changes in a market rate, such as changes in the Treasury bill rate, should work as well as changes in the discount rate in the specification of equation 4.4. This alternative hypothesis will also be tested. Second, the assumed exogeneity of the discount rate can be brought into question. That is, the discount rate may be responding to other factors, and, in particular, to changes in the commercial loan rate itself, in which case the interpretation of changes in the discount rate as a signal would be inappropriate. The short run timing of changes in the loan rate and changes in the discount rate, shown in Figure 4.1, provides persuasive, if not conclusive, evidence, however, that this is not the case.

4.3.2 THE DESIRED COMMERCIAL LOAN RATE

The specification of the desired commercial loan rate r_L^* is needed to complete the formulation of equation 4.4. Two alternative procedures

---

[2] A formal description and listing of the data for this variable is provided in the Appendix, Section A.1.

for this formulation are available. The first procedure directly specifies the determinants of r_L^* following the formulation used for the credit rationing equation in Chapter 3. This specification, it will be recalled, derived the desired loan rate as a function of three sets of variables:

1. the yield on an asset competing with commercial loans in the banks' portfolios;
2. a measure of the loan-asset or loan-deposit ratio;
3. an adjustment for the existence of the certificates of deposit market and the effect of Regulation Q ceilings.

In the specification adopted in Chapter 3, Treasury bills were used for 1, a nonlinear loan-asset variable was used for 2, and dummy variables were used for 3. Other variables that can be classified in these three categories have been used in earlier studies by Goldfeld [1966], Ando and Goldfeld [1968], and Hendershott [1968]. In the studies by Goldfeld, and Ando and Goldfeld, a long term government bond rate, as measured by a moving average of the Treasury bill rate, was used for 1, a simple loan-deposit ratio was used for 2, and a certificate of deposit-total deposit ratio was used for 3. The study by Hendershott used the long term corporate bond rate and the prime commercial paper rate for 1, but did not obtain a significant effect for the loan-deposit ratio and did not include any adjustments for the certificate of deposit market. The variables suggested by these studies will also be tested in the empirical tests in Section 4.4 below.

One further question with the direct specification procedure concerns the last term in equation 4.4, which multiplicatively interacts the spread between r_L^* and $(r_L)_{-1}$ with $|\Delta r_D|$. The problem is that the formulation of this term requires that we multiply the variable $|\Delta r_D|$ by each of the terms included in the specification of r_L^*, and that we include each of these terms in the estimated equation. Not surprisingly, multicollinearity precluded obtaining reasonable structural estimates for the coefficients of these variables. An alternative procedure is to use a single variable that stands proxy for the term $[r_L^* - (r_L)_{-1}]$ where it enters the multiplicative term of equation 4.4. As will be developed in the following analysis, the credit rationing proxy of Chapter 3 should be an adequate measure of the rate spread for this purpose.

The second procedure used for the specification of the desired loan rate relies on the earlier discussion in Chapter 3 on an empirical test for credit rationing. The basic structural equation in that chapter, equation 3.13, was written:

$$(4.5) \qquad H = a_o + a_1(r_L^* - r_L),$$

where all variables are measured in the current period and H is the principal component rationing proxy. Equation 4.5 can easily be transformed:

$$(4.6) \qquad r_L^* - r_L = \frac{H - a_0}{a_1},$$

and then by adding and subtracting $(r_L)_{-1}$ to both sides of (4.6), and rearranging terms, we obtain:

$$(4.7) \qquad r_L^* - (r_L)_{-1} = \Delta r_L + \frac{H - a_0}{a_1}.$$

Equation 4.7 implies that the spread, between the long run desired loan rate and the quoted rate of the previous period, is a linear function of the degree of rationing and the current change in the commercial loan rate. Substituting equation 4.7 into equation 4.4 and solving for Δr_L, then yields:

$$(4.8) \qquad \Delta r_L = \left[g_0 + g_1 \Delta r_D + b_0 \left(\frac{H - a_0}{a_1} \right) + b_1 \left(\frac{H - a_0}{a_1} \right) |\Delta r_D| \right] \Big/$$

$$\left[1 - b_0 - b_1 |\Delta r_D| \right] + \text{lagged terms.}$$

Equation 4.8 is, unfortunately, nonlinear in the variable $|\Delta r_D|$, and, to simplify, a linear approximation will be used:

$$(4.9) \qquad \Delta r_L = b_0 + b_1 H + b_2 \Delta r_D + b_3 H |\Delta r_D| + b_4 |\Delta r_D| + \text{lagged terms.}$$

The specification thus consists of the rationing proxy, changes in the discount rate, and the multiplicative interaction of the two terms. The main advantages of using the rationing proxy, rather than the direct specification of r_L^*, are that the various components of r_L^* can be compactly summarized in the single variable H and that the lagged dependent variable $(r_L)_{-1}$ does not have to be explicitly specified.[3] Indeed, as already indicated, the rationing proxy will be used, even when r_L^* is directly specified, in the multiplicative terms of equation 4.4.

4.4 | ESTIMATION OF THE COMMERCIAL LOAN RATE EQUATION

The results of testing the two specifications of the determinants of the commercial loan rate are discussed in this section. The equations were

---

[3] The principal advantage of suppressing the lagged dependent variable is that consistent coefficient estimates may still be obtained, even in the presence of serial correlation of the error terms.

fitted with two-stage least squares.[4] Interest rates are measured in percentage points and are not seasonally adjusted, while all other variables are seasonally adjusted. The change in the average rate on commercial loans is used as the dependent variable. Very similar results were obtained with changes in the prime rate, but the average rate was chosen because banks do vary the loan rate even in periods in which the prime rate is fixed. The sources for data are given in the Appendix, Section A.2.

The estimation period is 1952–3 to 1969–4. Although this is the same sample period used in other parts of this study, it should perhaps be discussed further in this context because Hendershott [1968] has argued that both the beginning and the end of this period are inappropriate for studies of the commercial loan rate.[5] With respect to the beginning of the period, Hendershott stressed that excess profits taxes made borrowing from the Federal Reserve unusually attractive until the end of 1953 and this reduced the opportunity cost of commercial loans. While there is no doubt that the excess profits taxes did effectively reduce the cost of borrowed funds for the banks, it is an empirical question whether this significantly affected the level of the commercial loan rate. Chow Tests (see Chow [1960]) performed over the first part of the sample indicated that, in fact, no structural changes had occurred. With respect to the end of the period, Hendershott argued that, starting in 1960 unusual government pressure made it difficult for banks to raise their loan rates. It has been already pointed out, however, that one reason banks may rely on the discount rate as a signal for determining the timing of loan rate changes would be to avoid such government pressure. To the extent this is true, the specification of the determinants of the loan rate should be as valid for the 1960s as it is for the 1950s.

4.4.1 RESULTS WITH THE CREDIT RATIONING PROXY SPECIFICATION

The results of testing the formulation of the commercial loan rate equation with the credit rationing specification for $r_L^* - (r_L)_{-1}$ are shown in Table 4.1. The lagged variables included are $\Delta \overline{r_D}$, which accounts for the secondary effects of a discount rate change as discussed above, and the multiplicative interaction term $(H_{-1} |\Delta r_D|_{-1})$. The term $b_4 |\Delta r_D|$ of equation 4.9 has been omitted from the final estimated equations because, in preliminary tests, its coefficient was small and not significant. This is not dis-

---

[4] For the results using the credit rationing proxy specification, Table 4.1, only the current value of the proxy is treated as endogenous. For the results using the direct specification of r_L^*, Table 4.2, both the credit rationing proxy and the quantity of outstanding commercial loans are treated as endogenous. The instruments remain as described in footnote 19 in Chapter 3.

[5] See Hendershott [1968], pp. 55–57.

turbing, and does not reflect on the hypotheses, however, because the coefficient of this variable is not identified in the specification.[6]

The results shown in Table 4.1 generally confirm the importance of changes in the discount rate as a signal for changes in the commercial loan rate and the usefulness of the credit rationing proxy as a measure of the spread between the desired and actual commercial loan rate. In equation 1, which shows the most complete specification, only the current value of the multiplicative interaction term and the secondary discount rate change are not significant; the former also has the wrong sign. The problem with these two variables appears, moreover, to be a result of multicollinearity. For example, in equation 2 in Table 4.1, the lagged value of the multiplicative term has been suppressed, with the effect that the T-statistic for the secondary discount rate change more than doubled and the sign of the current interaction term became positive. Similarly, in equation 3, in which the current multiplicative term is also suppressed, the standard error of estimate corrected for degrees of freedom is essentially the same as in equation 2. Finally, in equation 4, the change and the lagged change in the Treasury bill rate are used instead of the changes in the discount rate in equation 3. Although the current change in the Treasury bill rate has a large T-statistic, the goodness of fit of equation 4 is substantially poorer than the fit of equation 3, thus confirming the value of changes in the discount rate as the signal for the timing of loan rate changes.

The coefficient estimates of equation 1 indicate not only a significant, but also a large, effect from changes in the discount rate. Assuming the credit rationing proxy is at a value of 1.5, which is about the average level for the tight money periods of the late 1960s a one percentage point increase in the discount rate at the beginning of a quarter would result in an increase in the commercial loan rate of .36 percentage points in the current quarter and .33 percentage points in the following quarter. The total effect of a one percentage point change in the discount rate is thus approximately a .69 percentage point change in the commercial loan rate, given the assumed level for credit rationing.[7]

---

[6] The coefficient is not identified because the variable $|\Delta r_D|$ enters equation 4.9 not only linearly, but also as part of the multiplicative term $(H\,|\Delta r_D|)$. Since the rationing proxy H is an index number with an arbitrarily assigned mean (of zero), the coefficient b_4 of the variable $|\Delta r_D|$ will vary directly with the value selected for the mean of H. This same point is also true for the constant term in equation 4.9, since the proxy H also enters the equation linearly, and thus the estimated values for the constant cannot be given a behavioral interpretation.

[7] If the discount rate change occurred later in the quarter, more of the effect would be shifted to the following quarter because of the change in the secondary effect variable $\Delta \overline{r}_D$.

TABLE 4.1 ESTIMATED COEFFICIENTS FOR COMMERCIAL LOAN RATE EQUATION (*Credit Rationing Specification for* r_L^*; Δr_L *Dependent Variable*)

Equation	Const.	H	$H\lvert\Delta r_D\rvert$	$H_{-1}\lvert\Delta r_D\rvert_{-1}$	Δr_D	$\bar{r}_D$	Δr_T	$(\Delta r_T)_{-1}$	R^2	S_e	D.W.
(1)	.04 (2.1)	.08 (2.8)	−.09 (.52)	.22 (2.5)	.41 (3.5)	.08 (.69)			.579	.152	1.90
(2)	.04 (2.2)	.09 (3.2)	.01 (.03)		.29 (2.6)	.20 (1.8)			.540	.157	1.95
(3)	.04 (2.2)	.09 (4.6)			.29 (3.0)	.20 (1.8)			.540	.156	1.94
(4)	.05 (2.3)	.09 (4.0)					.26 (5.0)	.07 (1.3)	.481	.166	1.97

Notes: R^2 is not corrected for degrees of freedom; S_e is standard error of estimate corrected for degrees of freedom; D.W. is Durbin-Watson statistic; and absolute value of T-statistics shown in parentheses.

4.4.2 results with the direct specification of r_L^*

The results of using the second formulation for the commercial loan rate equation, the direct specification of r_L^*, are shown in Table 4.2. The formulation used in these equations can be derived from equation 4.4:

$$(4.10) \qquad \Delta r_L = g_0 + h_0 r_L^* - h_0(r_L)_{-1} + g_1 \Delta r_D + g_2 \overline{\Delta r_D} + h_1 H \left| \Delta r_D \right|$$
$$+ h_2 H_{-1} \left| \Delta r_D \right|_{-1}.$$

As already mentioned, the variable $\left| \Delta r_D \right|$ has been omitted because it was neither significant nor identified. The lagged terms for the discount rate change effects are again $\overline{\Delta r_D}$ and $H_{-1} \left| \Delta r_D \right|_{-1}$. The specification for r_L^*, it will be recalled, consists of three sets of variables. The preferred specification for these variables are shown in equation 1 in Table 4.2. The yield on an asset competing with commercial loans is Moody's AAA corporate bond rate, r_A. The loan-deposit ratio is the ratio of commercial loans to total bank deposits (demand and time), LD. The certificate of deposit and Regulation Q ceiling variables are specified in the same form used for the credit rationing equation in Chapter 3: The variable D is a dummy variable accounting for the existence of the CD market since 1962; its coefficient should be negative since the existence of the market lowers the opportunity cost of bank funds. The variables C_1 and C_2 are dummy variables accounting for the periods of a binding Regulation Q ceiling and the excess of the secondary market certificate of deposit rate over the Regulation Q ceiling respectively; the coefficients of both of these variables should be positive. The precise definitions of these variables are given in the Appendix to Chapter 3.

The results for equation 1 are generally reasonable and encouraging. The coefficients for all variables but the current interaction term have the expected sign and, except for the variables D and Δr_D, the coefficients are statistically significant. In terms of goodness of fit, the results compare favorably with the test using only the credit rationing proxy. The standard error of estimate of equation 1 of Table 4.2 is about .09 percentage points, while the standard error of estimate of equation 1 of Table 4.1 is about .15 percentage points.

The coefficient estimates are also reasonable in terms of magnitude. The effect of a change in the discount rate can be calculated the same way it was for equation 1 of Table 4.1. A one percentage point change in the discount rate at the beginning of a quarter, assuming a value of 1.5 for the credit rationing proxy, will result in a change in the commercial loan rate of .31 percentage points in the current quarter and .33 percentage points in the following quarter. The total effect in the short run is thus about .64 percentage points. In addition, the basic speed of adjustment, indicated by the coefficient of $(r_L)_{-1}$, is about 49 percent per quarter.

The coefficient estimates for the corporate bond rate, r_A, and the loan-deposit ratio, LD, are also easily interpreted. In the short run, a one percentage point increase in r_A will raise the loan rate by .26 percentage points, and a .10 increase in the loan-deposit ratio will increase the loan rate by .48 percentage points. In the long run, taking into account the partial adjustment of the loan rate of approximately 50 percent per quarter, these effects will be about doubled.

The last set of variables in equation 1 are the three dummy variables for certificates of deposit and the Regulation Q ceiling. The coefficient of D indicates that the existence of the certificate of deposit market reduced the loan rate by about .04 percentage points in the short run and about .08 percentage points in the long run. The coefficients of C_1 and C_2 indicate, respectively, that a binding Regulation Q ceiling raises the loan rate by .19 percentage points plus .28 percentage points times the spread between the secondary market rate and the ceiling rate; in the long run these effects are again doubled. One interesting feature of these results is they imply that a binding Regulation Q ceiling more than offsets the initial decline in the loan rate caused by the existence of the certificate of deposit market. This suggests that the banks' reliance on certificates of deposit for loanable funds may not be easily reversed, at least in the short or intermediate run. This conclusion must be taken as tentative, however, pending further observations of tight money periods without binding ceilings; fortunately, such observations will be available following the removal of the ceiling, for certificates of deposit of maturity less than 90 days, by the Federal Reserve on June 24, 1970.

In addition to the preferred specification of equation 1 in Table 4.2, a number of alternative specifications were also tested. First, instead of Moody's AAA bond rate, the long term rate on government bonds, the Treasury bill rate, and the prime commercial paper rate were tested. The results for these tests were similar to equation 1, but the significance of the interest rate variable and the goodness of fit of the estimated equation were reduced. Similarly, both a long term and short term rate were tested together, but the short term rate was then invariably not significant.

Second, instead of the linear loan-deposit ratio, nonlinear versions of the loan-deposit and loan-asset variables were tested. The rationale for testing these forms is the same as given in the discussion of the specification of the desired commercial loan rate in the credit rationing equation in Section 3.4.1 above. Again the results were similar to equation 1,

TABLE 4.2 Estimated Coefficients for Commercial Loan Rate Equation (*Direct Specification for* r_L^*; Δr_L *Dependent Variable*)

Equation	Const.	r_A	LD	D	G_1	G_2	$(r_L)_{-1}$	Δr_D	$\overline{\Delta r_D}$	Δr_T	$(\Delta r_T)_{-1}$	$H\lvert\Delta r_D\rvert$	$H_{-1}\lvert\Delta r_D\rvert_{-1}$	R^2	S_e	D.W.
(1)	.23 (1.6)	.26 (4.4)	4.8 (4.3)	−.04 (1.2)	.19 (2.9)	.28 (5.5)	−.49 (8.2)	.14 (1.8)	.18 (2.4)			−.01 (−.08)	.22 (3.9)	.853	.093	1.76
(2)	.12 (.93)	.28 (4.6)	4.9 (3.9)	−.06 (1.5)	.19 (3.5)	.29 (6.4)	−.48 (7.4)	.05 (.61)	.30 (3.9)					.815	.103	1.95
(3)	.24 (1.6)	.43 (7.1)	4.6 (3.0)	−.04 (.92)	.16 (2.4)	.34 (6.0)	−.63 (9.3)							.702	.129	1.55
(4)	.17 (1.1)	.37 (5.0)	4.7 (3.1)	−.05 (1.2)	.15 (2.4)	.31 (5.1)	−.56 (6.7)			.04 (.79)	.07 (1.8)			.724	.126	1.78

Notes: R^2 is not corrected for degrees of freedom; S_e is standard error of estimate corrected for degrees of freedom; D.W. is Durbin-Watson statistic; and absolute value of T-statistics shown in parentheses.

but the significance of the variable and the goodness of fit were best for the linear loan-deposit ratio.

Third, several tests were performed with alternative specifications for the discount rate signal effect. In equation 2 of Table 4.2, the multiplicative terms were suppressed to determine the contribution of the rationing proxy in this specification. It is apparent that the omission of these variables results in a substantial reduction in the goodness of fit. In equation 3, the two terms for the change in the discount rate have also been suppressed, and the reduction in the goodness of fit is even greater. In equation 4, the change in the discount rate variables have been replaced with the current and lagged changes in the Treasury bill rate. Comparing these results with equation 2, it is again clear that the change in the discount rate provides a considerably better fit.

4.5 | SUMMARY

The results presented in Section 4.4 have important implications for both the overall model of the loan market and the structural determinants of credit rationing. With respect to credit rationing, the theoretical and empirical results of Chapters 2 and 3 indicated that the spread, between the banks' desired commercial loan rate and the actual quoted rate, was the principal source of variations in the degree of credit rationing. The results presented here confirm that the loan rate will, in fact, adjust both slowly and sporadically toward the desired level, thus allowing for significant fluctuations in credit rationing. More specifically, the speed of adjustment, as estimated in equation 1 of Table 4.2, was about 50 percent per quarter. Thus, if the desired rate increases by one percentage point, the actual rate will adjust by only .50 percentage points, leaving a gap of .50 percentage points that will be the source of rationing. Furthermore, changes in the discount rate exert significant leverage in signaling for changes in the loan rate. The results indicated that a one percentage point change in the discount rate would cause approximately a .65 percentage point change in the commercial loan rate, with the distribution of the effect between the current and the following quarter depending on the specific timing of the discount rate change.

The use of the discount rate as the commercial bank signal for rate changes has an additional implication for the efficacy of Federal Reserve policy. It suggests that the Federal Reserve can have a direct and strong effect on the commercial loan rate, and thereby on credit rationing, by changing the discount rate at the appropriate time. It is worth repeating in this context, however, that the signal model is predicated on the assumption that both the Federal Reserve and the commercial banks continue to operate within an institutional structure that allows the discount rate to be used for this purpose. Furthermore, it should be stressed that these results do not indicate the discount rate is always the optimal policy instrument for Federal Reserve influence on the loan rate; the force of the argument is that the data indicate the Federal Reserve and commercial banks have *in fact* acted this way, but not that they necessarily *should* act this way.

The results presented here also reinforce the conclusion of Chapter 3 that the imposition and relaxation of the Regulation Q ceiling may have significant effects on the level of the desired commercial loan rate, and hence on credit rationing. By imposing a binding Regulation Q ceiling on certificate of deposit yields, the Federal Reserve can increase the desired commercial loan rate. Because the actual loan rate will adjust only slowly to this desired level in the absence of a discount rate change, a spread between the desired rate and the actual rate will develop in the short run, and this spread will be the source of dynamic credit rationing.

In terms of the complete model of the loan market introduced in Chapter 1, these results emphasize the importance of distinguishing between the long run and short run determinants of the loan rate. In the long run, the loan rate is determined as a function of the level of market rates and the loan-deposit ratio, with adjustment for the certificate of deposit market and the Regulation Q ceiling. The banks' customers will thus be able to obtain loan funds at this equilibrium rate, except for the existence of equilibrium credit rationing discussed in Chapter 3. In the short run, in contrast, the sluggishness of the loan rate is the cause of a more significant degree of dynamic rationing, and thus firms, particularly small and risky firms, may not be able to obtain loan funds regardless of the rate they are willing to pay.

The final confirmation of this mechanism can be developed by considering the volume of loan funds actually made available to loan customers. This facet of the market is considered in developing and testing the equations for the demand for loans, which is the subject of the following chapter.

APPENDIX ON DATA SOURCES

A.1 MEASURES OF THE DISCOUNT RATE

Two technical problems arise in obtaining appropriate measures of the discount rate. First, the timing of discount rate changes varies between regional Federal Reserve banks, creating the problem of which bank's discount rate to use. A more extended study might thus attempt to explain regional differences in the adjustment of the loan rate as a function of variations in discount rate changes among the regional banks.[8] For present purposes, however, the discount rate changes at the New York Federal Reserve bank have been used since it seems likely that most banks would look to this rate for the signal.

The second problem concerns the timing of discount rate changes. It arises because the commercial loan rate is obtained from the Federal Reserve's *Quarterly Interest Rate Survey*, which was taken during the first two weeks of the last month of the quarter through December 1966, and during the first two weeks of the middle month of the quarter thereafter. The result is that discount rate changes that occur after the two week period of the survey must be associated with the following quarter for our purposes. Furthermore, when discount rate changes occur during the two week period of the survey, an average rate for the period must be constructed. For the impact variable, r_D, we have weighted the rate by the number of days it was in effect during the two week survey period. For the secondary effect variable, $\bar{r}_D$, the average rate over the quarter was used, the weights being the number of days of the quarter the rate was in effect. The change in this variable, $\Delta\bar{r}_D$ is then equal to Δr_D, but with the effect distributed over two quarters.

In summary:

r_D: Average discount rate at the New York Federal Reserve bank during the two week period of the *Interest Rate Survey*.

$\bar{r}_D$ Average discount rate at the New York Federal Reserve bank based on quarters ending with the 14th day of the two week period of the *Interest Rate Survey*.

The data for the variables Δr_D, $\Delta\bar{r}_D$, and Δr_L are shown in Table 4.3 for the period 1952–2 to 1969–4. The variables Δr_D and Δr_L are graphed in Figure 4.1 above.

A.2 MEASURES OF OTHER VARIABLES

LD: Loan-deposit ratio $= L/(DEP)$;

r_A: Moody's AAA corporate bond rate, three month average.

All other variables are described in the Appendix to Chapter 3.

---

[8] See Carr [1961] for an interesting study of discount rate differentials at the regional Federal Reserve banks.

TABLE 4.3 CHANGES IN COMMERCIAL LOAN RATE AND DISCOUNT RATE

Quarter	Δr_L	Δr_D	$\Delta \overline{r}_D$	Quarter	Δr_L	Δr_D	$\Delta \overline{r}_D$
1952 2	0.06	0.0	0.0	1961 1	−0.02	0.0	0.0
1952 3	−0.02	0.0	0.0	1961 2	0.0	0.0	0.0
1952 4	0.02	0.0	0.0	1961 3	0.02	0.0	0.0
1953 1	0.03	0.25	0.16	1961 4	−0.03	0.0	0.0
1953 2	0.19	0.0	0.09	1962 1	0.02	0.0	0.0
1953 3	0.01	0.0	0.0	1962 2	0.03	0.0	0.0
1953 4	0.02	0.0	0.0	1962 3	−0.02	0.0	0.0
1954 1	−0.04	−0.25	−0.11	1962 4	0.03	0.0	0.0
1954 2	−0.12	−0.25	−0.30	1963 1	−0.02	0.0	0.0
1954 3	−0.04	0.0	−0.09	1963 2	0.01	0.0	0.0
1954 4	−0.01	0.0	0.0	1963 3	0.0	0.50	0.31
1955 1	−0.01	0.0	0.0	1963 4	−0.01	0.0	0.19
1955 2	0.02	0.25	0.16	1964 1	−0.01	0.0	0.0.
1955 3	0.21	0.34	0.21	1964 2	0.0	0.0	0.0
1955 4	0.16	0.41	0.46	1964 3	−0.01	0.0	0.0
1956 1	0.0	0.0	0.17	1964 4	0.02	0.50	0.11
1956 2	0.21	0.25	0.16	1965 1	−0.03	0.0	0.39
1956 3	0.21	0.25	0.14	1965 2	0.02	0.0	0.0
1956 4	0.03	0.0	0.20	1965 3	0.01	0.0	0.0
1957 1	0.0	0.0	0.0	1965 4	0.27	0.29	0.05
1957 2	0.02	0.0	0.0	1966 1	0.28	0.21	0.45
1957 3	0.43	0.50	0.12	1966 2	0.27	0.0	0.0
1957 4	0.02	−0.50	0.21	1966 3	0.48	0.0	0.0
1958 1	−0.36	−0.50	−0.51	1966 4	0.01	0.0	0.0
1958 2	−0.32	−0.75	−0.88	1967 1	−0.23	0.0	0.0
1958 3	0.04	0.04	−0.19	1967 2	−0.18	−0.50	−0.15
1958 4	0.29	0.71	0.46	1967 3	−0.01	0.0	−0.35
1959 1	0.01	0.29	0.33	1967 4	0.02	0.0	0.0
1959 2	0.36	0.71	0.55	1968 1	0.40	0.50	0.47
1959 3	0.40	0.11	0.42	1968 2	0.48	1.00	0.46
1959 4	0.09	0.39	0.49	1968 3	0.05	0.0	0.57
1960 1	−0.02	0.0	0.0	1968 4	−0.28	−0.25	−0.21
1960 2	0.01	−0.14	−0.03	1969 1	0.71	0.25	0.11
1960 3	−0.38	−0.86	−0.65	1969 2	0.54	0.50	0.32
1960 4	0.02	0.0	−0.32	1969 3	0.96	0.0	0.28
				1969 4	0.01	0.0	0.0

Chapter 5

The Demand for Commercial Loans

5.1 | Introduction

In the previous two chapters, equations were estimated for credit rationing and the commercial loan rate. This completed the specification of the supply side of the loan market. In this chapter, equations for the demand for commercial loans are developed and estimated.

The theoretical model for loan demand is formulated in Section 5.2. Three principal factors influence the loan demand of business firms and are incorporated in the model. First, the firm's total need for financing, which is a function of the production decisions and the resulting fixed and working capital requirements, must be met through either equity capital, long term debt, or short term loans, the latter category including commercial loans as the major part. Second, the proportion of the total need for funds that is financed by commercial loans will depend on the nature of the assets and on the cost and availability of loan funds relative to alternative sources of financing. Third, commercial loans serve an important short run *buffer* function; that is, commercial loans may finance a larger than normal percentage of the firm's new capital requirements in the short run, pending the increase in long term debt and equity to the desired long run level.

In Section 5.3 the impact of credit rationing on the firm's financial and real expenditures is considered. Because of the existence of credit rationing, the demand for loans must be distinguished from the actual volume of outstanding loans. *Loan demand* is defined as the firm's desired quantity of loans given that no credit rationing occurs. *Loans outstanding,*

124

on the other hand, refers to the quantity of loans actually received by the firm after taking account of any credit rationing. Thus formally, we have:

(5.1) $L = L^D - E,$

where L is outstanding loans, L^D is loan demand, and E is the amount of credit rationing as defined in equation 2.26 above.

The regression estimates of the model are provided in Sections 5.4 and 5.5. Section 5.4 provides the results of estimating the model using aggregate time series data, and Section 5.5 provides estimates using data disaggregated by the asset-size of firms. It is important to note that the dependent variable for the regression tests is the quantity of loans outstanding rather than loan demand itself because the latter is not observable. For this reason a variable incorporating the effect of credit rationing must be included in the estimated specification.

5.2 | THE MODEL FOR COMMERCIAL LOAN DEMAND

In this section we consider a firm that determines its demand for loans without concern for the possibility of credit rationing. The basic premise of the model, which follows the work of Locke Anderson [1964] and Stephen Goldfeld [1966], is that the firm first makes its production decision and determines its fixed and working capital requirements, and then adjusts its financial structure to meet the required need for funds. This means, in other words, that in the absence of credit rationing the financial structure adjusts to the predetermined fixed and working capital needs.

Table 5.1 contains a somewhat simplified corporate balance sheet which helps to clarify this point and also serves to define variables. The *asset* side of this balance sheet is referred to as *net assets* since it includes accounts payable, accrued tax liability, and other current liabilities, adjusted, of course, for sign. Also note that long term liabilities, T, include both the equity accounts and long term debt. The balance sheet has been divided in this way in order to emphasize that loans and long term liabilities finance the net assets shown on the left hand side of the balance sheet. The division of the financing between long term liabilities and commercial loans will depend on the structure of the firm's assets with respect to maturity, liquidity, and perhaps acceptability as collateral, and on the relative cost of the two liabilities. Furthermore, in the short run, adjustment and transactions costs may lead to a slow or partial adjustment of long term liabilities to the desired level, and commercial loans will then have the additional function of buffering this slack. In order to formalize these notions, it is helpful to consider first an abstract version of the model. The realistic details can then be filled in quite easily.

TABLE 5.1　CORPORATE BALANCE SHEET

Net Assets		Liabilities	
M	Cash	L	Commercial loans
G	Government securities	T	Long term liabilities (= long term debt and equity)
AR	Accounts receivable		
$-AP$	Accounts payable		
$-TAX$	Accrued tax liability		
OCA	Other current assets		
$-OCL$	Other current liabilities		
I	Inventory stock (book value)		
K	Fixed assets		

5.2.1 THE MODEL IN ABSTRACT

The net assets shown on the left hand side of the balance sheet in Table 5.1 can be separated into mutually exclusive and exhaustive classes with the dollar amount of assets in each class denoted by $P_i(i = 1, 2, \ldots, n)$. The distinguishing characteristic of each class is the proportion of the net assets in the class financed by commercial loans and long term liabilities. Letting $\hat{T}_i$ be the desired long term liabilities for class i and $\hat{L}_i$ the desired commercial loans for class i, the proportion of the assets financed by each of these liabilities is set equal to a constant term and a function of interest rates:

(5.2)　　$\hat{T}_i/P_i = \rho_i + f_i[r],$

　　　and

(5.3)　　$\hat{L}_i/P_i = 1 - \rho_i - f_i[r].$

The constant coefficients for each class, ρ_i, is distinct and depends on the characteristics of the assets in that class. The term $f_i[r]$ is a vector of interest rates that represents the effect of the relative cost of loan and long term liability financing on the proportion of the assets financed by each of the liabilities.

It is also useful to distinguish two special classes. The class P_1 consists of those net assets that are financed entirely by long term liabilities; that is $\rho_1 = 1$. Similarly, the class P_n represents the set of net assets that are financed entirely by commercial loans; that is $\rho_n = 0$. The interest rate coefficients for each of these two classes are assumed to be identically zero.

With this basis the total amount of desired long term liabilities $\hat{T}$ and commercial loans $\hat{L}$ can be written as:

$$(5.4) \qquad \hat{T} = P_1 + \sum_{i=2}^{n-1} \rho_i P_i + \sum_{i=2}^{n-1} f_i[r]P_i,$$

and

$$(5.5) \qquad \hat{L} = P_n + \sum_{i=2}^{n-1} (1 - \rho_i)P_i - \sum_{i=2}^{n-1} f_i[r]P_i.$$

The net asset group P_1 receives a weight of unity in (5.4) and zero in (5.5) because the assets in this group are financed solely by long term liabilities; similarly the net asset group P_n receives a weight of zero in (5.4) and unity in (5.5) because the assets in this group are financed solely by commercial loans.

It is now helpful to further simplify the specification by aggregating the interest rate terms in (5.4) and (5.5) into a single function:

$$(5.6) \qquad \hat{T} = P_1 + \sum_{i=2}^{n-1} \rho_i P_i + F[r]A,$$

and

$$(5.7) \qquad \hat{L} = P_n + \sum_{i=2}^{n-1} (1 - \rho_i)P_i - F[r]A.$$

The interest rate term is thus scaled by the level of total assets A, rather than by a weighted average of the interest rate terms, for each of the asset classes. It should be noted that this simplification does not significantly reduce the model's empirical implications because, in any case, it would be difficult to obtain accurate estimates of the weights for the individual asset classes.

There is also a balance sheet identity:

$$(5.8) \qquad A \equiv T + L \equiv P_1 + \sum_{i=2}^{n-1} P_i + P_n,$$

which simply notes that the total of the net assets in each group must equal the sum of long term liabilities and commercial loans. This identity is valid, of course, only for the actual quantities that exist at any time t. But if we assume that the firm's desired or planned financing is consistent in the sense that even planned values for L and T satisfy the balance sheet identity, then we have:

$$(5.9) \qquad \hat{T} + \hat{L} = P_1 + \sum_{i=2}^{n-1} P_i + P_n.$$

The principal behavioral assumption of the model is that the firm gradually adjusts its long term liabilities to the desired level given in equation 5.6. Thus, letting λ be the speed of adjustment, and using equation 5.8, we have:

$$(5.10) \qquad \Delta T = \lambda(\hat{T} - T_{-1}) = \lambda(P_1 + \sum_{i=2}^{n-1} \rho_i P_i + AF[r] - A_{-1} + L_{-1}).$$

Since the balance sheet identity is also valid in terms of flows,

$$(5.11) \qquad \Delta T = \Delta A - \Delta L,$$

by substituting (5.11) into (5.10), solving for L, and rearranging terms, we obtain:

$$(5.12) \qquad L^d = P_n + \sum_{i=2}^{n-1} (1 - \lambda\rho_i)P_i + (1 - \lambda)P_1 - \lambda AF[r]$$
$$- (1 - \lambda)(A_{-1} - L_{-1}),$$

where L^d refers to loan demand in contrast to loans actually received.

Equation 5.12 can be interpreted quite easily. A \$1 increase in the assets of class P_i results in an initial increase in long term liabilities in the amount \$$\lambda\rho_i$. In order to maintain the balance sheet identity, commercial loans must then adjust by the residual, that is by \$$(1 - \lambda\rho_i)$, and this is the effect included in the second term of (5.12). Similarly, for assets in the P_n or P_1 classes, commercial loans must adjust by \$1 or \$$(1 - \lambda)$ respectively, and these effects are included in the first and third terms in (5.12). The term $AF[r]$ accounts for any changes in the relative cost of loan and long term liability financing. Finally, the last term in equation (5.12), which can be written $(1 - \lambda)T_{-1}$, accounts for the replacement of commercial loans by long term liabilities as long term liabilities adjust toward the desired long run level following the initial disturbance.

It is thus apparent that commercial loans serve essentially two functions in the financial structure of business firms. In the long run, commercial loans finance some proportion of the firm's total financing need, the proportion depending on the nature of the assets and the relative cost of loan financing. In the short run, commercial loans serve an additional buffer function that is the result of the partial adjustment of long term liabilities toward the long run level. It is not possible to distinguish operationally these functions, however, and it is for this reason that the basic behavioral postulate of the model is set in terms of the gradual adjustment of long term liabilities to the desired level. In this context it is worth emphasizing that the coefficient λ refers to the speed of adjustment of long term liabilities rather than commercial loans.

It should also be noted that while commercial loans have been taken as the dependent variable in our formulation, there is no reason why the demand for other short term financial assets or liabilities, commercial paper for example, could not be similarly treated. In this way the entire short run dynamic financial behavior of the firm could be specified consistently with respect to both the budget constraint and long run equilibrium levels. Moreover, if an additional equation explicitly specifying the adjustment of long term liabilities were added, a complete model of corporate finance could be obtained.

5.2.2. SPECIFICATION FOR THE AGGREGATE EQUATION

We can now turn to the empirical specification of the loan demand equation formulated as equation 5.12. We shall restrict our attention in this section to the aggregate demand of all business firms; in Section 5.5 below the modifications that are necessary for the model when disaggregated data are used are discussed further.

The most general interpretation of the abstract model allows each of the net assets shown in the balance sheet in Table 5.1 to define a unique class P_i. These net assets would be included separately in the regression equations and the corresponding ρ_i coefficients would be estimated directly by the regression. A more restricted specification is suggested, however, by a priori information, and in some cases is made necessary by data limitations. The question that is posed then is which variables should be specified individually, and which can be aggregated and perhaps approximated by a summary measure.

Certainly the most important asset to specify individually is the inventory stock, since it is generally agreed to be the main determinant of loan demand.[1] The specification of the inventory variable should be the book value of the stock because this is the magnitude appearing on the balance sheet that must be financed. One would expect that the proportion of the inventory stock financed by commercial loans would be relatively large, indicating that, in terms of the formal analysis, the coefficient for the inventory stock in equation 5.2, say ρ_I, should be close to zero.

Fixed capital is a second variable that is important to separate in the specification. In contrast to the inventory stock, it can be expected that a relatively small percentage of fixed capital is financed in the long run

---

[1] See Goldfeld [1966], pp. 82–86, for further evidence on this point.

by commercial loans, and thus its coefficient in equation 5.2, call it ρ_K, should be close to unity. The fixed capital variable should enter the specification net of depreciation, since the depreciation reserves will provide an automatic source of financing for the asset, and thus the variable is included in the regression equations as the net capital stock.

The remaining net assets shown in the balance sheet of Table 5.1 are the firm's net liquid assets, and they will be denoted as V, where:

$$(5.13) \qquad V = M + G + AR + OCA - AP - TAX - OCL.$$

The net liquid assets, although financial in nature, are directly related to the level of the firm's sales, particularly when viewed as a composite.[2] They can thus be considered production or sales inputs that are to be financed by commercial loans or long term liabilities. It should be expected that the proportion of the net liquid assets financed by commercial loans will be less than the proportion for the inventory stock but more than the proportion for fixed capital. That is, letting ρ_V be the proportion of net liquid assets financed by long term liabilities, we have:

$$(5.14) \qquad 0 \leq \rho_I \leq \rho_V \leq \rho_K \leq 1.$$

A second reason for aggregating net liquid assets into a composite variable is that data for the individual components is difficult to obtain. As a proxy variable for the composite we propose to use the level of net business sales. This should provide an adequate measure since, as already noted, the firm's desired level of liquid assets is directly related to its sales. The operational measure of V is gross national product less inventory investment and fixed capital investment.[3]

With this part of the specification now completed, the operational form of the aggregate equation 5.6 for desired long term liabilities can be written as:

$$(5.15) \qquad \hat{T} = \rho_I I + \rho_K K + a_1 \rho_V V + AF[r],$$

where the coefficient a_1 is included in the term with V because the sales

---

[2] Since we are aggregating over all business firms, accounts receivable (AR) and accounts payable (AP) will cancel except for the amount of trade credit extended to the nonbusiness sector. This will not be true, however, when we work with the disaggregated data.

[3] The fixed capital investment has been subtracted in order to reduce multicollinearity with the separate specification of the fixed capital term. Regression equations were also fitted with the sales variable defined as gross national product less inventory investment, and the results are similar to those shown in Section 5.4 below except for a smaller coefficient on the fixed capital term.

Further verification of the reliability of the sales proxy is the high correlation, .96, between the sales proxy and net liquid assets for the manufacturing sector derived from FTC-SEC data (see Section 5.5 below).

variable is only a proxy for, and thus may only be proportional to, net liquid assets. It then follows from (5.12) that the operational equivalent of the derived loan demand equation is:

$$(5.16) \quad L^d = (1 - \lambda \rho_I)I + (1 - \lambda \rho_K)K + (1 - \lambda \rho_V)a_1 V$$
$$- (1 - \lambda)a_1 V_{-1} - \lambda AF[r] - (1 - \lambda)(L_{-1} + K_{-1} - L_{-1}).$$

Furthermore, since it is difficult to obtain reliable estimates of the stocks of inventory and fixed capital, it is desirable for the purposes of estimation to take the first difference of equation 5.16:

$$\Delta L^d = (1 - \lambda \rho_I) \Delta I + (1 - \lambda \rho_K) \Delta K + (1 - \lambda \rho_V)a_1 \Delta V$$
$$- (1 - \lambda)a_1 \Delta V_{-1}$$
$$(5.17) \quad - (1 - \lambda)(\Delta L_{-1} + \Delta K_{-1} - \Delta L_{-1})$$
$$- \lambda \Delta(AF[r]).$$

Equation 5.17 can be estimated using only the available data for the flows of inventory and fixed capital investment.[4]

Only the interest rate term in equation 5.17 remains to be given an empirical interpretation. Our hypothesis is that the demand for commercial loans is negatively related to its own rate r_L and is positively related to a weighted average of the commercial paper rate r_P and Moody's AAA corporate bond rate r_A. The specification thus takes the form:[5]

$$(5.18) \quad -\lambda \Delta(AF[r]) = b_1 \Delta[A(r_A - r_L)] + b_2 \Delta[A(r_P - r_L)].$$

The term with the corporate bond rate should, in principle, be more important, since all variables with the exception of long term liabilities and commercial loans have been specified directly. The commercial paper rate enters the formulation only because the proxy for net liquid assets, that is, sales, may not prove adequate in accounting for the substitution between commercial paper and commercial loans that arises from interest yield considerations. Furthermore, it is likely that firms will substitute commercial loans for long term debt when the long term bond rate is expected to fall. Since this expectation can be measured at least to a

---

[4] The lagged change in net sales (ΔV_{-1}) is not constrained to a coefficient of $(1 - \lambda)$, in contrast to ΔI_{-1} and ΔK_{-1}, because the conversion ratio of the proxy (a_1) is also a parameter that must be estimated.

[5] Equation 5.18 can also be written as

$$(b_1 + b_2) \left(\frac{b_1}{b_1 + b_2} \Delta[r_A A] + \frac{b_2}{b_1 + b_2} \Delta[r_P A] - \Delta[r_L A] \right)$$

to illustrate the weighted average of r_A and r_P.

rough approximation by the spread between the long term rate and the short term rate, we have additional reason to expect a relatively high weighting on the long term rate.[6]

With respect to data availability, the interest rate variables provide no difficulty. The scaling variable, total assets A, however, cannot be obtained on an aggregate basis. As a proxy, we propose to use nonfarm gross business product GBP, since both A and GBP should have similar time trends and only small short run variability.[7] Formally, the assumption is that:

$$(5.19) \qquad A = a_2 GBP.$$

Preliminary tests using the interest rate term as specified in equation 5.18 and the GBP proxy as specified in (5.19) did not, however, yield significant coefficient estimates. To consider the problem more closely, it is helpful, using the corporate bond rate term in equation 5.18 as an example, to note the following algebraic identity:

$$(5.20) \qquad \Delta[A(r_A - r_L)] = A_{-1}\Delta(r_A - r_L) + (r_A - r_L)\Delta A.$$

The interest rate term can thus be separated into two components. The first component represents the effect of a change in the interest rate spread, the level of total assets being given. The second component represents the effect of a change in total assets, the interest rate spread being given. The distinction between the two components is analogous to the distinction between *ex post* and *ex ante* substitution. The first component represents the *ex post* interest rate substitution for commercial loans given the total need for financing, while the second component represents the *ex ante* substitution that occurs when the total need for funds (represented by total assets) changes. Further regression tests indicated that only the second component, the *ex ante* substitution term, entered significantly in the equation. Similar results were also true for the commercial paper interest rate term in equation 5.18. Consequently, in the final empirical tests the interest rate terms are specified to include only the *ex ante* substitution component. The complete specification for the loan demand equation is then:

$$
\begin{aligned}
\Delta L^d = &(1 - \lambda \rho_I)\,\Delta I + (1 - \lambda \rho_K)\,\Delta K + (1 - \lambda \rho_V)a_1\,\Delta V \\
&- (1 - \lambda)a_1\,\Delta V_{-1} + b_1 a_2 (r_A - r_L)\,(\Delta\,GBP) \\
&+ b_2 a_2 (r_P - r_L)\,(\Delta\,GBP) - (1 - \lambda)\,(\Delta L_{-1} + \Delta K_{-1} - \Delta L_{-1}).
\end{aligned}
$$

(5.21)

Before testing this relationship, however, the issue of credit rationing

[6] This assumes regressive expectations for future values of the long term rate.
[7] The correlation between gross business product (GBP) and total assets of manufacturing corporations (see Section 5.5 below) is about .99.

must be considered in order to transform the dependent variable from the unobserved loan demand to the observed loans outstanding.

5.3 | THE EFFECT OF RATIONING ON THE DEMAND FOR LOANS

The mechanism of loan demand developed so far is quite simple. The firm first determines the desired level of its sales and production inputs—inventory stock, fixed capital stock, and net liquid assets. On the basis of these assets and the cost of alternative means of finance, the firm then calculates its demand for loans including any short run buffer component. If there is no rationing, the firm receives exactly the loan it requests; loan demand and loans outstanding are identical.

Now, however, we wish to include explicitly the possibility of nonprice credit rationing. In this case the firm will not be able to obtain the loan size it requests; any attempt by the firm to offer an interest rate higher than the rate quoted by the bank will be to no avail. Consequently, the firm returns from the bank with a smaller loan than it requested.

This suggests that the loan demand equation can be adjusted for the effects of rationing and transformed to a loans outstanding basis by simply subtracting the amount of rationing E. This procedure is incomplete, however, since it does not allow for the effects of rationing on the firm's net asset holdings. Indeed, the balance sheet identity implies that for any adjustment in commercial loans there *must* correspond an adjustment in either the firm's net assets or in its long term liabilities. Consequently, if commercial loans are rationed and the firm does not adjust its net assets, then the entire impact of the rationing must be taken up by increased issue of long term liabilities. It is reasonable to expect that more generally the firm will reduce its net assets, as well as increasing its long term liabilities, when the availability of commercial loans is limited. Since a reduction in net assets directly reduces the loan demand as specified in equation 5.21, the necessary adjustments for the effects of rationing are reduced to the extent that net assets adjust. In fact, in the polar case in which the firm adjusts only its net assets, long term liabilities remaining at their initial value, equation 5.21 is equivalent to a loans outstanding formulation and no further adjustment for rationing is needed.

To make this point in a more concrete setting, consider the case in which the firm adjusts for credit rationing by reducing its inventory investment by exactly the amount of the rationing; all other net assets remain at their initial values. From equation 5.21 it is apparent that a reduction in inventory investment of E reduces the demand for loans by $(1 - \lambda \rho_I)E$. This leaves a residual need for financing of $\lambda \rho_I E$, which must be met by increased issue of long term debt. Only in the case in which the adjusted asset (inventory in the example) is financed entirely by long term liabilities ($\rho_I = 1$) and the speed of adjustment of long term liabilities is unity ($\lambda = 1$) will it be correct to reduce the demand equation by the full amount of rationing. On the other hand, if the asset is financed entirely by commercial loans ($\rho_I = 0$), then no additional adjustment is needed (regardless of the speed of adjustment of long term liabilities).

In the general case, the introduction of rationing will cause the firm to adjust all its net assets. Using the asset categories distinguished in Section 5.2.2, these adjustments can be denoted as E_I for the inventory stock, E_V for net liquid assets, and E_K for the capital stock, where:

$$(5.22) \qquad E = E_I + E_V + E_K.$$

The reduction in loan demand "automatically" taken into account into equation 5.21 is then

$$(1 - \lambda\rho_I)E_I + (1 - \lambda\rho_V)E_V + (1 - \lambda\rho_K)E_K$$

and the additional amount of adjustment necessary for an equation using loans outstanding as the dependent variable is

$$(\lambda\rho_I)E_I + (\lambda\rho_V)E_V + (\lambda\rho_K)E_K.$$

This means that the amount of the correction for the effect of credit rationing depends on both the firm's demand parameters (ρ_I, ρ_V, ρ_K, and λ) and on the amount by which each of the net assets is adjusted. The parameters can be directly estimated by the regression equation, but additional information is needed to determine the amount by which the net assets adjust. Although this problem is discussed further in Chapter 6, the results are not sufficiently refined to be of value in the present context. It can be noted, however, that the quantitative effect at issue is probably very small, since the firm would tend to reduce those assets which are most dependent on commercial loans for their financing. In fact, in the polar case in which the firm reduces only assets financed entirely by commercial loans, no adjustment will be necessary as already noted.

This suggests that an approximate solution, in which the distribution of the effect of rationing on the various net assets is assumed to be constant over time, may be satisfactory. In this case the quantity of loans outstanding can be written:

$$(5.23) \qquad L = L^D - b_3 E,$$

where b_3 incorporates the effect of rationing on the various net asset classes. The credit rationing proxy variable can be used to specify the amount of rationing. It may be recalled from Chapter 3 that the rationing proxy H was defined as:

(5.24) $H = E/L^D$.

Substituting equation 5.24 into equation 5.23, then yields

(5.25) $L = L^D - b_3(HL^D)$,

and by taking first differences, we obtain:

(5.26) $\Delta L = \Delta L^D - b_3 \Delta(HL^D)$.

This formulation still leaves the practical problem of estimating the multiplicative interaction term of the rationing proxy with each component of loan demand. The analysis of a similar problem with interest rates in Section 5.2.2 above, suggests, however, that an acceptable approximation is:

(5.27) $\Delta L = \Delta L^D - b_3 a_3(H)(\Delta GBP)$,

where a_3, is the conversion factor for the use of gross business product (GBP) as a proxy for total assets.[8]

Finally, substituting the loan demand equation 5.21 into the loans outstanding equation 5.27, we obtain the specification to be tested:

(5.28)
$$\Delta L = (1 - \lambda \rho_I)\,\Delta I + (1 - \lambda \rho_K)\,\Delta K + (1 - \lambda \rho_V)a_1\,\Delta V$$
$$- (1 - \lambda)a_1\,\Delta V_{-1} - (1 - \lambda)\,(\Delta L_{-1} + \Delta K_{-1} - \Delta L_{-1})$$
$$+ a_2 b_1(r_A - r_L)\,(\Delta GBP) + a_2 b_2(r_P - r_L)\,(\Delta GBP)$$
$$- a_3 b_3(H)\,(\Delta GBP).$$

5.4 | Estimation of Loan Demand Equation: Aggregated Data

Table 5.2 presents the results of testing the specification for the loan demand equation. The equations were fitted for the period 1952–3 to 1969–4 using ordinary least squares.[9] Although all variables are defined in the Appendix, the derivation of the measures for inventory investment and fixed investment should be stressed. The proper measure for inventory investment, as already noted, is the change in the book value of the inventory stock. The inventory valuation adjustment was subtracted from

[8] It is important that the interest rate terms and the rationing variable have the same scaling since, from the viewpoint of the firm, every level of rationing has an analog in terms of interest rate levels. That is, the firm's unconstrained demand can be reduced to a given level (equal to the bank's supply) by charging a sufficiently high interest rate.

[9] Two-stage least squares was also used. The two-stage results are not shown because in the preferred specification all the endogenous variables are predetermined.

TABLE 5.2 ESTIMATED COEFFICIENTS FOR LOAN DEMAND EQUATION: AGGREGATED DATA[a,b] (ΔL *Dependent Variable*)

Equation	ΔI	ΔK	ΔV	ΔV_{-1}	LAG	$(r_A - r_L)$	$(r_P - r_L)$	H	R^2	S_e	D.W.
(1)	.60 (6.4)	.24 (2.1)	.46 (4.2)	-.11 (1.1)	-.22 (2.4)	.22 (1.9)	.09 (1.2)	-.02 (.34)	.715	.596	1.86
						$(r_A - r_L)_{-1}$	$(r_P - r_L)_{-1}$	H_{-1}			
(2)	.65 (6.8)	.31 (2.8)	.44 (4.3)	-.10 (1.1)	-.28 (3.0)	.25 (1.9)	.11 (1.6)	-.08 (1.6)	.728	.582	1.82
(3)	.56 (6.7)	.25 (2.3)	.45 (4.4)	-.07 (.69)	-.24 (2.6)		.18 (3.0)	-.10 (2.1)	.713	.593	1.86
(4)	.64 (6.7)	.30 (2.6)	.36 (4.0)	-.14 (1.5)	-.24 (2.6)	.37 (3.2)		-.03 (.78)	.717	.589	1.70

[a] R^2 is not corrected for degrees of freedom; S_e is standard error of estimate corrected for degrees of freedom; D.W. is Durbin-Watson statistic; and absolute value of T-statistics shown in parentheses.

[b] $LAG = \Delta I_{-1} + \Delta K_{-1} - \Delta L_{-1}$. Interest rate and rationing variables are scaled (multiplied) by ΔGBP.

the National Income Accounts definition of inventory investment to obtain an aggregate measure of this variable. The proper measure for the fixed investment variable is the net investment in nonresidential structures and producers' durable equipment. Although the National Income Accounts data can be used for the gross investment, the corresponding figures for depreciation are not directly available. As an approximation the capital consumption allowance figures in the National Income Accounts were adjusted as well as possible to obtain equivalent depreciation figures.

Equation 1 of Table 5.2 follows the specification of equation 5.28 directly. The overall fit appears quite good; the standard error of $596 million is about 1 percent of the sample mean of the outstanding stock of commercial loans. Although all coefficients have the correct sign, the principal weakness in the equation is that the rationing proxy and interest rate variable coefficients are not significant. Consequently, various lags for the effect of these variables were tested. The preferred specification is shown in equation 2 in which both the credit rationing proxy and interest rate spreads are lagged one quarter. Although the credit rationing proxy variable is still not significant, this may indicate that firms significantly adjust their net assets when faced with credit rationing so that only a small adjustment is needed in the loan demand formulation. The lack of significance of the interest rate variables appears, on the other hand, to be directly a function of multicollinearity. In equations 3 and 4 the corporate bond and commercial paper rate variables have been suppressed respectively, with the result that the remaining interest rate variable becomes significant without an appreciable change in the standard error of estimate.[10]

Using equation 2 further properties of the estimated equation can be derived. The speed of adjustment λ of long term liabilities is about 72 percent per quarter. While this is somewhat faster than one might expect, it is important to recall that retained earnings, which are part of long term liabilities by our definition, are a major source of the firms' financing and do in fact "adjust" very quickly. Using the estimated value of λ, the proportions of the inventory stock and the fixed capital stock that are financed by long term liabilities can be calculated to be 49 percent and 96 percent respectively.[11] Conversely, this implies that, in the long run, commercial loans finance 51 percent of the inventory stock and 4

---

[10] Additional regression equations were estimated with a constant added to the specification and with the inventory valuation adjustment separated from the inventory investment term. In both cases the added variable was not statistically significant.

[11] The long run coefficient can be calculated, using the inventory stock as an example, by setting the coefficient for inventory investment equal to the value given in equation 5.28; that is, $.65 = (1 - \lambda \rho_I)$ and thus $\rho_I = .49$.

percent of the fixed capital stock. Both of these results appear quite reasonable.

The equivalent long run effects of net liquid assets, and the interest rate and rationing variables, cannot be directly determined because of the use of proxy variables. The elasticity of loan demand with respect to sales can be evaluated, however, at the point of means to be about .45. Similarly, the impact effect of interest rates and credit rationing can be obtained by evaluating the change in gross business product at its sample mean, $1.8 billion per quarter. In this case, an increase in the spread between the prime commercial paper rate and the commercial loan rate of one percentage point would increase the quarterly change in commercial loans by $198 million, while a similar increase in the spread between Moody's AAA bond rate and the commercial loan rate would increase the quarterly change in commercial loans by $450 million.[12] Finally, an increase in rationing by 1.0 units, a change larger than any actually observed within one quarter, would reduce the quarterly change in commercial loans by $144 million. Since the mean quarterly change in commercial loans for the sample period is $1.2 billion and the mean of the stock of loans outstanding is over $50 billion, it is clear that the direct impact of rationing on commercial loans is quite small. (This does not take into account, however, the impact of rationing on other net assets.)

In summary, the model and coefficient estimates appear to provide a reasonable picture of the mechanism and structure of commercial loan demand. Perhaps the most telling criticism of the model is its complexity. For example, Hendershott [1968] has estimated a considerably more simple model in which the change in loans is regressed against inventory investment, the change in the commercial loan rate, and the lagged change in commercial loans. The results of estimating this specification over the sample period 1952–3 to 1969–4 are:[13]

$$\Delta L = \underset{(4.7)}{.38\,\Delta I} - \underset{(.39)}{.15\,\Delta r_L} + \underset{(4.2)}{.45\,\Delta L_{-1}}$$

$$R^2 = .631 \qquad S_e = .653 \qquad \text{D.W.} = 2.14.$$

(*T*-statistics shown in parentheses)
These results confirm the importance of inventory investment as a de-

---

[12] The greater importance of the long term rate (r_A) relative to the short term rate (r_P) is consistent with the expectations hypothesis mentioned earlier.

[13] Hendershott's original equation was estimated over the sample period 1953–1 to 1965–4. We have also reestimated the other specifications suggested by Hendershott and the results were essentially the same as the equation shown.

terminant of loan demand. However, the interest rate term is not significant and, more importantly, the standard error of estimate (.653) is over 10 percent greater than the standard error for equation 2 of Table 5.2. It thus appears that the complex model developed in this chapter does provide more accurate predictions of the movements in loan demand.

5.5 | Estimation of Loan Demand Equation: Disaggregated Data

To obtain further results on the demand for loans, we next turn to tests using data from the Federal Trade Commission-Securities and Exchange Commission (FTC-SEC) *Quarterly Financial Report for Manufacturing Corporations.* The principal advantages of the FTC-SEC reports are that the data contain a complete and consistent balance sheet for the universe of manufacturing corporations and that they are disaggregated by the asset size of the firms. These advantages are not obtained without cost, however, since the data are known to have error and are not suitable for time series analysis in raw form. The details of the adjustments that have been made are given in the Appendix, Section A.2.

The specification of the demand functions follows, with only minor changes, the model tested in the previous section. The notation, most of which is summarized in Table 5.1, is also unchanged, although it now, of course, pertains to the FTC-SEC data. We start by specifying the determinants of the desired level of long term liabilities in a form equivalent to equation 5.15:

$$(5.29) \qquad \hat{T} = \rho_I I + \rho_K K + \rho_N NAR + \rho_W W + AF[r],$$

where $NAR = AR - AP$ and $W = M + G + OCA - TAX - OCL$.
This equation differs from (5.15) only in that net trade credit (NAR) has been separated from other net liquid assets, reflecting the relative importance of trade credit on the disaggregated level as an important source of loan demand. Of course, both the trade credit and the remaining net liquid assets (W) can now be measured directly.

Preliminary tests of the loan demand equation that can be derived from equation 5.29 indicated the estimated coefficients for fixed capital (ρ_K) and other net liquid assets (ρ_W) were both slightly greater than unity. The result for the fixed capital coefficient is not surprising, since the estimated value for ρ_K from the aggregate data was almost unity. Consequently, in the results presented below, the coefficient ρ_K is constrained to be exactly unity. The result for the other net liquid assets is somewhat more surprising, however, because one would expect that at least the larger firms would finance part of their net liquid assets with commercial loans. Two points should be kept in mind, however.

First, the ρ coefficients are steady state parameters based, at least implicity, on a model with static expectations. Second, the model does not take into account the use of loans for smoothing seasonal variations in the need for liquid assets.[14] Consequently, it may not be unreasonable for firms to finance these assets, in equilibrium, entirely through long term liabilities, and hence the ρ_W coefficient will also be constrained to unity.[15]

Taking account of these constraints and following the analysis used in Section 5.2.2, a loan demand equation of the form of equation 5.16 can be derived:[16]

$$(5.30) \quad L^d = (1 - \lambda\rho_I)I + (1 - \lambda\rho_N)NAR - (1 - \lambda)(L_1 + NAR_{-1}$$
$$- \Delta W - \Delta K - L_{-1}) - \lambda AF[r].$$

With respect to the interest rate function, $F[r]$, the demand for loans is again assumed to be negatively related to its own rate r_L and positively related to a weighted average of the prime commercial paper rate r_P and the long term corporate bond rate r_A:

$$(5.31) \quad -\lambda F[r] = b_1(r_A - r_L) + b_2(r_P - r_L).$$

To transform the loan demand formulation into a loans outstanding equation, consideration must again also be given to rationing. The basic argument of Section 5.3 applies equally well for the disaggregated data: a substantial amount of the effect of rationing will be accounted for by changes in the firms' choice of assets, leaving only a small residual for the rationing proxy (H) when included separately.

Since the FTC-SEC balance sheets contain the proper stock values, there is no need to take first differences as was done for the aggregate data. One significant problem with the data, however, is that the asset classes are adjusted for the growth (and decline) of individual firms only in the first quarter of each year. This causes discontinuities in the first quarter for all the balance sheet variables. The problem can be avoided by working only with ratios of the balance sheet variables, as the FTC-SEC does in interpreting their own data. The natural scaling is total assets, and fortunately our formulation is amenable to this transformation since we need only divide through by total assets in equation

[14] The seasonal variations in loan demand are themselves of interest, and would provide an interesting area for future work.

[15] Jaffee [1967] shows results based on a very similar model without constraining the coefficient for the liquid assets to unity.

[16] The coefficients ρ_K and ρ_W are constrained to unity by including the variable K and W in the next to last term of equation 5.30 with a coefficient of $(1 - \lambda)$.

5.30. The final equation can then be written as:

$$(5.32) \quad L = (1 - \lambda \rho_I)\bar{I} + (1 - \lambda \rho_N)\overline{NAR} + b_1(r_A - r_L) + b_2(r_P - r_L)$$
$$- b_3 H - (1 - \lambda)(\bar{L}_{-1} + \overline{NAR}_{-1} - \Delta \bar{W} - \Delta \bar{K} - \bar{L}_{-1}),$$

where the bars indicate variables divided by total assets, and the dependent variable is loans outstanding, because the rationing proxy (H) is included.[17]

The estimated coefficients of this equation for six asset classes and the total are shown in Table 5.3.[18] The equations were fitted for the period 1952–3 to 1969–4 using ordinary least squares. In terms of goodness of fit the results are about on a par with the aggregate estimates of the previous section after adjustment to make units equivalent. The low Durbin-Watson statistics seem to be due to a sequence of quarters following the 1954 cyclical trough in which the volume of loans is overestimated, and a series of quarters preceding the 1960 cyclical peak in which the volume of loans is underestimated. The FTC-SEC data are suspect in these periods, however, since they deviate from the pattern of the aggregate data. Attempts to correct for the serially correlated disturbances with an autoregressive transformation were of no avail, probably because the serial correlation is centered only in the quarters just noted.

The estimated coefficients for the total of the manufacturing sector, shown in equation 7 of Table 5.3, can be compared with the results for the aggregate data shown in equation 2 of Table 5.2. The speed of adjustment of long term liabilities for total manufacturing is 35 percent per quarter, which is less than the adjustment of 72 percent per quarter estimated for the aggregate. The interest rate elasticities are very comparable for the two sets of estimates, and the long term rate is again more important than the short term rate.[19] The rationing proxy variable for

[17] Although the FTC-SEC data allow short term commercial loans to be separated from term loans, we have used the total as our dependent variable to maintain consistency with the aggregate results of the previous section. In addition, trials using only the short term loans were less successful, reflecting, perhaps, the high degree of substitution between the two forms of loans. Also, we have included "other noncurrent liabilities" with net fixed capital. With these two exceptions, all variables correspond directly to the FTC-SEC definitions.

[18] The asset classes are the largest number that can be consistently derived from the FTC-SEC data over the sample period. A larger number of classes are available for more recent data. The data are not seasonally adjusted, but seasonal dummies have been included in the estimated equations. Further details on the FTC-SEC data are given in the Appendix, Section A.2.

[19] The interest rate and rationing proxy variables have been lagged one quarter for the equations of Table 5.3 to maintain consistency with the results for the aggregate data shown in Table 5.2. The estimated coefficients were essentially unchanged when the current values of these variables were tested.

TABLE 5.3 ESTIMATED COEFFICIENTS FOR LOAN DEMAND EQUATION: DISAGGREGATED DATA[a] ($\bar{L}$ *Dependent Variable*)

Equation	Range of Assets ($ million)	$\bar{I}$	$\overline{NAR}$	$\overline{LAG}$[b]	$(r_A - r_L)_{-1}$	$(r_P - r_L)_{-1}$	H_{-1}	R^2	S_e	D.W.
(1)	Under 1	.45 (6.2)	.85 (22.8)	−.38 (4.9)	.002 (.67)	.002 (1.4)	.001 (.51)	.899	.005	1.34
(2)	1–5	.74 (13.7)	.92 (14.5)	−.71 (11.5)	.003 (1.1)	.002 (1.2)	.001 (1.3)	.873	.005	1.88
(3)	5–10	.70 (10.4)	.77 (9.0)	−.63 (8.1)	.002 (.54)	.003 (1.0)	.003 (1.6)	.805	.007	1.09
(4)	10–50	.76 (19.3)	.91 (17.5)	−.74 (15.4)	.001 (.38)	.004 (3.0)	.001 (.85)	.933	.004	1.15
(5)	50–100	.83 (20.7)	.89 (12.3)	−.79 (15.0)	.008 (2.4)	.001 (.78)	.003 (1.7)	.924	.005	1.58
(6)	Over 100	.69 (14.0)	.77 (10.6)	−.63 (10.8)	.006 (2.4)	.003 (1.8)	.002 (1.7)	.888	.004	1.13
(7)	Total	.70 (15.2)	.81 (11.8)	−.65 (11.5)	.004 (2.0)	.003 (1.9)	.002 (1.8)	.884	.004	1.05

[a] R^2 is not corrected for degrees of freedom; S_e is standard error of estimate corrected for degrees of freedom; D.W. is Durbin-Watson statistic; and absolute value of T-statistics shown in parentheses. Seasonal dummies, not shown in the table, were included in the estimated equations.

[b] $\overline{LAG} = \bar{L}_{-1} + \overline{NAR}_{-1} - \Delta\bar{W} - \Delta\bar{K} - \bar{L}_{-1}$.

total manufacturing has the wrong sign, although the coefficient is not significant. As stressed earlier, however, a strong effect was not expected from the rationing variable and thus the result is not too disturbing.

The primary differences between the results for total manufacturing and the aggregate are the estimated coefficients for inventory and net accounts receivable. The inventory stock variable is very significant for both estimates, but the coefficient for the percentage of the inventory stock financed by commercial loans is only 14 percent for the manufacturing sector, compared to 51 percent for the aggregate. While it is plausible that the manufacturing sector might finance a smaller percentage of its inventory stock with commercial loans, it is unlikely that a differential of this size can be fully explained on this basis. Instead, it appears that multicollinearity between the inventory stock and net accounts receivable has caused less weight to be placed on the inventory stock variable in the total manufacturing sector equation. Net accounts receivable cannot enter the aggregate equation because the variable is zero, of course, when summed over the entire economy.

It is also interesting to compare the estimated coefficients for the various asset classes. The effect of the spread between the long term bond rate and the commercial loan rate tends to increase with the size of the firm, and the variable is significant only for the two largest classes and the total. This result is reasonable since the smaller firms may have only limited access to the corporate bond market. The results for the effect of the spread between the prime commercial paper rate and the commercial loan rate are more mixed. The variable is significant only for the fourth asset class, assets $10 million to $50 million, and the magnitude of the estimated coefficient does not appear to vary with asset size.[20] The coefficient of the credit rationing proxy variable for the asset classes is similar to the result for the total of the manufacturing sector; in each case the coefficient has the wrong sign and is not statistically significant.

Perhaps the most interesting result for the asset classes is the relative importance of net trade credit, compared to the inventory stock, as a determinant of loan demand. The equilibrium coefficients for the percentage of net accounts receivable and the percentage of the inventory stock financed by commercial loans are tabulated in Table 5.4. In each case the coefficient for net accounts receivable is at least twice the coefficient for the inventory stock. Furthermore, the net accounts receivable variable

---

[20] The equations were also tested with each of the interest rate variables suppressed. In all cases the remaining interest rate variable became statistically significant and the fit of the equation remained essentially unchanged. This suggests strong multicollinearity between the two interest rate variables, as one might expect.

appears most important for the smallest firms. This has implications for the effect of credit rationing that are discussed in the following chapter.

Finally, the speed of adjustment of long term liabilities to the long run level for each of the asset classes is shown in the last column of Table 5.4. The most noteworthy result is the high speed of adjustment of the firms in the smallest asset class. Moreover, the speed of adjustment tends to be reduced as the size of the firms increases, although the relationship is not strictly monotonic to asset size. Since retained earnings will tend to adjust faster than the issue of long term debt or equity, this result may be explained by the greater reliance of the smaller firms on retained earnings financing.

TABLE 5.4   EQUILIBRIUM COEFFICIENTS FOR LOAN DEMAND:
DISAGGREGATED DATA[a]

Range of Assets ($ million)	$(1 - \rho_I)$ % of Inventory Stock Financed by Commercial Loans	$(1 - \rho_N)$ % of Net Trade Credit Financed by Commercial Loans	(λ) Speed of Adjustment of Long Term Liabilities
Under 1	.11	.76	.62
1–5	.20	.72	.29
5–10	.19	.38	.37
10–50	.08	.65	.26
50–100	.19	.48	.21
Over 100	.16	.38	.37
Total	.14	.46	.35

[a] The arithmetic derivation of the coefficients is described in footnote 11, p. 137.

5.6 | SUMMARY

In this chapter a model of the demand for commercial loans was formulated and estimated. Three main assumptions were used in developing the model. First, it was assumed that the real expenditure decisions of business firms are made prior to the financial decisions except in periods of unexpected credit rationing. Second, it was assumed that the short run adjustment of the firm's long term liabilities is imperfect and the adjustment takes place at a constant rate. Third, it was assumed that the net assets of the firm could be separated into meaningful aggregates including inventory stock, fixed capital, net liquid assets, and trade credit.

Further assumptions, which have been only implicit in the analysis, concern the use of the commercial loan interest rate as the relevant yield for the firm's financing decision. It should be noted that the use of the interest rate for this purpose must be considered only an approximation because compensating balances are also typically required of the borrowing firm. Furthermore, by assuming a constant rate of adjustment of long term liabilities, we have abstracted from term structure considerations that might cause variations in the speed of adjustment depending on the borrowing firm's expectations for future movements in the long term interest rate.

The results of testing the model were generally reasonable and encouraging. Inventory investment and trade credit appear to be the main determinants of long run equilibrium loan demand. Fixed capital investment may also be financed by commercial loans, but this occurs primarily in the short run when commercial loans are buffering the adjustment of long term liabilities. The substitution between commercial loans and long term liabilities and between commercial loans and other short term net assets appears significant. The interest elasticity of loan demand is substantial, with the long term rate being more important than competing short term interest rates. Finally, the effect of credit rationing, which is included in the loan demand formulation in order to adjust the estimated equation to a loans outstanding basis, is quite small. This suggests that the major impact of credit rationing is on the firm's net asset holdings. This point is considered in more detail in the next chapter in which the direct effects of credit rationing on real capital markets and other financial markets are developed.

APPENDIX ON DATA SOURCES

A.1 VARIABLES USED IN SECTION 5.4

Dollar values are measured in billions of dollars in current prices and interest rates are measured in percentage points. All flow variables are measured at *quarterly* rates. All variables with the exception of interest rates are seasonally adjusted.

SCB = *Survey of Current Business,* August-September, 1965 as revised by March, 1970.

FRB = *Federal Reserve Bulletin*, various issues.

ΔI = Change in book value of the non-farm inventory stock; calculated as inventory investment (in current dollars) less inventory valuation adjustment; SCB.

ΔK = Net non-residential fixed investment; calculated as gross non-residential fixed investment less depreciation. Depreciation is the sum of corporate and non-corporate capital consumption allowances less the capital consumption allowance for the real estate industry; *SCB*.

GBP = Gross private business product; *SCB*.

GNP = Gross national product; *SCB*.

$V = GNP - \Delta I - \Delta K$

r_P = Prime commercial paper rate, 3 month average; *FRB*.

All other variables are described in the Appendix to Chapter 4.

A.2 NOTES ON THE FEDERAL TRADE COMMISSION (FTC)-SECURITIES AND EXCHANGE COMMISSION (SEC) *Quarterly Financial Report for Manufacturing Corporations*

The FTC-SEC *Quarterly Financial Reports* provide consistent balance sheets and income statements for the universe of manufacturing corporations derived from a selected sample.[21] The coverage is essentially complete for firms with assets over $5 million, but decreasingly smaller samples are used for the smaller firms. The official FTC-SEC view is that the data provide the best available estimate for the universe covered at the time of publication. Little attempt is made to revise the data or maintain consistency over time. Consequently, a significant amount of noise is found in the data and to some degree must just be accepted. Several problems are too important to ignore, however, and adjustments are noted here:

1. Splicing Sample Change Quarters. In 1951 and 1956 new samples were introduced (primarily for the smaller firms) to eliminate drifting which had arisen with the old sample. The introduction of the new samples resulted in substantial discontinuities in the transitional quarters. Overlap observations were provided, however, for 1951–3 and 1951–4, and for 1956–2. To smooth this transition, the ratio between the new sample and the old sample was first calculated for the overlap period for each series. This ratio was linearly interpolated to unity at the point where the sample was first used. The interpolated ratio was then used to correct the old sample.[22] The primary problem with this procedure is that the derived series need not satisfy the balance sheet identity, although in practice the inconsistency is very small.

2. Certificates of Deposit. Until the first quarter of 1964 a substantial

---

[21] Anderson [1964], p. 29, and Frazer [1965], p. 509, both provide summaries of the nature and problems of the data.

[22] Anderson, *op. cit.,* has used the same splicing method. Evans [1968] has suggested an alternative technique.

percentage of the certificates of deposit were included in "other current assets" and "government securities" as well as "cash." Starting in 1964–1, all CDs were supposed to be included in cash. To make 1963–4 consistent with the new data, the FTC-SEC suggested increasing 1964–1 cash by 15 percent and reducing government securities and other current assets by 5 percent and 18 percent, respectively. Private correspondence with a SEC official indicated that it was reasonable to assume that the entire adjustment belonged to the over $100 million asset group. No information on the amount of adjustment necessary for quarters prior to 1963–4 was available however. To solve the problem for the earlier period, the ratio between the amount of adjustment necessary in 1963–4 and a series of total CDs outstanding for that quarter was calculated. Assuming the ratio was constant, an implicit adjustment was derived for earlier quarters by multiplying the ratio by the CD series for each quarter. The adjustment extends back to 1960–1, before which CDs are assumed zero.

3. *"Reserves Not Reflected Elsewhere."* Starting in 1965–1, the FTC-SEC discontinued the category "reserves not reflected elsewhere" in the capital accounts. For that quarter they estimated that 10 percent of this category went to earned surplus and surplus reserves, and the other 90 percent went to "other noncurrent liability." We assumed that these percentages were correct for the earlier quarters also and made the adjustments on this basis.

4. *Accounts Receivable and Accounts Payable.* Effective in 1965–1 the FTC-SEC announced that certain nontrade items were being excluded from accounts payable and accounts receivable and were being shifted to other current assets and liabilities. On the basis of figures obtained from the SEC, adjustments were made to the pre-1965 data to maintain consistency with the later observations.

CHAPTER 6

The Effects of Credit Rationing on Firm Behavior

6.1 | INTRODUCTION

The discussion of credit rationing has so far been exclusively concerned with the existence and effects of rationing within the commercial loan market. In Chapters 2 and 3, the existence of credit rationing was discussed and verified as an important factor in the supply of loans by commercial banks. In Chapters 4 and 5, the determinants of the commercial loan rate and the demand for commercial loans were developed and estimated taking into account credit rationing. The result is that a complete and consistent model of the commercial loan market, including the effects of credit rationing, has been developed.

In this chapter, the effects of credit rationing on other sectors of the economy are considered. From the standpoint of economic policy, the major concern is with the effects of credit rationing on the investment expenditures of business firms. The access of rationed firms to alternative sources of funds, however, is an important determinant of the importance of credit rationing for investment expenditures, and thus the effects of credit rationing on other capital markets must also be taken into account. The theoretical considerations pertaining to this issue are introduced in Section 6.2. The following three sections then review and develop the available evidence for the effects of credit rationing on financial and real markets. In Section 6.3, the access of rationed firms to the debt and equity capital markets is considered as a possible offset to credit rationing in the loan market. In Section 6.4, the availability of trade credit is considered in a similar light. In Section 6.5, the empirical evidence on the

148

direct effects of credit rationing on business investment expenditures is reviewed.

6.2 | CREDIT RATIONING, INVESTMENT EXPENDITURES, AND OTHER FINANCIAL MARKETS

The implicit assumption in almost all earlier discussions of the availability doctrine and credit rationing was that a limited availability or rationing of loan funds would be directly transmitted to the real sectors of the economy in the form of reduced expenditures by business firms.[1] The most complete and consistent model of such a transmission process is provided by Tucker [1968].[2] Credit rationing develops in the loan market of Tucker's model as the result of lags in the adjustment of the commercial loan rate to the desired level.[3] The transmission process is then viewed as very direct. A firm desiring to increase its fixed or working capital stock approaches a bank for a loan. Finding the loan is not available, the firm has no choice but to reduce its expenditures to a level that is consistent with the funds that it does have on hand.

Tucker also introduces further assumptions which allow for what he terms a *credit contraction multiplier*. The principle assumption is that the response of investment to credit rationing is faster and greater than the response of investment to the corresponding interest rate change that would occur in the long run. Alternatively, it can be assumed that the response of investment to credit rationing occurs at the same speed as the response to the interest rate change, but then a lag in production decisions must also be introduced. The central notion of Tucker's argument for a credit multiplier is that credit rationing will immediately reduce the sales of investment goods, but that production may be reduced with only a lag. This will create an increase in the inventory stock of investment goods. If firms producing investment goods must then use their available funds to finance this unexpected inventory accumulation, the result may be additional cancellations of investment expenditures. The impact of the multiple contraction of expenditures occurs primarily, however, in the short run. Over a longer period the unintended inventory could be sold, thus creating a cash flow to finance the desired fixed capital investment. Even so, the credit contraction multiplier does offer a plausible explanation for the destabilizing credit squeezes that have been observed.

[1] See the literature discussed and cited in Section 2.2 above.

[2] Related issues are also discussed in Modigliani [1963], Tussing [1966], and Silber [1969].

[3] Tucker's concept of credit rationing is thus closely akin to what was defined as *dynamic* credit rationing in Chapter 2 above.

The critical premise underlying Tucker's mechanism for a direct effect of rationing on investment expenditures is the assumed absence of alternative means for the rationed firm to finance its desired investment. Otherwise, if rationed firms were allowed access to funds in other financial markets, then it would appear that the impact of loan market rationing would be reduced, if not completely avoided. Tucker recognizes, of course, that alternative means of finance may exist, but he leaves the empirical verification of this offset to credit rationing as an open question.

For present purposes, however, it is important to try to draw more definitive conclusions concerning the likely degree of the offset to credit rationing that is due to the availability of funds in other markets. Two principal modes of such financing can be distinguished: funds available in the capital markets and trade credit. The capital markets are defined here to include the markets for short term debt (other than commercial loans), long term debt, and equity issues. Trade credit is the direct financing of sales by business firms. Trade credit, unlike capital market financing, is offered only in conjunction with a purchase from the lending firm, and can thus be viewed as essentially a redistribution of funds within the business sector. In the following two sections the degree of the offset to credit rationing that might be attributed to the availability of funds from these two sources is considered.

6.3 | THE CAPITAL MARKETS AS ALTERNATIVE SOURCES OF FUNDS

The first issue that must be considered is the availability of capital market funds for the firms rationed in the commercial loan market. It is certainly going to occur that firms rationed by commercial banks will also be rationed in their attempts to obtain capital market financing. The inability of a firm to obtain bank credit, for example, might itself strongly prejudice the chances of the firm obtaining capital market funds. Furthermore, even when funds from the capital markets are available, the terms may not be acceptable to the borrowing firm. A particularly clear case occurs when the only available funds are in the form of an equity interest, and the borrowing firm views the dilution of ownership as too high a cost. Regardless of the form of the capital market rationing, however, it is clear that when it does occur, commercial loan credit rationing will continue to have an important and direct effect on business investment.

It is not difficult, on the other hand, to develop cases in which capital market funds will be available although the firm has been rationed by commercial banks. First, firms that cannot obtain funds on a loan basis may still attract and accept funds on an equity basis. It is clear, in fact, that in many cases an "adequate" equity base may be a necessary condition for obtaining a bank loan. The equity markets thus serve the function of providing the risk capital, in return for which the lender receives a higher expected return. Second, the rationing of firms by commercial banks will generally take the form of a limit on the size of the loan made available, rather than a complete rejection of the loan request. The firm would thus enter the capital markets in need of only supplemental financing, with the remainder of the financing already provided or guaranteed by the bank. In this case, the likelihood of rationing in the capital markets is less certain.

Even when funds are available in the capital markets, however, there remains the question of whether the entry of the rationed firms into these markets might not still have an effect on aggregate investment expenditures. One possible channel for such an effect would occur if the level of interest rates in the capital markets increases because of the entry of the bank rationed firms. It is clear, for example, that firms rationed at commercial banks are likely to be required to pay higher than average interest rates for capital market funds. Any reduction in investment that is due to the higher interest rates paid by these firms should not, however, be attributed to credit rationing. To the extent that such firms are not willing to pay the higher rates, it is the cost rather than the availability of the funds that is at issue.

A more significant effect occurs when the entire level of interest rates is higher because of the entry into the capital markets of the additional demand of the firms rationed by the banks. In this case even firms not rationed by banks will find their interest costs higher. This suggests that bank rationing, even if it does not affect firms directly, could still have an indirect influence through higher interest rates in the capital markets.

It is to be stressed, however, that this interest rate effect is likely to be damped, if not eliminated, by substitution on both the demand and supply sides of the capital markets. On the demand side, nonrationed firms may react to the higher interest costs by transferring more of their financing to the commercial loan market. The empirical results in the previous chapter on loan demand, for example, indicated significant substitution between both corporate bonds and commercial loans and commercial paper and commercial loans. Furthermore, it can be noted that the additional loan demand of these firms may be accepted by commercial banks, even though the banks are rationing smaller and riskier customers. The net effect of the higher interest rates in the capital markets can thus be simply a redistribution of funds in which small and risky firms use the open capital markets while larger firms substitute commercial loans for the more costly capital market funds.

The interest rate effect will also be damped by an increase in the supply of funds by the commercial banks to the capital markets. That is, the banks may invest the funds, made available by commercial loan rationing, in open market securities such as municipal and government bonds. Although these funds would not be directly available to corporate borrowers, the U.S. capital markets are sufficiently perfect that an increase in the flow of funds to one sector of the market is likely, via substitution, to increase the supply in other sectors.

In summary, it is apparent that if firms rationed in the c mmercial loan market are also rationed in the capital markets, then commercial loan credit rationing should have a direct and important effect on the investment expenditures of the rationed firms. If capital marl t rationing does not occur, on the other hand, then even if the bank rationed firms must pay higher interest rates for the capital funds, these funds will still be available for investment expenditures. Furthermore, the effects of higher capital market interest rates on nonrationed firms are likely to be small because these firms will substitute commercial loans for the capital market funds and because the commercial banks will also increase their supply of funds to the capital markets. The question of whether commercial loan market credit rationing can be offset by the availability of funds in the open capital markets reduces then, perhaps obviously, to the question of whether the firms rationed by banks will also be rationed in the capital markets. Unfortunately, very little direct empirical evidence is available on the extent to which capital market credit rationing occurs. Pending further work in this area, one must then evaluate the effect of credit rationing from the available evidence, summarized in Section 6.5 below, from survey studies and from regression studies of the impact of credit rationing on the final investment expenditures themselves.

6.4 | TRADE CREDIT AS AN ALTERNATIVE SOURCE OF FUNDS

Trade credit obtained from other business firms provides a second alternative source of funds for firms rationed by commercial banks. The analysis of trade credit as a substitute for loans follows the same basic lines used for capital market funds. The major issue again concerns the availability of trade credit to the rationed firms. Variations in the cost of trade credit are less important because the terms at which trade credit is granted have generally remained fixed over time.

Several factors suggest that trade credit may be more readily available than capital market credit for firms that are rationed by commercial banks. First, trade credit is an expensive source of funds for a firm that has alternatives in the form of either commercial loans or capital market borrowing. Trade credit is usually granted in the form of a *discount*

from the quoted price if the firm pays within a stated period (typically
10 days); otherwise the firm is expected to pay the full price within
some *net* period (typically 30 days). If the discount period is 10 days,
the net period is 30 days, and the discount rate is 2 percent, then the
implicit cost of foregoing the discount to obtain credit for 20 days is
an annual interest rate of 36 percent ($[(360 \text{ days}) (2 \text{ percent})]/[20 \text{ days}]$). It would thus appear that only rationed firms would wish to
make use of this form of credit. Furthermore, assuming competition be-
tween business firms in the granting of trade credit, the high cost must
be interpreted as an indication that the borrower has a high default risk.

Second, the available data indicate that small firms do, in fact, make
relatively more intense use of trade credit than large firms. In the last
column of Table 6.1 below, the average ratios of net trade credit granted
(accounts receivable minus accounts payable) to sales are shown for six
asset-size categories and the total of manufacturing corporations. It is
apparent that the smallest firms (under $1 million in assets) grant the
smallest amount of net trade credit. Furthermore, although the relationship is not monotonic for the two largest classes, there is also clear evidence that the amount of net trade granted increases with the asset size
of the firms. In addition, as shown in the last row of the table, the
corporate manufacturing sector as a total issues a significant amount of
trade credit to the rest of the economy. Since the noncorporate, nonmanufacturing sector of the economy generally consists of smaller firms, this
is additional evidence of the use of trade credit by such firms.

Finally, the results on loan demand in Chapter 5 indicated that trade
credit was an important determinant of loan demand for small firms.
This implies that, in periods of credit rationing, small firms can decrease
their need for commercial loans by increasing the amount of trade credit
obtained from large firms. The large firms will, in turn, finance the trade
credit through either bank loans or the capital markets. The net effect
is thus a redistribution of funds from the large firms to the small firms,
with the large firms bearing the burden of obtaining the funds from
banks or the capital markets.[4]

This redistribution of trade credit may substantially dampen the effect
of credit rationing on real expenditures. The small firms will change
their expenditure decisions only to the extent that the cost of trade credit
is substantially higher than the cost of the rationed commercial loans,
assuming ample trade credit is provided. Even then, if the interest elasticity of investment decisions by small firms is low, and there is certainly

[4] This mechanism has also been discussed in Meltzer [1960], Meltzer [1963],
Brechling and Lipsey [1963], and Schwartz [1970].

evidence in this direction, small firms may be relatively unaffected by rationing. Similarly, large firms will change their behavior only if the cost of the bank loans, or long term liabilities, used to finance the additional trade credit exceeds the return on the trade credit. Although the implicit interest rate on trade credit is very high, the risk is also great, and thus it is difficult to determine a reasonable rate of return.[5]

6.4.1 CREDIT RATIONING AND THE REDISTRIBUTION OF TRADE CREDIT: A DIRECT TEST

The likely importance of trade credit in offsetting the effects of credit rationing makes it desirable to test the hypothesis directly that trade credit is redistributed from large firms to small firms in periods of rationing. Aggregate data are of little value in this case, since trade credit sums to zero when aggregated over the entire business sector.[6] The FTC-SEC data for the manufacturing sector, on the other hand, are disaggregated by asset-size classes, and thus provide a good source for such estimates. Also, there is supporting evidence from survey data, which is discussed in Section 6.4.2 below.

The test for the redistribution of trade credit in periods of credit rationing takes the form of estimating equations, for each of the FTC-SEC data asset-size classes, explaining the ratio of net accounts receivable (NAR) to sales (S). Net accounts receivable are taken as the dependent variable, rather than accounts receivable or accounts payable separately, because our concern is with the distributional effects on the *net credit* extended by the firms. The scaling by sales assumes that the *net average collection period*[7] is constant except as modified by the independent variables indicated below.

The strongest version of the hypothesis to be tested is that the amount of net trade credit (relative to sales) extended by large firms rises, and the amount extended by small firms falls, in periods of credit rationing. It is important to distinguish, however, between the redistribution of trade credit within the corporate manufacturing sector (that is, the universe for the FTC-SEC data sample) and the redistribution between this sector and the remainder of the business sector. Since the noncorporate, nonmanufacturing sector consists primarily of very small firms, one would expect to find this sector receiving additional net trade credit from the

---

[5] See, for example, Goldfeld [1966], p. 83.

[6] This abstracts from credit granted by the business sector to the household sector.

[7] In equilibrium the net average collection period is $NAR/(S/90)$; that is the ratio of net receivables outstanding to daily sales (assuming S is measured at a quarterly rate). The dependent variable is scaled this way to avoid the problem of heteroskedastic error terms which would otherwise be likely.

manufacturing sector in periods of rationing. In addition, small corporate manufacturers may be indistinguishable from large corporate manufacturers in this respect.[8] That is, in periods of rationing, the small firms in the FTC-SEC universe will not only obtain additional credit from the large firms in this group, but they also will extend further credit to the remainder of the business sector. Since the net results of these two forces cannot be determined a priori, a weaker proposition is suggested: in periods of tight money and credit rationing, large firms tend to extend relatively more trade credit than small firms in the corporate manufacturing sector.

Turning now to the specification of the net trade credit equation, it is to be expected that net trade credit will respond to changes in the degree of credit rationing primarily with a lag. In periods of increased rationing, for example, firms may at first maintain their previous standards for accepting accounts receivable. But if faced with a continuing problem of a loss of sales if receivable standards are not revised, they may then reevaluate their credit terms. This effect is incorporated in the tested equation by using a four quarter distributed lag on the credit rationing variable.[9]

A second important factor for the specification of the net trade credit equation is the existence of a large time trend in the ratio of net trade credit to sales. Although both accounts receivable and accounts payable have risen relative to sales over the sample period, accounts receivable have grown faster, leading to a time trend in the net receivable ratio. To some extent this trend may be the result of a similar trend in monetary tightness over the sample period. Other explanations, however, may also be suggested. First, the favorable experience with trade credit over the post-war period may have led firms to be more willing to grant such credit. Second, increased competition may have forced the terms or availability of trade credit to be more favorable. Third, industries with high net trade credit to sales ratios may have expanded faster than the average.[10] A simple linear time trend is used as a proxy variable for these effects, although this is clearly only an indication of the problems in directly specifying the true structural determinants.

Other variables could also be added to the equation. For example, high capacity utilization rates or low profit margins might make firms

---

[8] The work of Meltzer [1963] and Frazer [1965] also points strongly in this direction.

[9] Alternatively, Nadiri [1969] has used a lagged trade credit variable in the specification of his equations. This form was also tested, but the results were slightly poorer. The results of Nadiri's study are discussed below.

[10] The issues relating to the time trend in trade credit are discussed in greater detail in Federal Reserve Bank of Kansas City [1957] and [1959].

reluctant to extend additional credit, since the profit from additional sales will then be low. The ratio of costs of production to sales could be included since the level of accounts payable should be more closely related to the firm's expenditures than its sales. Meltzer [1960], working with a similar model, has included both liquidity and sales variables. Finally, Nadiri [1969] has included variables for the opportunity cost of credit and general indicators of monetary tightness.

These variables have all been tested as additions to the basic specification with credit rationing. In general the estimated coefficients had correct signs, but the estimates were typically neither significant nor robust to other changes in the specification. This may be the result of either multi-collinearity or the poor quality of the data. In any case, these variables have been omitted in the results presented here, and this does serve to emphasize the very simple structure of the model.

The specification for the estimated equation is thus given by:

$$(6.1) \qquad \frac{NAR}{S} = a_0 + a_1 T + a_2 H + a_3 H_{-1} + a_4 H_{-2} + a_5 H_{-3},$$

where T is a linear time trend and H is the credit rationing proxy. The coefficient for the time trend is expected to be positive. The coefficient of the constant term is not identified in terms of behavioral significance because both the credit rationing proxy and the time trend have arbitrary origins. The expected signs for the coefficients of the credit rationing terms depend on the form of the hypothesis. The strong version of the hypothesis would indicate that the net trade credit extended by large firms should rise with credit rationing. Small firms, on the other hand, should extend less trade credit in periods of high credit rationing. The weaker version of the hypothesis, which takes into account net trade credit extended outside the corporate manufacturing sector, suggests a modification in these expectations. The net trade credit issued by small firms in the corporate manufacturing sector may actually rise in periods of credit rationing, but the net effect should still be less than for the large firms.

The results of testing equation 6.1 for 6 asset classes and the total of the corporate manufacturing sector are shown in Table 6.1. The data, with the exception of the credit rationing proxy, are not seasonally adjusted.[11] Seasonal dummies, not shown in the table, were included in the estimated equations and were very significant. The equations were

---

[11] The FTC-SEC data was also used for the estimation of the loan demand equation in Chapter 5, and the data is described in the Appendix to Chapter 5. The credit rationing proxy is the H_a principal component form described in the Appendix to Chapter 3. The net trade credit ratio is measured in percentage points.

TABLE 6.1 ESTIMATED COEFFICIENTS FOR NET TRADE CREDIT EQUATION (NAR/S Dependent Variable)

Eq.	Range of Assets ($ Million)	Constant	T	H	H_{-1}	H_{-2}	H_{-3}	ΣH	ρ	R^2	S_e	D.W.	Mean of Dependent Variable (Percentage)
(1)	Under 1	4.5 (6.7)	.14 (12.5)	-.14 (.71)	-.16 (2.3)	-.14 (1.2)	-.09 (.87)	-.53 (2.4)	.46	.933	.724	2.10	12.5
(2)	1-5	18.3 (11.6)	.04 (1.5)	-.04 (.14)	-.06 (.44)	-.06 (.30)	-.04 (.23)	-.20 (.43)	.64	.704	1.178	2.21	20.5
(3)	5-10	28.2 (5.6)	.01 (.06)	-.51 (1.6)	-.11 (.53)	.11 (.45)	.15 (.75)	-.36 (.53)	.89	.885	.842	2.19	27.6
(4)	10-50	31.5 (4.6)	.01 (.39)	-.31 (1.5)	-.21 (1.5)	-.12 (.77)	-.05 (.43)	-.69 (1.6)	.95	.974	.751	1.89	30.9
(5)	50-100	13.4 (5.8)	.29 (7.9)	-.57 (2.2)	-.12 (.77)	.13 (.68)	.17 (1.1)	-.39 (.78)	.81	.976	.954	2.13	30.1
(6)	Over 100	9.7 (9.7)	.25 (15.0)	-.23 (.97)	.12 (1.2)	.27 (1.8)	.23 (1.8)	.39 (1.4)	.57	.977	.877	2.10	24.1
(7)	Total	12.8 (8.5)	.19 (7.9)	-.13 (.85)	.02 (.22)	.09 (.81)	.08 (.93)	.06 (.30)	.83	.985	.551	2.18	23.7

Notes: R^2 is not corrected for degrees of freedom; S_e is standard error of estimate corrected for degrees of freedom; D.W. is Durbin-Watson statistic; and absolute value of T-statistics in parentheses.

fitted for the period 1953–1 to 1969–4 using ordinary least squares. The distributed lag on the credit rationing proxy was estimated using the Almon [1965] technique for a second-degree polynomial with the far end constrained to zero. Because the error terms in the original equations indicated significant serial correlation, the final equations were estimated also using the Cochrane and Orcutt [1949] iterative procedure for relationships involving first-order serially correlated errors.

The estimated equations appear to fit quite well given the rough nature of the data. The time trend has the expected positive sign in all equations, although it is not significant for the three middle asset categories. The estimated coefficients for the serial correlation of the error terms, shown as ρ in the table, are generally quite high. This may be due, however, to the method of sample revision used in the FTC-SEC surveys (see Appendix to Chapter 5).

With respect to the credit rationing effects, the results generally confirm the weak hypothesis for the effect of credit rationing on trade credit, and they are consistent with the strong hypothesis. Looking first at the sum of the lagged rationing variables, shown in the column marked ΣH, it is clear that credit rationing has a significant negative effect on the issue of net trade credit by the smallest firms (assets under $1 million). This indicates that the existence of rationing causes these firms to increase their accounts payable more than they increase (or possibly decrease) their accounts receivable. In contrast, the results indicate that for the class of largest firms, assets over $100 million, the effect of the credit rationing variable is positive (though not quite significant). This implies that the large firms increase their issue of net trade credit in periods of credit rationing. The results for the asset-size categories between the two extremes are more mixed as one would expect. The total effect for these classes is always negative, but there is only one case of a T-statistic greater than one.

Turning next to the distribution of the effect of rationing over time, the results are again quite reasonable. For the two smallest classes, the maximum effect of credit rationing is reached with a one-quarter lag; for all the larger classes the maximum effect is obtained in the concurrent quarter. In three cases the distributed lag includes both negative and positive terms. In equations 3 and 5, the effect is negative for the first two quarters and positive for the last two. This is not disturbing, however, since in terms of magnitude the total effect is still distinctly negative. In equation 6, for the largest class, the effect of rationing is negative in the first quarter, but is then positive in the last three quarters. The total effect, as already noted, is distinctly positive. The negative effect in the concurrent quarter can be interpreted as an impact of credit rationing in which even the large firms reduce their issue of net trade credit. Then, as the effects of credit rationing persist, the large firms begin to actually increase their issue of trade credit.

The results thus appear consistent with the hypothesis that credit rationing causes a redistribution of trade credit from large firms to small firms. This conclusion also provides additional confirmation of the earlier studies by Meltzer [1960], Meltzer [1963], and Brechling and Lipsey [1963] that have argued for a similar effect of tight money, as distinct from credit rationing, on the issue of trade credit. The results stand in contrast, however, with the conclusions of Nadiri [1969] who found no effect of general monetary tightness on the net extension of trade credit. Several explanations can be offered for this difference in results. First, Nadiri used only the money supply and related monetary aggregates as measures of monetary tightness.[12] Second, his sample extended only through 1964–4 and thus did not contain the important period of tight money that began in 1965 and has extended through the present. Third, and perhaps most important, his equations were estimated only for the aggregate of the FTC-SEC corporate manufacturing sample. It thus seems fair to conclude that the preponderance of the evidence still indicates a significant effect of credit rationing and tight money on the issue and distribution of trade credit.

6.4.2 CREDIT RATIONING AND THE REDISTRIBUTION OF TRADE CREDIT: SURVEY DATA

Surveys of the reactions of business managers to high interest rates and credit rationing provide an additional source of data for evaluating the hypothesis that net trade credit is redistributed toward smaller forms in periods of tight money. A particularly interesting survey for this purpose was undertaken jointly by the Federal Reserve-M.I.T. econometric model project and Donaldson, Lufkin & Jenrette, Inc., New York investment bankers. Questionnaires were sent to a sample of 1000 small-to-medium sized firms (assets ranging from $1 million to $50 million) in December 1966 to determine the firms' adjustments to the tight money conditions of 1966.

---

[12] In particular, Nadiri argued that interest rates are not an appropriate measure of the effect of monetary tightness on trade credit because (1) they are endogenous variables and (2) they are part of the user cost of trade credit. This argument appears quite forced. First the endogeneity of interest rates does not preclude a *structural* relationship with trade credit, although it may present statistical problems. Indeed, the money supply suffers from the same problem of endogeneity without there being an obvious structural link. Second, the emphasis on the user cost of trade credit ignores the effect of interest rate costs on the *demand* for this credit. This effect is likely to be quite pronounced since the actual cost of trade credit is generally institutionally fixed.

The first part of the questionnaire was concerned with determining the proportion of firms in the sample that could not obtain bank credit in the desired amount. A summary of these results (on the basis of 343 acceptable responses) is shown in Table 6.2. Of the firms in the sample, 275 actively sought bank credit during 1966, while 45 of these firms could not obtain the desired amount from the first bank which they approached. In terms of percentages (row 4 of the table), it is clear that the smallest firms experienced relatively more rationing, as would be expected. It is perhaps surprising that 19 percent of the largest firms in the sample were also denied loan requests, but it should be noted the survey did not include firms with assets over $50 million.[13]

The most important and relevant portion of the survey is the response to the question, "Have you been able to secure at least part of the desired

TABLE 6.2 PERCENTAGE OF BANK CUSTOMERS RATIONED[a]

	Asset Size ($ Millions)				
	1–5.2	5.3–10.0	10.1–21.3	21.4–49.8	Total
(1) Total number of firms in sample	57	64	116	106	343
(2) Firms actively seeking credit	45	51	100	79	275
(3) Firms denied initial loan request	12	7	11	15	45
(4) Percentage of firms denied initial loan request (row 3/row 2)	26.7%	13.7%	11.0%	19.0%	16.4%

[a] The data for Tables 6.2, 6.3, and 6.4 were obtained from the tabulation of the Year End Survey in Donaldson, Lufkin & Jenrette, Inc. [1967], p. 44. It should be pointed out that the number of observations for data cells, particularly in Tables 6.3 and 6.4, is very small and at best these data can provide only supporting evidence. The four asset classes we have distinguished were chosen to provide a comparison with the data from the FTC-SEC *Quarterly Financial Report;* a more complete classification is available in the source.

[13] The survey also asked the firms to give the bank's reason for rationing. By far the most frequent response was "very little or no money available for new loans." Presumably this is merely a euphemism used by the banks and supports the contention (discussed in Chapter 3) that survey data cannot successfully determine the existence or source of credit rationing.

funds from other sources?"[14] A tabulation of these results is shown in Table 6.3. The numbers represent the percentage of firms, not granted their desired amount of bank credit at the original bank, that succeeded in obtaining at least some additional funds from other sources. "Other banks" are, in general, the most important of these additional sources, not too surprisingly. It is of interest, moreover, that the small firms had about as much success as the large firms in obtaining bank credit after being rationed at one bank.

TABLE 6.3 ADDITIONAL SOURCES OF FINANCE FOR RATIONED FIRMS
(*Percentage of Rationed Firms Relying on Various Alternative Sources*)

	Asset Size ($ Millions)				
	1–5.2	5.3–10.0	10.1–21.2	21.3–49.8	Total
Other banks	25.0	28.6	27.3	26.7	26.7
Trade credit (payables)	33.0	14.3	9.1	20.0	20.0
Finance company	16.7	14.3	9.1	6.7	11.1
Insurance company	8.3	14.3	0.0	20.0	11.1
Long term debt	8.3	0.0	0.0	20.0	8.9
Other	25.0	42.9	0.0	13.3	17.8

Our primary interest is related to the second row of the table, which shows the percentage of firms relying on trade credit as a substitute for bank credit. In terms of magnitude, it is clear from the table that trade credit does rank among the most important substitutes for bank credit. Furthermore, 33 percent of the smallest firms used this source, making it the most important substitute for this asset class. In addition, the small firms relied more heavily on trade credit than any of the larger classes, although the relationship is not monotonic to asset size. The fact that 20 percent of the largest firms relied on additional long term debt offerings suggests that firms (or at least large firms with access to the open market) may be able to substitute long term debt for commercial loans in periods of credit rationing, thus not disturbing the rest of their asset holdings. Each of these results, the reliance on trade credit, especially by small firms, and the reliance on long term debt, especially by large firms, is consistent with the view that the impact of credit rationing on real ex-

[14] A copy of the questionnaire is reproduced in Donaldson, Lufkin & Jenrette, Inc., *op. cit.*, pp. 8–9.

penditures is reduced by an intra-business sector redistribution of funds from large firms to small firms.

The final set of data of interest from the survey concerns the reduced spending of business firms caused by credit rationing.[15] The tabulation in Table 6.4 shows the percentage of rationed firms that reduced spending on the assets shown. Somewhat surprisingly, the strongest effect was related to expenditures associated with fixed capital, that is, modernization, additions to capacity, and acquisitions. The reduction in expenditures on accounts receivable was the least important of the five assets shown, although in terms of absolute magnitude (24 percent for the total) it still is significant. In addition, the smallest firms reduced trade credit receivables substantially more than the largest class, although the relationship is not monotonic to asset size.

TABLE 6.4 REDUCED EXPENDITURES FOR RATIONED FIRMS (*Percentage of Firms Reducing Expenditures on Alternative Assets*)

	Asset Size ($ Millions)				
	1.0–5.2	5.3–10.0	10.1–21.2	21.3–49.8	Total
Reduced expenditures on:					
Inventory	50.0	71.4	45.5	53.3	53.3
Trade credit (receivables)	25.0	28.6	36.4	13.3	24.4
Modernization of facilities	50.0	71.4	27.3	39.9	44.4
Additions to capacity	58.3	100.0	100.0	20.0	62.2
Acquisitions of other companies	41.7	85.7	72.3	46.7	57.8
Other	0.0	0.0	9.1	6.7	4.4

6.5 | THE DIRECT EFFECTS OF CREDIT RATIONING ON INVESTMENT EXPENDITURES

The preceding discussion of the possible offsets to credit rationing from the availability of capital market funds and trade credit indicates that the principal case for a direct effect of credit rationing on business firm

[15] The question, as actually stated in the survey, did not distinguish between reductions in spending caused specifically by high interest rates and those reductions related directly to credit rationing.

investment must rest with empirical findings. Unfortunately, until quite recently no attempts had been made to develop such studies. The main problem was the absence of an explicit measure of credit rationing, an issue already discussed in Section 3.2 above. A subsidiary problem was the difficulty of differentiating between the effects of tight money, such as high interest rates, and the effects of credit rationing per se.

Within the last several years, however, a number of exploratory studies have been undertaken, many using the credit rationing proxy described in Chapter 3, to determine the impact of credit rationing on the investment expenditures of business firms. The principal center of this activity has been the Federal Reserve-M.I.T.-Penn. econometric model project. Michael Evans has also incorporated the credit rationing proxy variable in his econometric model developed for Philadelphia Research Associates. In addition, a survey of the effects of tight money conditions during 1966 was undertaken by the Office of Business Economics (OBE) of the Department of Commerce, and there have been several studies of the effects of rationing within the mortgage and housing markets.

6.5.1 FIXED CAPITAL INVESTMENT

There have been four studies, in addition to the OBE survey, of the effects of credit rationing on the fixed capital investment of business firms: Charles Bischoff [1970], Steven Elgart [1969], John Hand [1968], and Michael Evans [1970]. The results of these studies are quite mixed. Bischoff's study involved including the rationing proxy, with various lags, in his equations for aggregate nonresidential construction expenditures. The results are generally negative—Bischoff finds that the rationing proxy typically enters with the correct sign but the coefficient is never statistically significant.[16]

The other studies all use disaggregated data. Elgart's study estimated total investment equations for firms disaggregated by two-digit industry classifications. His results are similar to Bischoff's in that the rationing proxy is significant with the correct sign in only one industry group (textiles). More encouraging results are found in the studies by Evans and Hand. Evans obtained a significant effect for the credit rationing proxy in his equations for commercial structures and other structures.[17] In addition to the disaggregation, the most notable feature of Evans' work is that the credit rationing variable is entered in the equations nonlinearly. Hand estimated equations for the total fixed investment of manufacturing corporations using data disaggregated by the asset size of firms. His re-

[16] In unpublished work, Bischoff has also obtained similar results for investment in producers' durable equipment.
[17] See Evans [1970], pp. 13 and 17.

sults are encouraging in that for large firms and for the total of manufacturing corporations, the rationing proxy enters significantly with a negative sign. In his preferred equations for the total of manufacturing corporations, a 1.0 increase in the credit rationing proxy (approximately the standard deviation of the series) results in a reduction in the annual rate of investment of about $300 million.

This latter result of Hand's is also broadly consistent with the findings and evaluation of the OBE survey by Crockett, Friend, and Shavell [1967]. They estimate that the monetary tightness in 1966 resulted in a reduction in annual fixed capital investment of about $500 million. Their estimates include not only the effects of rationing, but also other monetary conditions such as high interest rates and the decline in the stock market, that occurred during this period. It is thus reasonable that their estimate is somewhat higher than Hand's.

The OBE survey also indicated the number of firms affected by various aspects of monetary tightness. These aspects include the rise in interest rates, the decline in the stock market, credit rationing by financial institutions, and credit rationing in the capital markets. Of the firms indicating a decrease in investment expenditures during 1966 and 1967, between 60 and 90 percent (depending on asset size) attribute high interest rates as a source. Between 30 and 47 percent of the firms attribute credit rationing by financial institutions as a source. The percentages attributing the decline in the stock market and capital market rationing as a source are much lower.

6.5.2 INVENTORY INVESTMENT

There have been three studies of the effect of credit rationing on inventory investment. The first study was undertaken directly as part of the Federal Reserve-M.I.T.-Penn. model project.[18] The results were quite similar to the findings of Bischoff and Elgart on fixed investment, namely that the credit rationing proxy typically enters with the correct sign, but it is rarely statistically significant. Only slightly more encouraging results are obtained by Hand [1968]. He tested the credit rationing proxy in equations for the inventory investment of manufacturing corporations disaggregated by asset-size categories. He found that the credit rationing proxy enters the equations for the small firms with the correct sign, but the variable appears to be collinear with other variables, particularly unfilled orders.

The evaluation of the OBE survey by Crockett, Friend, and Shavell

---

[18] Frank de Leeuw had primary responsibility for the inventory investment equation of the model at the time the credit rationing tests were performed.

indicated more significant effects of tight money on inventory investment. They estimate a total reduction in inventory investment of $500 million due to monetary sources during 1966. The distribution of the number of firms affected by the various aspects of the tightness is similar to the results for fixed investment. Between 57 and 100 percent of the firms (depending on asset size) attribute interest costs as one source for the reduction in inventory investment. Between 21 and 51 percent of the firms attribute credit rationing by financial institutions as a source. The percentages for the decline in the stock market and capital market rationing are again distinctly smaller.

6.5.3 OTHER EXPENDITURES

Effects of credit rationing have also been indicated in several other sectors of the economy. Perhaps the clearest case is in the markets for mortgages and housing. In the Federal Reserve-M.I.T.-Penn. model, for example, the effect of rationing on housing investment is estimated by including the advance mortgage commitments of financial intermediaries in the housing starts equation (see Gramlich and Jaffee [1970]). The mortgage market in that model also incorporates the possibility of disequilibrium (see Jaffee [1970]). A more structural approach to the estimation of the effects of rationing in the mortgage and housing market has also been developed in Fair and Jaffee [1970]. In this model, the disequilibrium structure of the market is specified explicitly and the equations are then estimated accordingly (see also discussion in Section 3.2 above).

An impact of credit rationing on consumer durable expenditures has been suggested by the work of Evans [1970]. Evans included the credit rationing proxy variable in his equations for personal consumption of furnishings and new automobile registrations, and found it had a negative and significant effect. Although it is difficult to attribute a credit rationing effect on consumer durables directly to the commercial loan market, it is plausible that credit rationing might occur in consumer credit markets with about the same timing that it occurs in the commercial loan market.

Finally, the work of William Branson [1970] has indicated that the credit rationing proxy variable can be usefully incorporated in equations explaining international financial flows. An important premise of the Branson study is that interest rates by themselves are not adequate indicators of the yields and opportunity costs that influence international portfolio allocations. Consequently, the credit rationing proxy is used, along with interest rates and a measure of the velocity of the money, to obtain a more comprehensive measure of these yields.

6.5.4 SUMMARY

The results reviewed here for the effect of credit rationing on investment and other expenditures are quite varied. Furthermore, many of the studies are distinctly exploratory in nature and many features of the specification of the tested equations, in addition to the credit rationing variable, remain in question. As a consequence, it is not possible to provide a simple summary evaluation of the results. In particular, the evidence for an effect of rationing on the investment expenditures of large firms is especially mixed. Because large firms represent the major share of the assets and sales of the total economy, this also indicates that an effect of rationing on aggregate investment expenditures must similarly remain in doubt. On the other hand, the evidence for an effect of rationing on the investment expenditures of small firms is more convincing. Therefore, in concluding the study in the following chapter, we shall emphasize the policy implications for the case in which the major effect of credit rationing is on the investment expenditures of small firms. It is again stressed, however, that these conclusions must remain tentative pending further empirical research on the direct effects of credit rationing.

CHAPTER 7

Conclusions

7.1 | INTRODUCTION

The discussion in the preceding chapters has concentrated on two topics: an analysis of the structure of the commercial loan market; and a more specific investigation of the existence and effects of credit rationing in the commercial loan market. In this chapter, the main conclusions with respect to these topics are summarized.

7.2 | THE STRUCTURE OF THE COMMERCIAL LOAN MARKET

The model of the commercial loan market that has been formulated and estimated in this study can be usefully separated into its supply and demand components. On the supply side, the commercial banks' two decision variables are the commercial loan interest rate and the degree of credit rationing. On the demand side, business firms determine the demand for commercial loans. These three variables—the loan rate, the degree of rationing, and loan demand—together with the identity determining loans outstanding as loan demand minus credit rationing, then form the full system.

The principal determinant of the equilibrium level of the commercial loan rate is the opportunity cost of funds to the banks. This opportunity cost can be measured as the interest yield on competing assets such as Treasury bills or long term bonds, but liquidity considerations based on the status of the certificate of deposit market, and loan-deposit and liquid asset-deposit ratios, must also be taken into account. These variables were included in the formulation by specifying them explicitly in one test and by using the credit rationing proxy variable in an alternative test.

A somewhat more innovative approach has been used in the specification of the short run dynamics of commercial loan rate determination. The actual level of the commercial loan rate is first assumed to be determined by a partial adjustment process in which the change in the rate is proportional to the spread between the desired level and the quoted level. In contrast to the usual procedure, however, the parameters of the adjustment process are not assumed to be constant, but instead they depend on an exogenous signal that determines the short run timing of rate changes. More specifically, the signal was assumed to take the form of changes in the Federal Reserve's discount rate, and the estimated equations indicated that changes in the discount rate did, in fact, explain a significant percentage of the variation in the commercial loan rate.

A second important factor determining short run variations in the commercial loan rate is the level of the Regulation Q ceiling on certificate of deposit interest rates. Because the certificate of deposit market increases bank access to capital market funds, the existence of this market has lead to lower commercial loan rates on average. Conversely, however, when the Regulation Q ceiling is sufficiently low, relative to market rates of interest, to hinder the issue of new CDs by the commercial banks, then the benefit of the existence of the CD market in terms of lower commercial loan rates is lost.

The importance of changes in the discount rate and the level of the Regulation Q ceiling as determinants of the commercial loan rate implies that the Federal Reserve may have considerable direct control over the level of the commercial loan rate. In this respect, the Federal Reserve's control over the commercial loan rate may more closely resemble the direct control of, say, the Bank of England over the British bank rate, than is normally assumed. This direct control of the commercial loan rate has two important implications for the efficacy of Federal Reserve monetary policy. First, to the extent that investment expenditures are elastic with respect to the commercial loan rate, control of the commercial loan rate by the Federal Reserve will obviously imply some measure of control over investment expenditures. Second, given that credit rationing is a function of the spread between the banks' desired commercial loan rate and the loan rate actually being quoted, control of the quoted rate by the Federal Reserve implies control over the degree of credit rationing. It should be emphasized, however, that there is a basic conflict between these two effects of Federal Reserve control over the commercial loan rate. While an increase in the quoted loan rate would be expected to decrease investment expenditures due to the interest elasticity assumed in the first effect, an increase in the quoted loan rate would also decrease the degree of credit rationing and thus increase investment expenditures. The short run effects of a change in the quoted loan rate might thus well cancel. Consequently, although there remains an important question concerning the effects of short run changes in the loan rate on the distribution of investment expenditures between rationed and nonrationed firms (see discussion in Section 7.3 below), the main force of Federal Reserve monetary policy would still appear to reside primarily in the influence of Federal Reserve policy on the level of the desired commercial loan rate.

Given the level of the commercial loan rate and the degree of credit rationing determined by the commercial banks, the actual quantity of loans outstanding is then determined by the demand for loans by business firms. The model of the demand for commercial loans can also be usefully separated into its equilibrium and dynamic components. In equilibrium, and abstracting from credit rationing, it is assumed that business firm loan demand is a function of the assets the firms want to finance and of the relative cost of the available modes of financing. The main determinants of loan demand are the firms' inventory stock and net trade credit, the latter appearing only on a disaggregated basis. The firms' other net liquid assets and fixed capital stock also appear in the final formulation, but they are much less important. In terms of the relative cost of financing, the results indicated significant substitution, on the basis of interest yield spreads, between both long term debt and commercial loans and commercial paper and commercial loans.

The dynamic adjustments of commercial loan demand are based on the assumption that the firm's long term liabilities adjust only gradually to the desired level. In order to maintain the balance sheet identity in the short run, commercial loans must then serve a buffer function. For example, if total financing needs rise, perhaps due to an increase in inventory investment, then if long term liabilities increase less than the long run desired amount, commercial loan demand will then increase by more than the expected amount to take up this slack. An important implication of this buffer function of commercial loans for business financing is that it provides a concrete illustration of the principle that Federal Reserve monetary policy in the commercial loan market may have more leverage than the quantitative amounts involved would otherwise indicate.

7.3 | THE EXISTENCE AND EFFECTS OF CREDIT RATIONING

An important distinction has been drawn in this study between the existence and effects of credit rationing within the commercial loan market and the effects of credit rationing on other sectors of the economy. Within the theoretical framework of Chapters 2 and 3, credit rationing was viewed as a limit on the availability of loan funds primarily to small and risky firms. On the other hand, the analysis indicated that risk-free firms would generally be supplied the quantity of loans they demanded at the ruling commercial loan rate. The results of the empirical tests on the structure of the commercial loan market confirmed this conclusion. In particular, the fluctuations in the credit rationing proxy, which is a principal component of series representing the percentage of loans granted to prime and large bank customers, were satisfactorily explained by the rate differential between the desired commercial loan rate and the loan rate actually being quoted.

In Chapter 6 we then proceeded to consider the effects of rationing on other sectors of the economy. Taking into account the possible offsets to credit rationing from the availability of capital market funds and trade credit, it appeared that the primary effect of credit rationing was on the investment expenditures of small firms. In particular, the following mechanism may be at work. The primary impact of credit rationing within the commercial loan market is directed at the small and risky firms. To some extent these firms may avoid revising their expenditures plans on account of the rationing by obtaining access to other capital markets. Perhaps even more significantly, the small firms may rely on additional trade credit from the large firms. But even with these offsets to credit rationing, the net effect on small firms is still likely to be at least some reduction in their expenditures. For the large firms, on the other hand, the primary burden of credit rationing is that it necessitates their financing an additional volume of trade credit. In order to do this they must obtain additional funds in either the capital markets or from the commercial banks. Although one result of the additional demand of the large firms for funds may be a general increase in market interest rates, and thus a reduction in investment demand, this effect is likely to be matched by an additional supply of funds to the capital markets by banks and other suppliers who have rationed the small firms.

Given the existence of such a mechanism, the next question then concerns the implications in such a setting for the efficiency of the flow of funds through the financial markets and for the efficacy of monetary policy. With regards to efficiency, the discussion in Chapter 2 indicated that the two necessary conditions for credit rationing in the loan market were the risk of default on the loan and the imperfect competitive structure of the banking industry. On the theoretical level, the problem may thus be posed in terms of the allocation of resources under uncertainty. Although important work in this area is now available,[1] the analysis re-

---

[1] See, for example, Arrow [1965] and Arrow and Lind [1970] and the literature cited therein.

mains quite abstract. On a more practical level, two issues appear to be involved. Assuming that trade credit is the main alternative open to rationed firms, one issue concerns the relative efficiency of business firms compared to commercial banks in providing credit to small and risky enterprises. Although banks have an obvious expertise in evaluating loan requests, business firms may have an advantage in determining the likely success of the investment projects of small firms in closely related fields; the question thus remains unsettled. The second issue concerns the more general problem of stimulating competitive entry and innovation into areas in which large initial investments are required. The problem here is mainly that the value of competition and innovation accrues to the economy in general in the form of an externality, and thus the returns to an individual lender may have to be subsidized if the funds are to be available. This leaves open, of course, the question of the magnitude of the subsidy, an answer to which would require a substantial cost and benefit analysis.

With respect to the efficacy of monetary policy, the main question concerns the magnitude of the effect of credit rationing on large firms. If the impact of credit rationing centers solely on small firms, then the main effect may simply be a redistribution of flows wi: in the financial markets. The efficacy of monetary policy in this case will still depend on the interest elasticity of investment demand. On the other hand, if it can be shown that credit rationing also significantly affects the investment expenditures of large firms, then the implications for monetary policy become more important. In particular, monetary policy could continue to have an impact even when faced with inelastic investment demand. In addition, the Federal Reserve would have reason to take the volume of bank credit, as well as its cost, into account in evaluating the degree of tightness in the financial markets.

7.4 | SUGGESTIONS FOR FUTURE RESEARCH

On the basis of these conclusions, two main directions for further research can be suggested. The first direction would concern empirical research on the effects of credit rationing on investment expenditures and on the degree to which these effects can be offset by the availability of funds in other markets. The limited amount of empirical evidence on the availability of capital market funds to bank rationed firms was already mentioned in an earlier discussion (Section 6.3). In addition, research in this area would have the benefit of providing information on the effects of credit rationing on the timing of corporate long term debt issues. Similarly, further research on the effects of credit rationing on the distribution and magnitude of trade credit is desirable, although as the discussion in Section 6.4 indicated, some important research on this topic is already available. Finally, and perhaps most importantly, empirical studies of the direct effects of credit rationing on the various expenditures of business firms and household units is needed. The available studies in this area were summarized in Section 6.5.

The second direction for future research would concern simulations of the commercial loan market as part of a complete econometric model of the economy. Although an attempt has been made in this study to develop the policy implications in a general equilibrium setting, it is apparent that quantitative analysis of the various policy multipliers can be achieved only with the other equations of the system specified. As already mentioned, the results of such a simulation study using the Federal Reserve-M.I.T.-Penn. econometric model should be available quite soon. Looking perhaps even further into the future, however, one would hope for the development of models that explicitly incorporate the markets for corporate debt instruments such as commercial paper and corporate bonds. An important benefit of developing such models would be an improved understanding of the dynamic relationships that underlie the various debt markets of the financial system.

Bibliography

Alhadeff, David A., *Monopoly and Competition in Banking,* Berkeley, University of California Press, 1954.

Almon, Shirley, "The Distributed Lag between Capital Appropriations and Expenditures," *Econometrica,* January, 1965, pp. 178–196.

American Bankers Association, *The Commercial Banking Industry,* Englewood Cliffs, Prentice-Hall, Inc., 1962.

Anderson, W. H. L., *Corporate Finance and Fixed Investment,* Division of Research, Harvard Graduate School of Business Administration, 1964.

Ando, Albert and Stephen M. Goldfeld, "An Econometric Model for Evaluating Stabilization Policies," in Albert Ando, E. Cary Brown, and Ann F. Friedlaender, editors, *Studies in Economic Stabilization,* Washington, D.C., The Brookings Institution, 1968.

———— and Franco Modigliani, "Econometric Analysis of Stabilization Policies," *American Economic Review,* May, 1969, pp. 296–314.

Andrews, P. W. S., "A Further Inquiry into the Effects of Rates of Interest," *Oxford Economic Papers,* March, 1940, pp. 32–73.

Arrow, Kenneth J., *Aspects of the Theory of Risk-Bearing,* Yrjo Jahnsson Lecture Series, Helsinki, 1965.

———— and Robert C. Lind, "Uncertainty and the Evaluation of Public Investment Decisions," *American Economic Review,* June, 1970, pp. 364–378.

Bach, G. L. and C. J. Huizenga, "The Differential Effects of Tight Money," *American Economic Review,* March, 1961 (a), pp. 52–80.

——— and ———, "The Differential Effects of Tight Money: Reply," *American Economic Review*, December, 1961 (b), pp. 1042–1044.

——— and ———, "The Differential Effects of Tight Money: Reply," *American Economic Review*, September, 1963, pp. 743–745.

Bischoff, Charles W., "A Model of Nonresidential Construction in the United States," *American Economic Review*, May, 1970, pp. 10–17.

Blitz, Rudolph C. and Millard F. Long, "The Economics of Usury Regulation," *Journal of Political Economy*, December, 1965, pp. 608–619.

Board of Governors of the Federal Reserve System, *Federal Reserve Bulletin*, various issues.

Branson, William H., "The New View of International Capital Movements and Its Implications for Monetary Policy," *Brookings Papers on Economic Activity*, No. 2, 1970.

Brechling, F. P. R. and R. G. Lipsey, "Trade Credit and Monetary Policy," *Economic Journal*, December, 1963, pp. 618–641.

Brunner, Karl, "A Schema for the Supply Theory of Money," *International Economic Review*, January, 1961, pp. 79–109.

——— and Allan H. Meltzer, "Some Further Investigations of Demand and Supply Functions for Money," *Journal of Finance*, May, 1964, pp. 240–283.

Budzeika, G., "Commercial Banks as Suppliers of Capital Funds to Business," in *Essays on Money and Credit*, Federal Reserve Bank of New York, 1964.

Burgess, W. R., *The Reserve Banks and the Money Markets*, New York, Harper and Bros., 1927.

Burstein, Meyer L., *Money*, Cambridge, Schenkman Publishing Company, 1963.

Carr, Hobart C., "A Note on Regional Differences in Discount Rates," *Journal of Finance*, March, 1960, pp. 62–68.

Carson, Deane, "The Differential Effects of Tight Money: Comment," *American Economic Review*, December, 1961, pp. 1039–1042.

Chase, Sam B., Jr., "Credit Risk and Credit Rationing: Comment," *Quarterly Journal of Economics*, May, 1961, pp. 319–327.

Chow, Gregory C., "Tests of Equality between Sets of Coefficients in Two Linear Regressions," *Econometrica*, July, 1960, pp. 591–605.

Cleveland, Federal Reserve Bank, "Continuous Borrowing Through 'Short-Term' Bank Loans," *Business Review*, September, 1956.

Cochrane, D. and G. H. Orcutt, "Application of Least Squares Regression to Relationships Containing Auto-Correlated Errors," *Journal of the American Statistical Association*, March, 1949, pp. 32–61.

Crockett, Jean, Irwin Friend, and Henry Shavell, "The Impact of Monetary Stringency on Business Investment," *Survey of Current Business,* September, 1967.

de Leeuw, Frank, "A Model of Financial Behavior" in J. S. Duesenberry, *et al.,* editors, *The Brookings Quarterly Econometric Model of the United States,* Chicago, Rand McNally & Co., 1965.

———— and Edward Gramlich, "The Federal Reserve-MIT Econometric Model," *Federal Reserve Bulletin,* January, 1968, pp. 11–40.

———— and Edward Gramlich, "The Channels of Monetary Policy," *Federal Reserve Bulletin,* June, 1969, pp. 472–491.

Donaldson, Lufkin & Jenrette, Inc., *Timely Review of 1966 Credit Shortage Effects on Business Financing and Spending Decisions,* July, 1967.

Elgart, Steven J., "Credit Rationing and Distributed Lag Investment Functions for Two-Digit Industries," Discussion Paper Number 131, The Wharton School of Finance and Commerce, Department of Economics, University of Pennsylvania, 1969.

Ellis, Howard S., "The Rediscovery of Money" in *Money, Trade, and Economic Growth; in Honor of John Henry Williams,* New York, The Macmillan Company, 1951.

Evans, Michael, "An Industry Study of Corporate Profits," *Econometrica,* April, 1968, pp. 343–364.

————, *Macro-Economic Model,* Philadelphia Research Associates, 1970.

———— and Lawrence R. Klein, "The Wharton Econometric Forecasting Model," Studies in Quantitative Economics, No. 2, Wharton School of Finance and Commerce, University of Pennsylvania, 1968.

Fair, Ray C. and Dwight M. Jaffee, "Methods of Estimation for Markets in Disequilibrium," forthcoming, *Econometrica.*

Fforde, J. S., "The Monetary Controversy in the U.S.A.," *Oxford Economic Papers,* October, 1951, pp. 221–239.

Fisher, Franklin M., "Dynamic Structure and Estimation in Economy-Wide Econometric Models," in J. S. Duesenberry, *et al.,* editors, *The Brookings Quarterly Econometric Model of the United States,* Chicago, Rand McNally & Co., 1965.

Frazer, William J., Jr., *The Liquidity Structure of Firms and Monetary Economics,* University of Florida Monographs, Social Sciences No. 27, Gainesville, Florida, University of Florida Press, Summer, 1965.

Freimer, Marshall and Myron J. Gordon, "Why Bankers Ration Credit," *Quarterly Journal of Economics,* August, 1965, pp. 397–416.

Goldfeld, Stephen M., *Commercial Bank Behavior and Economic Activity*, Amsterdam, North-Holland Publishing Company, 1966.

Goudzwaard, Maurice B., "Price Ceilings and Credit Rationing," *Journal of Finance*, March, 1968, pp. 177–185.

Gramley, Lyle E., "Interest Rates and Credit Availability at Commercial Banks," in *Essays on Commercial Banking*, Federal Reserve Bank of Kansas City, 1962.

Gramlich, Edward, and Dwight M. Jaffee, *Savings Deposits, Mortgages, and Residential Construction*, forthcoming, Heath-Lexington, 1971.

Guttentag, Jack, "Credit Availability, Interest Rates, and Monetary Policy," *Southern Economic Journal*, January, 1960, pp. 219–228.

Hand, John, *The Availability of Credit and Corporate Investment*, unpublished doctoral dissertation, M.I.T., 1968.

Hendershott, Patric H., "Recent Development of the Financial Sector of Economic Models," *The Journal of Finance*, March, 1968, pp. 41–66.

Henderson, H. D., "The Significance of the Rate of Interest," *Oxford Economic Papers*, October, 1938, pp. 1–13.

Hester, Donald D., "An Empirical Examination of a Commercial Bank Loan Offer Curve Function," *Yale Economic Essays, Spring*, 1962; reprinted in Donald D. Hester and James Tobin, editors, *Studies of Portfolio Behavior*, Monograph 20, New York, John Wiley & Sons, Inc., 1967, pp. 118–170.

Heston, Alan W., "An Empirical Study of Cash, Securities, and Other Current Accounts of Large Corporations," *Yale Economic Essays*, Spring, 1962, pp. 116–168.

Hodgman, Donald R., "In Defense of the Availability Doctrine: A Comment," *Review of Economics and Statistics*, February, 1959, pp. 70–73.

———, "Credit Risk and Credit Rationing," *Quarterly Journal of Economics*, May, 1960, pp. 258–278.

———, "Credit Risk and Credit Rationing: Reply," *Quarterly Journal of Economics*, May, 1961 (a), pp. 327–329.

———, "The Deposit Relationship and Commercial Bank Investment Behavior," *Review of Economics and Statistics*, August, 1961 (b), pp. 257–268.

———, "Credit Risk and Credit Rationing: Reply," *Quarterly Journal of Economics*, August, 1962, pp. 488–493.

———, *Commercial Bank Loan and Investment Policy*, Champaign, Bureau of Economic and Business Research, University of Illinois, 1963.

Huang, David S., "The Short Run Flows of Nonfarm Residential Mortgage Credit," *Econometrica*, April, 1966, pp. 433–459.

Jaffee, Dwight M., "The Commercial Loan Market and Credit Rationing," unpublished paper presented at the December 29, 1967 meetings of the Econometric Society.

————, "An Econometric Model of the Mortgage Market: Estimation and Simulation," forthcoming in E. Gramlich and D. Jaffee, editors, *Savings Deposits, Mortgages, and Residential Construction.*

———— and Franco Modigliani, "A Theory and Test of Credit Rationing," *American Economic Review,* December, 1969, pp. 850–872.

Johnson, Harry G., "Monetary Theory and Policy," *American Economic Review,* June, 1962, pp. 335–384.

Kane, E. J. and B. G. Malkiel, "Bank Portfolio Allocation, Deposit Variability, and the Availability Doctrine, *Quarterly Journal of Economics,* February, 1965, pp. 113–134.

Kansas City, Federal Reserve Bank of, "Trade Credit: A Factor in the Rationing of Credit," *Monthly Review,* June, 1957, pp. 3–8.

————, "Forces Behind the Growth in Tràde Credit," *Monthly Review,* October, 1959, pp. 3–8.

Kareken, John H., "Lenders' Preferences, Credit Rationing, and the Effectiveness of Monetary Policy," *Review of Economics and Statistics,* August, 1957, pp. 292–302.

————, "In Defense of the Availability Doctrine: Reply," *Review of Economics and Statistics,* February, 1959, pp. 73–74.

Keynes, John Maynard, *A Treatise on Money,* Volumes I and II, London, MacMillan & Co., Ltd., 1930.

————, *The General Theory of Employment Interest and Money,* New York, Harcourt, Brace and Company, 1936.

Lindbeck, Assar, *The "New" Theory of Credit Control in the United States,* Stockholm Economic Studies, Pamphlet Series 1, Stockholm, Almquist and Wiksell, 1959.

Lutz, Friedrich A., "The Interest Rate and Investment in a Dynamic Economy," *American Economic Review,* December, 1945, pp. 811–830.

Maisel, Sherman J., "Nonbusiness Construction," in J. S. Duesenberry, *et al.,* editors, *The Brookings Quarterly Econometric Model of the United States,* Rand McNally and Company, Chicago, 1965.

Malinvaud, E., *Statistical Methods of Econometrics,* Chicago, Rand McNally & Co., 1966.

Meade, J. E., and P. W. S. Andrews, "Summary of Replies to Questions on Effects of Interest Rates," *Oxford Economic Papers,* October, 1938, pp. 14–31.

Meigs, A. James, *Free Reserves and the Money Supply,* Chicago, University of Chicago Press, 1962.

Meltzer, Allan H., "Mercantile Credit, Monetary Policy, and Size of Firms," *Review of Economics and Statistics,* November, 1960, pp. 429–437.

———, "Monetary Policy and the Trade Credit Practices of Business Firms," in Commission on Money and Credit, *Stabilization Policies,* Englewood Cliffs, N.J., Prentice-Hall, 1963.

Miller, Merton H., "Credit Risk and Credit Rationing: Further Comment," *Quarterly Journal of Economics,* August, 1962, pp. 480–488.

Modigliani, Franco, "The Monetary Mechanism and Its Interaction with Real Phenomena: A Review of Recent Developments," *Review of Economics and Statistics,* a supplement to the February 1963 issue, pp. 79–107.

———, Robert Rasche, and Philip Cooper, "Central Bank Policy, The Money Supply and the Short-Term Rate of Interest," *Journal of Money, Credit and Banking,* May, 1970, pp. 166–218.

Musgrave, Richard A., "Credit Controls, Interest Rates, and Management of Public Debt," in *Income, Employment and Public Policy; Essays in Honor of Alvin H. Hansen,* New York, W. W. Norton and Company, 1948.

——— and Evsey D. Domar, "Proportional Income Taxation and Risk-Taking," *Quarterly Journal of Economics,* May, 1944, pp. 480–488.

Nadiri, M. I., "The Determinants of Trade Credit in the U.S. Total Manufacturing Sector," *Econometrica,* July, 1969, pp. 408–423.

Orr, D. and W. J. Mellon, "Stochastic Reserve Losses and Expansion of Bank Credit," *American Economic Review,* September, 1961, pp. 614–623.

Rasche, Robert H. and Harold T. Shapiro, "The F.R.B.-M.I.T. Model: Its Special Features," *American Economic Review,* May, 1968, pp. 123–149.

Riefler, W. W., *Money Rates and Money Markets,* New York, Harper and Bros., 1930.

Roosa (Rosa), Robert V., "Interest Rates and the Central Bank," in *Money, Trade and Economic Growth; in Honor of John Henry Williams,* New York, The Macmillan Company, 1951.

Ryder, Harl E., Jr., "Credit Risk and Credit Rationing: Comment," *Quarterly Journal of Economics,* August, 1962, 471–479.

Samuelson, Paul, "Hearings before the Subcommittee on General Credit Control and Debt Management of the Joint Committee on the Economic Report," 82nd Congress, 2nd Session, Washington, D.C., Government Printing Office, 1952, pp. 691–698.

Sayers, R. S., "Business Men and the Terms of Borrowing," *Oxford Economic Papers,* March, 1940, pp. 23–31.

Schwartz, Robert A., "Delayed Payment and the Marshallian Demand Curve—An Analytic View of Trade Credit," unpublished, mimeo, 1970.

Scott, Ira O., Jr., "The Availability Doctrine: Theoretical Underpinnings," *Review of Economic Studies,* October, 1957 (a), pp. 41–48.

———, "The Availability Doctrine: Development and Implications," Quarterly Journal of Economics, November, 1957 (b), pp. 532–539.

Shapiro, Harold, *The Canadian Monetary Sector, An Econometric Analysis,* unpublished doctoral dissertation, Princeton University, 1964.

Silber, William L., "Monetary Channels and the Relative Importance of Money Supply and Bank Portfolios," *Journal of Finance,* March, 1969, pp. 81–87.

——— and Murray E. Polakoff, "The Differential Effects of Tight Money; An Econometric Study," *Journal of Finance,* March, 1970, pp. 83–97.

Smith, Lawrence B., "A Model of the Canadian Housing and Mortgage Markets," *Journal of Political Economy,* September/October, 1969, pp. 795–816.

Smith, Vernon L., "The Theory of Credit Rationing—Some Generalizations," forthcoming, *American Economic Review.*

Smith, Warren L., "On the Effectiveness of Monetary Policy," *American Economic Review,* September, 1956, pp. 588–606.

Sparks, Gordon R., "An Econometric Analysis of the Role of Financial Intermediaries in Postwar Residential Building Cycles," in Robert Ferber, editor, *Determinants of Investment Behavior,* New York, Columbia University Press, 1967.

———, "A Model of the Mortgage Market and Residential Construction Activity," *American Statistical Association Proceedings,* 1968.

Teigen, Ronald L., "Demand and Supply Functions for Money in the United States: Some Structural Estimates," *Econometrica,* October, 1964, pp. 476–509.

Tobin, James, "Monetary Policy and the Management of the Public Debt: The Patman Inquiry," *Review of Economics and Statistics,* May, 1953, pp. 118–127.

Tucker, Donald P., "Credit Rationing, Interest Rate Lags, and Monetary Policy Speed," *Quarterly Journal of Economics,* February, 1968, pp. 54–84.

———, "Macroeconomic Models and the Demand for Money Under Market Disequilibrium," forthcoming, *Journal of Money, Credit and Banking.*

Tussing, A. Dale, "The Differential Effects of Tight Money: Comment," *American Economic Review,* September, 1963, pp. 740–743.

———, "Can Monetary Policy Influence the Availability of Credit," *Journal of Finance,* March, 1966, pp. 1–13.

U.S. Congress, Joint Committee on the Economic Report, "Monetary Policy and the Management of the Public Debt: Their Role in Achieving Price Stability and High Level Employment," Hearings before the Subcommittee on General Credit Control and Debt Management, 82nd Congress, 2nd Session, Washington, 1952 (a).

————, "Monetary Policy and the Management of the Public Debt: Their Role in Achieving Price Stability and High Level Employment," Replies to Questions and other Material for the Use of the Subcommittee on General Credit Control and Debt Management, 82nd Congress, 2nd Session, Washington, 1952 (b).

————, Report to Committees on Banking and Currency and the Select Committees on Banking and Currency, *Financing Small Business,* 85th Congress, 2nd Session, by the Federal Reserve System, Parts 1 and 2, 1958.

Viner, Jacob, *Studies in the Theory of International Trade,* New York, Harper and Bros., 1937.

Williams, John N., "The Implications of Fiscal Policy for Monetary Policy and the Banking System," *American Economic Review,* March, 1942, Supplement, pp. 234–249.

Willis, P. B., "The Secondary Market for Negotiable Certificates of Deposits," paper prepared for the Committee for the Fundamental Reappraisal of the Discount Mechanism, appointed by the Board of Governors of the Federal Reserve System.

Wojnilower, Albert M. and Richard E. Speagle, "The Prime Rate" in *Essays on Money and Credit,* Federal Reserve Bank of New York, 1964.

Index